الحقّ المبين

في

علاج الصَّرعِ والسِّحرِ والعين

THE JINN, MAGIC AND THE EVIL-EYE

DR. ABDULLAH AL-TAYYAR
SHAYKH SAMI AL-MUBARAK

INTRODUCTION BY
SHAYKH ABDUL AZIZ IBN ABDULLAH IBN BAZ

ISBN 978-1-898649-78-6

British Library Cataloguing in Publication Data.
A catalogue record for this book is available from the British Library.

Published & distributed by

Al-Hidaayah Publishing & Distribution Ltd

PO Box 3332, Birmingham B10 0UH, United Kingdom.
T: 0121 753 1889 : F: 0121 753 2422
E-mail: mail@al-hidaayah.co.uk : www.al-hidaayah.co.uk

Printed in Turkey by Mega Printing

Table of Contents

Translator's Foreword

All Praise is due to Allāh, the Creator of the heavens with its stars, moon and sun, the Creator of the earth with its mountains and seas, trees and rivers, and all those who inhabit it. May the peace and blessings of Allāh be upon the best of creation, His slave and final Messenger Muḥammad, his family, companions and all those who follow in their footsteps until the Day of Accounting. To Proceed:

Indeed Allāh the Most High created us all for His worship. He has promised those who fulfil His commandments with the most eternal and pleasing of rewards, and has warned those who choose a path other than His that their abode will be in the most evil and dreaded of places. The one who chooses to tread the Straight Path will without doubt face many challenges and have to overcome many trials, as Allāh says:

الٓمٓ ﴿١﴾ أَحَسِبَ ٱلنَّاسُ أَن يُتۡرَكُوٓاْ أَن يَقُولُوٓاْ ءَامَنَّا وَهُمۡ لَا
يُفۡتَنُونَ ﴿٢﴾ وَلَقَدۡ فَتَنَّا ٱلَّذِينَ مِن قَبۡلِهِمۡۖ فَلَيَعۡلَمَنَّ ٱللَّهُ ٱلَّذِينَ
صَدَقُواْ وَلَيَعۡلَمَنَّ ٱلۡكَٰذِبِينَ ﴿٣﴾

Alif Lām Mīm. Do people think that they will be left alone because they say: "We believe," and will not be tested. And we indeed tested those who were before them. And Allāh will certainly make (it) known (the truth of) those who are true, and will certainly make (it) known (the falsehood of) those who are liars, (although Allāh knows all that before putting them to test).

Sūrah al-'Ankabūt, Verses 1-3

From the greatest of these trials is the constant planning and plotting of Satan and his helpers from the devils of *jinn* and men, who tirelessly stand in the way of the believer and obstruct him from taking the path of good, and urge him to take the path of desires and evil. The successful one is he who knows with certainty that they only call to that which has harmful results, and will only succeed in causing a person to distance himself from his Lord.

The use of magic and its likes by people who only wish to cause harm has become widespread in our times. It is rare to find a person who does not know someone who has been inflicted with these problems, or at the very least heard about these incidents. Problems related to the spirits and the unknown cause more grief to its victims than most physical ailments, for in most cases people are unaware of how to cure such illnesses. Modern medicine rejects the notion of evil spirits possessing others. Instead, these are considered to be psychological illnesses; this may be the case in some cases but not in all instances.

It is important for the Muslim in general to know what Islām mentions as being the truth with regards to the *jinn*, magic, evil-eye and such similar affairs. It is especially important for those who have been afflicted with such illnesses to know what the *sharī'ah* says concerning the causes and cures to these illnesses. This will mean that a person is fully aware of what he is dealing with, is able to use the lawful means which have been prescribed by Allāh in seeking a cure, and is not in need of those deceivers and impostors from the fortune tellers, soothsayers and their likes who claim to have knowledge of the unseen, and who will only cause a person to fall into the major sins when approached.

Due to their not being, to the best of my knowledge many Muslims, especially in the West, who have sufficient insight into these topics, nor many suitable sources of information in the English language, many Muslims are at a loss as to what to do in the event of such a calamity befalling. In times like this, many people refer to those who have no more experience in these cases than the afflicted. This is why it is important that something simple and comprehensive is made available to everyone, so that the rulings of the *sharīʿah* are made clear to the Muslims. So, when I heard of the increase in the amount of cases of this type, I asked Allāh that He assist me in bridging this gap and filling this hole.

This book is perhaps one of the most comprehensive, simple and practical books on this subject, as the authors have tried their utmost in not only mentioning the theoretical aspects of the issues discussed, but also the practical steps one can take in the prevention, protection and removal of these illnesses. Also, the book was read to and recommended by the late Shaykh Ibn Bāz, which gives the book more weight. He placed additional footnotes in the book, as well as adding two small treatises of his own, which can be found at the end.

It should be noted here, that due to there not being a direct translation for some of the Arabic terminology, I have sufficed with using a rough translation in the book and placed footnotes in the appropriate places (at the beginning of the chapters on convulsions and possession). I have mentioned what is meant by the Arabic in detail; the following words are from this category: '*al-ṣarʿ*' which is referred to as convulsions, and '*al-mass*' which is referred to as possession. In both cases what is being referred to in the translations is what comes about from the possession and touching of the *jinn*, and not conventional convulsions and insanity. The reader should therefore bear this in mind throughout the book.

It is only appropriate here that I thank Allāh the Most High for enabling me to undertake and complete this project, for He is the One who grants success. I would also like to thank the authors for their assistance in the translation, and for allowing me to add certain footnotes and summarise certain parts of the book. These were all necessary in making the translation more understandable; any mistakes in the translation are mine and not the authors. May Allāh reward all those who in any way assisted in this book.

Finally, I ask Allāh that He makes this work sincerely for His sake, beneficial to the Muslims, and that He bestows faith and health upon us and all the Muslims, guides us to the truth, keeps us firm upon this religion, and gathers us all in Paradise on the Day when the successful will rejoice and the disbelievers will wish they were dust.

وَمَا تَوْفِيقِيْ إِلَّا بِاللهِ عَلَيْهِ تَوَكَّلْتُ وَإِلَيْهِ أُنِيبُ

وَاللهُ الْمُسْتَعَانُ، وَمَنْ بِغَيْرِهِ اسْتَعَانَ لَا يُعَانُ

Ahsan Hanif
City of the Prophet
Al-Madinah al-Nabawiyyah
17/5/1427 AH
13/6/2006 AD

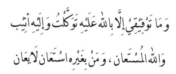

Recommendation
By
Shaykh ʿAbdul-ʿAzīz bin ʿAbdullāh bin Bāz

(May Allāh have mercy upon him)

[Below are two of the three letters the Shaykh wrote to the authors. The third is a recommendation for the title of the book, which the authors agreed to.]

All Praise is due to Allāh alone, and may the peace and blessings of Allāh be upon the final Prophet. To proceed:

I have read the book written by Shaykh ʿAbdullāh al-Ṭayyār and Shaykh Sāmī al-Mubārak. I consider it to be a beneficial book on the topic in which the authors have gathered evidence from the *sharīʿah* with regards to the cures of that which they have mentioned. May Allāh reward them both, make this book beneficial and cure the Muslims from all evil. I recommend this book to all those who want to prepare themselves to cure these illnesses.

To Shaykh ʿAbdullāh al-Ṭayyār: I request that you place my two treatises entitled: *'The clarification of the truth regarding the jinn entering humans, and the refutation of those who deny it,'* and *'Seeking cures from magicians and fortune tellers poses a great danger for Islām and the Muslims,'* into your book. May Allāh reward you.

ʿAbdul-ʿAzīz bin ʿAbdullāh bin Bāz
Grand Mufti, Kingdom of Saudi Arabia
Head of the Institute of Research, *Fatāwā* and Guidance.

Introduction

All praise is due to Allāh, the One who cures and gives health, the One who benefits and harms, the One, the Majestic, the One who is unique in His Oneness (*tawḥīd*). He is the One who creates and to Him all things return. He created everything with His power, and arranged all affairs by His will. We testify that none has the right to be worshipped except Allāh, and we testify that Muḥammad is His slave and messenger. He conveyed the message, fulfilled his obligation, and strove for the sake of his Lord, so may the peace and blessings of Allāh be upon him, his family, companions and all those who follow him until the Last Day. To proceed:

Indeed the conscious and familiar world is known to a person's soul; he is accustomed to it, and hence is only surprised by that which is new or strange. On the other hand a person is driven to explore that which is unknown and unseen to him, and for this reason the world of the *jinn* is a world that the soul wishes to learn about, and to know what has been mentioned regarding it from the texts of the Qur'ān and *Sunnah*, and that which the scholars have mentioned in their books. It is for this reason that some scholars dedicated books to this topic and in particular to the possession of people by the *jinn*. Allāh says:

وَأَنَّهُۥ كَانَ رِجَالٌ مِّنَ ٱلْإِنسِ يَعُوذُونَ بِرِجَالٍ مِّنَ ٱلْجِنِّ
فَزَادُوهُمْ رَهَقًا ۝٦

And verily, there were men among mankind who took shelter with the males among the jinn, but they (jinn) increased them (mankind) in sin and transgression.

Sūrah Jinn, verse 6

From that which is well known and accepted is that a person is vulnerable to dangers and illnesses; very few people live their whole lives without afflictions. These afflictions do not befall a person except by the will of Allāh, and due to His infinite wisdom which may or may not be known to the afflicted. For every affliction there is reward if that person is patient and seeks the reward from Allāh. This is why the Prophet (ﷺ) said: *"How amazing is the affair of the believer. Verily, all his affairs are good for him; if some good comes to him he is grateful and that is better for him, and if some evil befalls him he is patient and that is better for him."*[1]

However, this affliction may be prevented or lifted or eased by the will of Allāh; this occurs when the Muslim takes the necessary steps to prevent such afflictions from befalling, such as:

1. The protection of Allāh for His servant, as is in the *ḥadīth*: *"Preserve Allāh (by constantly remembering him) and He will preserve you"*[2]

2. Remembering Allāh in times of ease by following His orders and staying away from His prohibitions. The Prophet (ﷺ) said: *"Remember Allāh in times of ease and He will remember you in times of hardship"*[3]

---

[1] Collected by Imām Muslim in his *Ṣaḥīḥ* 2999.

[2] Authentic, collected by al-Tirmidhī, see *Ṣaḥīḥ Sunan al-Tirmidhī*, no. 2043.

[3] Authentic, collected by al-Tirmidhī.

3. Giving in charity, for charity prevents misfortunes from befalling or eases them: "*Good actions protect from evil hardships*"[4]

4. Turning to Allāh, trusting in Him, entrusting all your affairs to Him knowing that He alone possesses benefit and harm. To realise no matter how much strength mankind possesses it will not benefit or harm him unless it has been decreed by Allāh. However, when a person is befallen by an illness, he begins to seek a cure using all means [possible]. This may be obligatory upon him, recommended or allowed, as long as that cure does not harm others, and is something lawful in the *sharī'ah* and not *ḥarām*. The Prophet (ﷺ) said: "*Cure yourselves O servants of Allāh, but do not cure with that which is ḥarām*"[5]

He also said (ﷺ): "*Allāh has not sent an illness except that he has sent with it a cure. Know it those who know it and be ignorant of it those who are ignorant of it.*"[6]

Reasons for choosing this topic:

1. The thought of writing this book first came whilst sitting with Shaykh 'Abdul-'Azīz ibn 'Abdullāh ibn Bāz in his house and discussing the topic of incantations (*ruqyah*), and how to cure magic and the evil eye (*'ayn*). The shaykh requested that I write something on this topic; I considered that an honour. May Allāh gather us with him in Paradise.

I was then visited by my friend, Shaykh Sāmī al-Mubārak, and we discussed this topic. I mentioned to him what the shaykh had recommended, and he proposed that he and I should both write this book together. This increased my desire to embark upon this project, especially since he has a lot of valuable experience with this topic.

---

[4] Authentic, collected by al-Ṭabarānī.

[5] Authentic, collected by Abū Dāwūd and al-Tirmidhī, no. 2039.

[6] *Ṣaḥīḥ al-Bukhārī* no. 5678.

2. This topic is of the utmost importance, especially since the *jinn* are a living and intellectual creation who live with us on this earth and mix with us in our lives. For this reason they have been mentioned in the texts of the Qur'ān and *Sunnah*. Indeed, the Qur'ān has dedicated a whole *Sūrah* to them. This book then, is like a foundation in this topic. In it we have tried to mention everything with its evidence and we have left out that which is exaggerated by people and has no truth to it.

3. Indeed the knowledge of the plans and plots of *Shayṭān* and his army from the impious and the evil *jinn* is a means of protecting oneself from their harm. This is done by fearing Allāh and turning to Him, obeying His commands and refraining from His prohibitions, and reciting the necessary *adhkār*.

4. The majority of books dealing with this topic do not focus on the practical side. That is, they do not focus on the description of the illness and how to cure it. This is what we have tried to do in this book, since everything mentioned has come from personal experience and not just narrations from others; the one who witnesses is not like the one who hears.

5. There is an increasing amount of people who are afflicted by psychological illnesses, epilepsy, magic and the evil eye. The consequences of these afflictions place the afflicted and their family in a very difficult situation.

6. The need to strengthen our faith (*īmān*) and our connection with Allāh, for there is no refuge except with Allāh, no dependence except upon Him, and no cure except from Him alone, for He is the one who possesses all cures, as He says:

وَإِذَا مَرِضْتُ فَهُوَ يَشْفِينِ ﴿٨٠﴾

And when I am ill, it is He who cures me.
Sūrah al-Shu'arā', verse 80

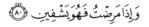

If Allāh has not willed for a person to be cured then he must be patient with this and seek the reward from Allāh.

7. There is an increase in the number of soothsayers, fortune tellers and their likes. They possess deception and there is nothing behind it except evil.

8. To explain the prescribed (*shar'ī*) form of incantations '*ruqyah*'[7] and to advise our readers.

Finally, we must give credit to those who deserve it. We thank his eminence, Shaykh 'Abdul-'Azīz ibn 'Abdullāh ibn Bāz, as he was the reason after Allāh that compelled us to write this book. We also thank all those who assisted in any way. We apologise to the reader for any shortcomings, for perfection is for Allāh alone and His messenger in that which he conveyed from his Lord and no book is perfect save the Book of Allāh:

وَلَوْ كَانَ مِنْ عِندِ غَيْرِ ٱللَّهِ لَوَجَدُوا۟ فِيهِ ٱخْتِلَٰفًا كَثِيرًا ﴿٨٢﴾

Had it been from other than Allāh, they would surely have found therein many a contradiction.
Sūrah al-Nisā', verse 82

But our excuse is that we tried our best, and success is from Allāh. We ask Allāh that He benefits all who read this book, hear of it or come across it. Verily He alone is capable of all things. May the peace and blessings of Allāh be upon our Prophet Muḥammad, his family and companions.

The authors,
Dr. 'Abdullāh bin Muḥammad al-Ṭayyār
Shaykh Sāmī bin Salmān al-Mubārak
Makkah, by the Sacred House, the Ka'bah, the evening of Monday 23/2/1412AH

---

[7] Translator's note: *Ruqyah* is to recite upon oneself or upon others, and this recitation can be with that which is *ḥalāl* or *ḥarām*. This is why the authors mention *shar'ī ruqyah* i.e. permissible incantations. In English, *ruqyah* is commonly translated as, incantations.

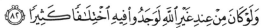

Preface

This preface centres upon three topics: Belief in the unseen, submission to the will of Allāh, and patience upon the decree of Allāh. One may ask, 'What is the relation between belief in the unseen, pre-decree, patience and the topic of this book?' The answer to this question is that these matters are essential in the life of the Muslim as they give him respite and comfort in all his affairs:

Belief in the unseen, as well as being an essential part of faith (*īmān*), causes a Muslim to submit to that which Islām has told him despite not having the full knowledge of those hidden matters such as the angels and the *jinn*. Likewise, belief in the pre-decree of Allāh is one of the six pillars of *īmān*, and if the Muslim submits to this pillar he realises that all that happens is by the will of Allāh, hence he does not grieve over that which has befallen him or passed him. Patience with the decree of Allāh is from the means that enables the Muslim to have peace at heart. The one who has been exposed to magic, the evil eye, physical or psychological illnesses, may try to search for a cure, and he may or may not succeed; he can only be patient in all this.

Firstly: Belief in the unseen

Indeed, from the pivotal aspects of the Islamic *'aqīdah* is belief in the unseen. This belief is considered fundamental for the Muslim;

it is from the characteristics of the pious, as Allāh says:

الٓمٓ ﴿١﴾ ذَٰلِكَ ٱلْكِتَٰبُ لَا رَيْبَ فِيهِ هُدًى لِّلْمُتَّقِينَ ﴿٢﴾ ٱلَّذِينَ يُؤْمِنُونَ بِٱلْغَيْبِ وَيُقِيمُونَ ٱلصَّلَوٰةَ وَمِمَّا رَزَقْنَٰهُمْ يُنفِقُونَ ﴿٣﴾

Alif Lām Mīm. This is the Book (the Qur'ān) whereof there is no doubt, a guidance to those who are al-Muttaqūn (pious believers). Who believe in the unseen and perform ṣalāt and spend out of what we have provided for them (zakāt)

Sūrah al-Baqarah, verse 1-3

So, it is obligatory upon the Muslim to submit to that which has been mentioned from the unseen in the Qur'ān and authentic *Sunnah*, whether it is conceivable to him or not, and regardless of whether he has seen any of that world or not. It is incumbent upon him to fully submit. Allāh says:

فَلَا وَرَبِّكَ لَا يُؤْمِنُونَ حَتَّىٰ يُحَكِّمُوكَ فِيمَا شَجَرَ بَيْنَهُمْ ثُمَّ لَا يَجِدُوا فِي أَنفُسِهِمْ حَرَجًا مِّمَّا قَضَيْتَ وَيُسَلِّمُوا تَسْلِيمًا ﴿٦٥﴾

But no, by your Lord, they can have no Faith until they make you (O Muḥammad) judge in all disputes between them, and find in themselves no resistance against your decisions, and accept (them) with full submission.

Sūrah al-Nisā', verse 65

This is why the methodology of the companions (ﷺ) was to completely submit to that which the Prophet (ﷺ) told them. From that is belief in the angels; this is one of the pillars of *īmān*, and the world of the angels is from the unseen. Is it therefore allowed for the Muslim to deny it because he has not seen or comprehended it?

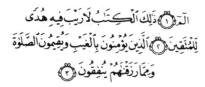

The denial of many matters that have been established in the Qur'ān and *Sunnah* are as a result of denying the unseen. Due to this, many people have rejected the creation of angels and *jinn*, and the only evidence for this denial is that they have not witnessed them or have not been able to experiment on them, even though at the same time they speak of magnetic fields and gravity and such things which are also unseen.

Secondly: Belief in pre-decree, the good of it and the bad of it
This is one of the six pillars of *īmān* without which a person is not a believer. It is obligatory upon the Muslim to submit to this decree, the good of it and the bad of it, and to know with certainty that what has befallen him would not have passed him, and that which has passed would not have befallen him. That which takes place in the universe is only by the will and decree of Allāh. Allāh says:

مَآ أَصَابَ مِن مُّصِيبَةٍ فِي ٱلْأَرْضِ وَلَا فِيٓ أَنفُسِكُمْ إِلَّا فِي
كِتَٰبٍ مِّن قَبْلِ أَن نَّبْرَأَهَآ ۚ إِنَّ ذَٰلِكَ عَلَى ٱللَّهِ يَسِيرٌ
﴿٢٢﴾ لِّكَيْلَا تَأْسَوْا۟ عَلَىٰ مَا فَاتَكُمْ وَلَا تَفْرَحُوا۟ بِمَآ
ءَاتَىٰكُمْ ۗ وَٱللَّهُ لَا يُحِبُّ كُلَّ مُخْتَالٍ فَخُورٍ ﴿٢٣﴾

No calamity befalls on the earth or in yourselves but it is inscribed in the Book of Decrees before We bring it into existence, verily, that is easy for Allāh. In order that you may not grieve at the things which you fail to get, nor rejoice over that which has been given to you. And Allāh likes not prideful boasters.

Sūrah al-Ḥadīd, verse 22-23

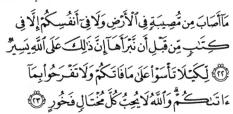

The Prophet (ﷺ) said to Ibn 'Abbās: "*...and know that if the whole of mankind was to gather to benefit you in something, they would not benefit you except in that which has already been written for you, and were they to gather to harm you, they would not harm*

you except in that which has already been written against you. The pens have been lifted and the pages have dried."[8]

Thirdly: Patience upon the decree of Allāh
Allāh says:

وَبَشِّرِ ٱلصَّٰبِرِينَ ١٥٥ ٱلَّذِينَ إِذَآ أَصَٰبَتۡهُم مُّصِيبَةٞ
قَالُوٓاْ إِنَّا لِلَّهِ وَإِنَّآ إِلَيۡهِ رَٰجِعُونَ

But give glad tidings to the patient. Who, when afflicted with calamity, say: "Truly to Allāh we belong and truly, to Him we shall return.

Sūrah al-Baqarah, verse 155-156

Umm Salamah said: I heard the Prophet (ﷺ) say: "*There is not a single Muslim who is befallen by a calamity and he says that which Allāh ordered him to: 'Indeed to Allāh we belong and to Him we shall return, O Allāh reward me in my calamity and replace it with that which is better,' except that Allāh will reward him for that calamity and replace it with that which is better.*"[9]

So a person's life is full of calamities and pain; for every day you laugh, you will cry for days. In a world like this, it is necessary to be equipped and ready with a weapon, and that weapon is patience with the decree of Allāh. Allāh says:

وَلَئِن صَبَرۡتُمۡ لَهُوَ خَيۡرٞ لِّلصَّٰبِرِينَ ١٢٦

But if you endure patiently, verily, it is better for the patient.

Sūrah al-Naḥl, verse 126

Patience is to *īmān* what a head is to the body. On the authority of Abū Yaḥyā, Ṣuhayb ibn Sinān (رضي الله عنه) who said that the Prophet

[8] Authentic, collected by al-Tirmidhī.

[9] Collected by Muslim.

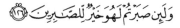

(ﷺ) said: "*How amazing is the affair of the believer. Verily all his affairs are good for him, and that is not for anyone except the believer. If some good comes to him he is grateful and that is better for him, and if some evil befalls him he is patient and that is better for him.*"[10]

The Muslim should know that the greatest calamity is that which befalls a person in his religion; this is the greatest calamity in this world and the hereafter. It is a loss with which there is no profit, and the deprivation with which there is no success.[11]

---

[10] Collected by Muslim.

[11] *Tasliyat Ahlul-Maṣā'ib*, Muḥammad al-Manbajī al-Ḥanbalī p. 24.

Chapter 1

Jinn: The Reality

The world of the *jinn* is a different one from the worlds of mankind and the angels, but the *jinn* are similar to men in that they have intellect, willpower, and the ability to choose whether to do good or bad. They like men are also ordered with the worship of Allāh alone, as Allāh says:

وَمَا خَلَقْتُ ٱلْجِنَّ وَٱلْإِنسَ إِلَّا لِيَعْبُدُونِ ﴿٥٦﴾

And I (Allāh) created not the jinn and mankind except that they should worship Me (Alone).

Sūrah al-Dhāriyāt, verse 56

The *jinn* differ from men in their nature and appearance. Their reality is that they are intellectual spirits with willpower like men, but with no physical substance. They are hidden from our senses, and cannot be seen in their true form, nor upon their true nature, but they have the ability to take different forms. They eat, marry, have offspring, and will be held to account for their actions in the hereafter.[12]

[12] *'Ālam al-Jinn fī Ḍaw' al-Kitāb wal-Sunnah*, 'Abdul-Karīm 'Ubaydāt, p. 8-9.

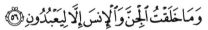

Imām al-Shawkānī said: "They are an intellectual and hidden being that is mostly from fire."[13] Also, it is not possible to see them in the original form in which they were created. Allāh says:

يَٰبَنِيٓ ءَادَمَ لَا يَفْتِنَنَّكُمُ
ٱلشَّيْطَٰنُ كَمَآ أَخْرَجَ أَبَوَيْكُم مِّنَ ٱلْجَنَّةِ يَنزِعُ عَنْهُمَا لِبَاسَهُمَا
لِيُرِيَهُمَا سَوْءَٰتِهِمَآ ۗ إِنَّهُۥ يَرَىٰكُمْ هُوَ وَقَبِيلُهُۥ مِنْ حَيْثُ لَا تَرَوْنَهُمْ ۗ
إِنَّا جَعَلْنَا ٱلشَّيَٰطِينَ أَوْلِيَآءَ لِلَّذِينَ لَا يُؤْمِنُونَ ﴿٢٧﴾

O children of Adam! Let not shayṭān deceive you as he got your parents (Adam and Hawwa) out of Paradise, stripping them of their raiments, to show them their private parts. Verily, he and his tribe see you from where you cannot see them. Verily, We made the shayāṭīn Awliyā' (protectors and helpers) for those who believe not.

Sūrah al-Aʿrāf, verse 27

The *jinn* are less honourable and lower in standing than men, Shaykh Abū Bakr al-Jazāirī said:

> Indeed the *jinn*, even the pious from amongst them are less honourable and lower in standing than men, for the Creator the Most High, has emphasised the honour of mankind in Sūrah al-Isrā':

وَلَقَدْ كَرَّمْنَا بَنِيٓ ءَادَمَ وَحَمَلْنَٰهُمْ
فِي ٱلْبَرِّ وَٱلْبَحْرِ وَرَزَقْنَٰهُم مِّنَ ٱلطَّيِّبَٰتِ وَفَضَّلْنَٰهُمْ عَلَىٰ
كَثِيرٍ مِّمَّنْ خَلَقْنَا تَفْضِيلًا ﴿٧٠﴾

And indeed We have honoured the Children of Adam, and We have carried them on land and sea, and have provided them with al-Ṭayyibāt (lawful good things), and have preferred them

[13] *Fatḥ al-Qadīr*, vol. 5, p. 303.

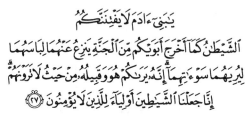

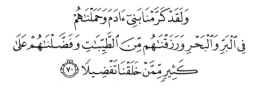

above many of those whom We have created with a marked preferment.

Sūrah al-Isrā', verse 70

This prestige has not been mentioned for the *jinn* in any of the Holy Books, nor by the tongue of any of the Messengers, so from this, it is known that man is of a higher standing than *jinn*. This is also shown through the way the *jinn* feel weak and inferior in the presence of men. However, when men seek refuge with the *jinn* they feel superior and proud because of the way men glorify them, but the truth is the opposite; they only increase in tyranny and disbelief, as Allāh mentions concerning them:

وَأَنَّهُۥ كَانَ رِجَالٌ مِّنَ ٱلْإِنسِ يَعُوذُونَ بِرِجَالٍ مِّنَ ٱلْجِنِّ فَزَادُوهُمْ رَهَقًا ﴿٦﴾

And verily, there were men among mankind who took shelter with the males among the jinn, but they (jinn) increased them (mankind) in sin and transgression.

Sūrah Jinn, verse 6

Another proof for this is that when men seek assistance from them and swear by them they immediately answer this call, due to the weakness and inferiority they feel in the presence of the righteous son of Adam who believes in Allāh and worships Him alone. As for those of mankind who disbelieve in Allāh, then the righteous of the *jinn* are better than them.[14]

Indeed, the disbelievers are more astray than cattle, as Allāh says:

إِنْ هُمْ إِلَّا كَٱلْأَنْعَٰمِ بَلْ هُمْ أَضَلُّ سَبِيلًا ﴿٤٤﴾

[14] *'Aqīdat al-Mu'min*, p. 228.

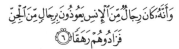

They are only like cattle-nay, they are even further astray from the Path.

Sūrah al-Furqān, verse 44

The Reason they are Called *Jinn*

They are known as *jinn* because they are invisible and hidden from the naked eye. They see men but men do not see them, as Allāh says:

إِنَّهُۥ يَرَىٰكُمْ هُوَ وَقَبِيلُهُۥ مِنْ حَيْثُ لَا تَرَوْنَهُمْ

Verily, he and his tribe see you from where you cannot see them.

Sūrah al-A'rāf, verse 27

The point being that men cannot see the *jinn* in their original form, however they may see them in other forms, such as certain animals.

When were the *Jinn* Created?

The *jinn* were created before mankind as is mentioned in the clear text of the Qur'ān:

وَلَقَدْ خَلَقْنَا ٱلْإِنسَـٰنَ مِن صَلْصَـٰلٍ مِّنْ حَمَإٍ مَّسْنُونٍ ﴿٢٦﴾
وَٱلْجَآنَّ خَلَقْنَـٰهُ مِن قَبْلُ مِن نَّارِ ٱلسَّمُومِ ﴿٢٧﴾

And indeed, We created man from dried (sounding) clay of altered mud. And the jinn, we created aforetime from the smokeless flame of fire.

Sūrah al-Ḥijr, verse 26-27

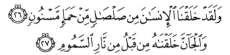

The Origin of their Creation

Allāh created the *jinn* from fire, as this is what has been revealed in the Qur'ān:

وَٱلْجَآنَّ خَلَقْنَٰهُ مِن قَبْلُ مِن نَّارِ ٱلسَّمُومِ ﴿٢٧﴾

And the jinn, we created aforetime from the smokeless flame of fire.

Sūrah al-Ḥijr, verse 27

Allāh also says:

وَخَلَقَ ٱلْجَآنَّ مِن مَّارِجٍ مِّن نَّارٍ ﴿١٥﴾

And the jinn: He created from a smokeless flame of fire.

Sūrah al-Raḥmān, verse 15

The Prophet (ﷺ) said: "*The angels were created from light, and the jinn from the smokeless flame of fire and Adam was created from that which has been described to you.*"[15]

The Types of *Jinn*

It has been reported in a *ḥadīth* that the Prophet (ﷺ) said: "*The jinn are of three types: a type which flies in the air, a type which are snakes and dogs and a type which resides and wanders.*"[16]

If one wishes to refer to a particular or single *jinn* he says: '*jinnī*', and if he is referring to those of the *jinn* who live with people he says: "*āmir*', and if he is discussing those of the *jinn* who present themselves to children he says: '*arwāḥ*'. If they are evil and impious they are known as: '*shayṭān*', and if they increase in their evil they are: '*mārid*', and if it has the ability to move rocks etc it is: "*ifrīt*'.[17]

---

[15] Muslim 2996.

[16] Authentic, collected by Ḥākim and al-Bayhaqī.

[17] *Maṭālib Ulin-Nuhā: Sharḥ Ghāyat al-Muntahā*, Muṣṭafā al-Suyūṭī al-Ruhaybānī, vol. 1, p. 642.

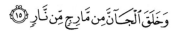

Ibn Taymiyyah said: "The *jinn* take the forms of men and animals, so they come in the appearance of snakes and scorpions and other than it, and in the form of camels, cows, sheep, horses, mules, donkeys and in the form of birds and men."[18]

He also says: "...and the *jinn* take its appearance often, meaning a black dog, likewise the appearance of a black cat, for the colour black agrees more with the strength of *shayṭān* than other colours, and it also has hotness to it."[19]

Have the *Jinn* been Ordered to Follow the *Sharīʿah* of Islām?

The only religion accepted by Allāh is Islām, and the message of the Prophet Muḥammad (ﷺ) is the final and everlasting message. It is a message for both mankind and the *jinn*, hence they have been ordered to follow it. From them are both believers and disbelievers, as Allāh says:

وَأَنَّا مِنَّا ٱلصَّٰلِحُونَ وَمِنَّا دُونَ ذَٰلِكَ كُنَّا طَرَآئِقَ قِدَدًا ﴿١١﴾

There are among us some that are righteous, and some the contrary, we are groups having different ways (religious sects)

Sūrah Jinn, verse 11

And Allāh says:

هَٰذِهِۦ جَهَنَّمُ ٱلَّتِى يُكَذِّبُ بِهَا ٱلْمُجْرِمُونَ

﴿٤٣﴾ يَطُوفُونَ بَيْنَهَا وَبَيْنَ حَمِيمٍ ءَانٍ ﴿٤٤﴾ فَبِأَىِّ ءَالَآءِ رَبِّكُمَا تُكَذِّبَانِ

This is the Hell which the Mujrimūn (polytheists, criminals, sinners) denied. They will go between it (Hell) and the fierce boiling water! Then which of the blessings of you Lord will you both (jinn and men) deny?

Sūrah al-Raḥmān, verses 43-45

---

[18] *Īḍāḥ al-Dalālah fī ʿUmūm al-Risālah.*

[19] *Majmūʿ Fatāwā*, vol. 19, p. 52.

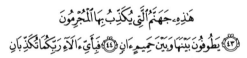

The Prophet (ﷺ) conveyed this message to the *jinn* and warned them, as Allāh has mentioned in His Book:

وَإِذْ صَرَفْنَآ إِلَيْكَ نَفَرًا مِّنَ ٱلْجِنِّ يَسْتَمِعُونَ ٱلْقُرْءَانَ فَلَمَّا
حَضَرُوهُ قَالُوٓا۟ أَنصِتُوا۟ فَلَمَّا قُضِىَ وَلَّوْا۟ إِلَىٰ قَوْمِهِم مُّنذِرِينَ

And (remember) when We sent towards you (Muḥammad) a group (three to ten persons) of the jinn, (quietly) listening to the Qur'ān. When they stood in the presence thereof, they said: "Listen in silence!" and when it was finished, they returned to their people, as warners.

Sūrah al-Aḥqāf, verse 29

The purpose of creation for mankind and the *jinn* is the worship of Allāh alone, as He says:

وَمَا خَلَقْتُ ٱلْجِنَّ وَٱلْإِنسَ إِلَّا لِيَعْبُدُونِ ﴿٥٦﴾

And I (Allāh) created not the jinn and mankind except that they should worship Me (Alone).

Sūrah al-Dhāriyāt, verse 56

So from this it is known that the believing *jinn* will enter Paradise just like the believers from mankind, and their disbelievers will enter the Fire like the disbelievers from mankind. This has been mentioned by Allāh in the Qur'ān:

وَلِمَنْ خَافَ مَقَامَ رَبِّهِۦ جَنَّتَانِ ﴿٤٦﴾

But for him who fears the standing before his Lord, there will be two gardens (i.e. in Paradise)

Sūrah al-Raḥmān, verse 46

This is something we ourselves have seen from those who have been possessed. Some of the *jinns* were disbelievers, but when we recited over them, they accepted Islām, and some of them were disobedient Muslims so we advised them.

Can Men and *Jinn* marry?

This is a difficult question, and the scholars differ greatly over it. Some say it is possible whilst others say it is not, and what seems to be the case is that this is something very rare if not impossible, and if it takes place it may be by force, for were this door to be opened there would be many evils as a result of it.[20]

Ibn Taymiyyah stated: "And it is possible for men to marry from the *jinn* and they can have offspring, and this is well known, and the scholars have mentioned it and disliked it..."[21]

Proof that the *Jinn* exist:

We have already mentioned that from the integral parts of the *ʿaqīdah* is belief in the unseen, from that which has been established in the Qur'ān and authentic *Sunnah*, and from that which has been mentioned from the unseen is the *jinn*, and here are some of those texts proving their existence:

Firstly, from the Qur'ān:

1.

يَٰمَعۡشَرَ ٱلۡجِنِّ وَٱلۡإِنسِ أَلَمۡ يَأۡتِكُمۡ رُسُلٞ مِّنكُمۡ يَقُصُّونَ
عَلَيۡكُمۡ ءَايَٰتِي وَيُنذِرُونَكُمۡ لِقَآءَ يَوۡمِكُمۡ هَٰذَاۚ قَالُواْ
شَهِدۡنَا عَلَىٰٓ أَنفُسِنَاۖ وَغَرَّتۡهُمُ ٱلۡحَيَوٰةُ ٱلدُّنۡيَا وَشَهِدُواْ عَلَىٰٓ
أَنفُسِهِمۡ أَنَّهُمۡ كَانُواْ كَٰفِرِينَ ١٣٠

O you assembly of jinn and mankind! Did not there come to you Messengers from amongst you, reciting unto you My verses and warning you of the meeting of this Day of yours? They will say: We bear witness against ourselves. It was the life of this

---

[20] Shaykh Ibn Bāz said: This is the only correct opinion for many reasons.

[21] *Majmūʿ Fatāwā*, vol. 3, p. 39.

world that deceived them. And they will bear witness against themselves that they were disbelievers.

Sūrah al-Anʿām, verse 130

2.

وَلَٰكِنْ حَقَّ ٱلْقَوْلُ مِنِّى لَأَمْلَأَنَّ جَهَنَّمَ مِنَ ٱلْجِنَّةِ
وَٱلنَّاسِ أَجْمَعِينَ ﴿١٣﴾

But the Word from Me took effect (about evil-doers), that I will fill Hell with jinn and mankind together.

Sūrah al-Sajdah, verse 13

3.

وَٱلْجَآنَّ خَلَقْنَٰهُ مِن قَبْلُ مِن نَّارِ ٱلسَّمُومِ ﴿٢٧﴾

And the jinn, we created aforetime from the smokeless flame of fire.

Sūrah al-Ḥijr, verse 27

4.

وَمَا خَلَقْتُ ٱلْجِنَّ وَٱلْإِنسَ إِلَّا لِيَعْبُدُونِ ﴿٥٦﴾

And I (Allāh) created not the jinn and mankind except that they should worship Me (Alone).

Sūrah al-Dhāriyāt, verse 56

5.

يَٰمَعْشَرَ ٱلْجِنِّ وَٱلْإِنسِ إِنِ ٱسْتَطَعْتُمْ أَن تَنفُذُوا۟ مِنْ أَقْطَارِ
ٱلسَّمَٰوَٰتِ وَٱلْأَرْضِ فَٱنفُذُوا۟ ۚ لَا تَنفُذُونَ إِلَّا بِسُلْطَٰنٍ ﴿٣٣﴾

O assembly of jinn and men! If you have power to pass beyond the zones of the heavens and the earth, then pass beyond (them)! But you will never be able to pass them, except with authority (from Allāh)!

Sūrah al-Raḥmān, verse 33

6.

قُلْ أُوحِيَ إِلَيَّ أَنَّهُ اسْتَمَعَ نَفَرٌ مِّنَ الْجِنِّ فَقَالُوا إِنَّا
سَمِعْنَا قُرْآنًا عَجَبًا ﴿١﴾

Say (O Muḥammad): "It has been revealed to me that a group (from three to ten in number) of jinn listened (to this Qur'ān). They said: Verily we have heard a wonderful Recitation (this Qur'ān)!

Sūrah Jinn, verse 1

These and other verses clearly mention the *jinn* and certain aspects concerning them. The Qur'ān does not mention something which does not exist even if we are unable to see it, for verily with Allāh is the most perfect wisdom.

Secondly, from the Sunnah:

1. The *ḥadīth* of ʿAbdullāh ibn Masʿūd (ؓ): "*We were with the Prophet (ﷺ) one night, and we lost sight of him, so we searched for him in the valleys and mountain passes. We thought he had been kidnapped and spent the worst night a (group of) people can spend. The following morning he returned, and we said to him: 'O Messenger of Allāh, we lost sight of you, then began to search for you but could not find you, and ended up spending the worst night a (group of) people can spend.' He (ﷺ) replied: 'A caller from the jinn came to me, so I went with him and recited the Qur'ān to them.' Ibn Masʿūd continued: So he took us and showed us the traces and signs of them and their fire. They had asked him for provisions, so he said: 'For every bone over which the name of Allāh is mentioned, it will be for you the most plentiful of meat, likewise the droppings of animals for your animals.' He (ﷺ) said: 'Do not clean yourselves with them, for they are food for your brothers.'*"[22]

---

[22] *Ṣaḥīḥ Muslim bi Sharḥ al-Nawawī*, vol. 4, p. 170.

2. The *ḥadīth* of ʿĀ'ishah that the Prophet (ﷺ) said: *"The angels were created from light, and the jinn from a smokeless flame of fire and Adam was created from that which has been described to you."*[23]

Thirdly, from the intellect:

Our intellect does not prevent us from accepting an unseen world, for there are many things in this universe which are unseen to man, but their presence is felt. Just because one is unable to see them it does not imply that they do not exist.[24]

Muḥammad Rashīd Riḍā said: "...and were the invisibility of matters a sufficient evidence for their absence, one would not search in this world for those matters which were unknown, nor would micro bites - which have allowed medicine and surgery to reach modern levels - have been discovered..."[25]

It is a mistake in western and other civilisations to only believe in intellect and reject all else. How many Muslims have fallen into dangerous beliefs when they have changed the Holy texts with their own intellect, thus falling into dangerous traps which almost remove them from Islām.

The Dwellings of the *Jinn* and where they are Found:

Some people believe that the *jinn* live underground, but what is correct is that they live on the face of the earth. They have many places of dwelling, however they are most commonly found in the following places:

---

[23] *Ṣaḥīḥ Muslim bi Sharḥ al-Nawawī*, vol. 18, p. 123.

[24] *ʿĀlam al-Jinn fī Ḍaw' al-Kitāb wal-Sunnah*, pp. 82-83.

[25] *Tafsīr al-Manār*, vol. 8, p. 366.

1. Valleys, mountain passes, wildernesses and deserts - we have already mentioned the *ḥadīth* of Ibn Mas'ūd, and how the Prophet (ﷺ) met the *jinn* in these kinds of places and preached Islām to them.

2. Rubbish heaps, bins and places where food is generally found.

3. Toilets - due to the *ḥadīth* of Zayd ibn Arqam, in which the Prophet (ﷺ) said: "*Verily these spaces are occupied, so when one of you wants to relieve himself then let him say: O Allāh, I seek refuge in You from all evil and evil-doers.*"[26]

4. Caves, cleaves and burrows - for it is narrated that the Prophet (ﷺ) said: "*Do not urinate into a burrow.*" Qatādah was asked: "Why is it disliked to urinate into a burrow?" He replied: "It is said they are the dwellings of the *jinn*."[27]

5. In people's houses - these *jinn* are referred to as "*'āmir*'. The evidence for this is the story of the young man who found a *jinnī* in his house in the form of a snake. The Prophet (ﷺ) said: "*Indeed in Madīnah there are a number of jinn who have accepted Islām, so whoever sees one of these 'āmirs then let him ask it to leave thrice. If it appears to him after this then let him kill it, for verily it is a devil (shayṭān).*"[28]

6. Camel pens - this is reported in the *ḥadīth* of Abū Hurairah (ﷺ) that the Prophet (ﷺ) said: "*Pray in sheep pens but do not pray in camel pens.*"[29] Another narration states "*...for verily they (i.e. the camels) have been created from the shayāṭīn.*"[30]

---

[26] Authentic, collected by Abū Dāwūd, no. 60.

[27] Authentic, collected by al-Nasā'ī, see *Mukhtaṣar al-Targhīb wa al-Tarhīb*, p. 62.

[28] *Sahih Muslim*, vol. 2, p. 1757.

[29] Authentic, collected by Tirmidhī, authenticated by al-Albānī, *Irwā' al-Ghalīl*, vol. 1, p. 194.

[30] Authentic, collected by Aḥmad, authenticated by al-Albānī, *Irwā' al-Ghalīl*, vol. 1, p. 164

7. Abandoned places.

8. Graveyards.

Ibn Taymiyyah stated: "...and this is why they are commonly found in ruins, wildernesses, and in places of filth such as toilets, and where rubbish is found. This is why those who co-operate with the *shayāṭīn* increasingly go to these places which are the shelters of the *shayāṭīn*."[31]

9. Market places - this is because sins such as lying, cheating, women uncovering etc. are common in these places. For this reason, the Prophet (ﷺ) advised Salmān (رضي الله عنه): "*If you are able, do not be the first to enter the market, nor the last to leave it for verily it is the battlefield of shayṭān and in it his flag is raised.*"[32]

Times when the *Jinn* Spread

On the authority of Jābir (رضي الله عنه), the Prophet (ﷺ) said: "*When it is the beginning of the night, withhold your children for indeed it is during this time the shayāṭīn disperse, so when a portion of the night passes then leave them, close the doors and mention the name of Allāh, for indeed shayṭān cannot open a closed door. Tie the mouth of your water-skins and mention the name of Allāh, and cover your vessels and mention the name of Allāh. Cover them even by placing something across it, and extinguish your lights.*"[33]

Another narration states: "*Do not send your cattle and your children out once the sun has set until the blackness of the evening disappears, for indeed the shayāṭīn spread once the sun has set until the blackness of the evening disappears.*"[34]

---

[31] *Majmū' Fatāwā*, vol. 19, pp. 40-41.

[32] Collected by Muslim.

[33] *Sahih al-Bukhari* 5623 and *Sahih Muslim* 2012.

[34] *Sahih Muslim* 2013.

These are the places in which the *jinn* dwell, and the times in which they spread, so if a person passes by any of these places or comes across one of these times then he should protect himself by reciting the appropriate *du'ās*. These will be mentioned soon *Inshā Allāh*.

Chapter 2

Protective Shields

Indeed, people are very keen and eager to protect and preserve themselves from the many calamities and problems of life, whether it is disease, fire or accidents. The *sharīʿah* does not disallow this; rather the *sharīʿah* has come to preserve the five essential necessities: religion, life, intellect, honour and wealth.

However, the major problem today is that even though people have followed the means to protect themselves with regards to material things, they have become negligent of protecting themselves from that Day when they will be called to answer for their deeds. Allāh says:

فَكَيْفَ تَتَّقُونَ إِن كَفَرْتُمْ يَوْمًا يَجْعَلُ ٱلْوِلْدَٰنَ شِيبًا ﴿١٧﴾

Then how can you avoid the punishment, if you disbelieve, on a Day (i.e. the Day of Resurrection) that will make the children grey-headed?

Sūrah al-Muzzammil, verse 17

So it is obligatory upon the Muslim to take the necessary steps to protect himself on that Day. This is achieved by believing in Allāh and being upright upon His obedience and performing righteous actions. Allāh says:

يَٰٓأَيُّهَا ٱلَّذِينَ ءَامَنُواْ هَلْ أَدُلُّكُمْ
عَلَىٰ تِجَٰرَةٍ تُنجِيكُم مِّنْ عَذَابٍ أَلِيمٍ ﴿١٠﴾ تُؤْمِنُونَ بِٱللَّهِ وَرَسُولِهِۦ وَتُجَٰهِدُونَ
فِي سَبِيلِ ٱللَّهِ بِأَمْوَٰلِكُمْ وَأَنفُسِكُمْ ذَٰلِكُمْ خَيْرٌ لَّكُمْ إِن كُنتُمْ تَعْلَمُونَ ﴿١١﴾

O you who believe! Shall I guide you to a trade that will save you from a painful torment? That you believe in Allāh and His Messenger, and that you strive hard and fight in the Cause of Allāh with your wealth and your lives: that will be better for you, if you but know!

Sūrah al-Ṣaff, verses 10-11

إِنَّ ٱلَّذِينَ قَالُواْ رَبُّنَا ٱللَّهُ ثُمَّ ٱسْتَقَٰمُواْ تَتَنَزَّلُ عَلَيْهِمُ
ٱلْمَلَٰٓئِكَةُ أَلَّا تَخَافُواْ وَلَا تَحْزَنُواْ وَأَبْشِرُواْ بِٱلْجَنَّةِ
ٱلَّتِي كُنتُمْ تُوعَدُونَ ﴿٣٠﴾

Verily those who say: "Our Lord is Allāh (Alone)," and they stand firm, on them the angels will descend (at the time of their death) (saying): "Fear not, nor grieve! But receive the glad tidings of Paradise which you have been promised!

Sūrah Fuṣṣilat, verse 30

مَنْ عَمِلَ صَٰلِحًا مِّن ذَكَرٍ أَوْ أُنثَىٰ وَهُوَ مُؤْمِنٌ فَلَنُحْيِيَنَّهُۥ
حَيَوٰةً طَيِّبَةً وَلَنَجْزِيَنَّهُمْ أَجْرَهُم بِأَحْسَنِ مَا كَانُواْ
يَعْمَلُونَ ﴿٩٧﴾

Whoever works righteousness –whether male or female- while he (or she) is a true believer verily, to him We will give a good life, and We shall pay them certainly a reward in proportion to the best of what they used to do.

Sūrah al-Naḥl, verse 97

So if a person takes the necessary steps to protect himself on the Day of Accounting, then there is no harm in seeking protection from the evils of this world. One of the main reasons behind these evils is sins, for sins are the cause of all evil in this world and the Hereafter, as Ibn al-Qayyim said: "Is there an evil or illness in this life or the Hereafter except that the reason for it is sin?"[35]

The means of protecting oneself from the worldly evils are of two types:

1. Materialistic means.
2. Divine means.

That which concerns us here is the second category, as it is the beneficial one Inshā Allāh. For indeed, the *Sunnah* has mentioned the cure for all illnesses, but people neglect this, and were the Muslim to pay heed to them and ensure his family paid attention to them then they would be safe from all evil by the will of Allāh.

Everything which has been mentioned in the *Sunnah* as being beneficial for a certain illness is without doubt beneficial even if the afflicted doubts its benefit due to personal experience. The reason for this maybe himself, as the Prophet (ﷺ) said: "*Allāh has spoken the truth, and the stomach of you brother has lied.*"[36]

From our own experience, we have found that most people who are afflicted [with illnesses] have been negligent of these *du'ās* which are a fortress by the will of Allāh against all apparent and hidden evils.

---

[35] *Al-Jawāb al-Kāfī*, p. 46.

[36] Collected by al-Bukhārī.

Ways of Repelling Evil before it Befalls, and Driving it Away after it Befalls

They are as follows:

1. Attaining sincere *Tawḥīd*, which is of three types:

Firstly: *Tawḥīd al-Rubūbiyyah* (the Oneness of Allāh's Lordship) - this is to know and accept that Allāh is the Lord and Master of all that exists, so this universe with its heavens, earth, planets, stars, animals, trees, land, sea, *jinn*, angels and humans all submit to the will of Allāh, as He says:

وَلَهُۥٓ أَسْلَمَ مَن فِى ٱلسَّمَٰوَٰتِ وَٱلْأَرْضِ
طَوْعًا وَكَرْهًا

...while to Him submitted all creatures in the heavens and the earth, willingly or unwillingly. And to Him they shall all be returned.

Sūrah Āl-ʿImrān, verse 83

When the slave realises that everything which takes place; all good that comes or evil that befalls, is by the will and permission of Allāh, he will make *duʿā* to Allāh in every situation. Allāh says:

وَإِن يَمْسَسْكَ ٱللَّهُ بِضُرٍّ فَلَا كَاشِفَ لَهُۥٓ إِلَّا هُوَ ۖ وَإِن
يُرِدْكَ بِخَيْرٍ فَلَا رَآدَّ لِفَضْلِهِۦ ۚ يُصِيبُ بِهِۦ مَن يَشَآءُ مِنْ عِبَادِهِۦ ۚ
وَهُوَ ٱلْغَفُورُ ٱلرَّحِيمُ ﴿١٠٧﴾

And if Allāh touches you with harm, there is none who can remove it but He, and if He intends any good for you, there is none who can repel His favour which He causes it to reach whomsoever of His slaves He wills. And He is the Oft-Forgiving, the Most Merciful.

Sūrah Yūnus, verse 107

Secondly: *Tawḥīd al-Ulūhiyyah* (the Oneness of Allāh's Worship) – this is to sincerely worship Allāh alone, without any partner. This relates to the sayings and actions of the slave, whether apparent or hidden.[37] This category of *tawḥid* was the first thing that all the Prophets called to, as Allāh says:

وَلَقَدْ بَعَثْنَا فِي كُلِّ أُمَّةٍ رَّسُولًا أَنِ اعْبُدُوا اللَّهَ وَاجْتَنِبُوا الطَّاغُوتَ

And verily, We have sent among every Ummah (nation) a Messenger (proclaiming): "Worship Allāh (Alone), and avoid Ṭāhgūt (all false deities).

Sūrah al-Naḥl, verse 36

The slave does not become a *muwaḥḥid* (monotheist) unless he testifies that none has the right to be worshipped except Allāh alone, acknowledges that He alone deserves all types of worship, and associates no other partners with Him. Allāh says:

وَمَا خَلَقْتُ الْجِنَّ وَالْإِنسَ إِلَّا لِيَعْبُدُونِ ﴿٥٦﴾

And I (Allāh) created not the jinn and mankind except that they should worship Me (Alone).

Sūrah al-Dhāriyāt, verse 56

This category of *tawḥīd* necessitates that the slave make all his *du'ā*, sacrifice, oaths, his hope, fear and trust for Allāh alone, because making any act of worship for other than Allāh is *shirk* (polytheism). Examples of acts which consist of shirk include the one who sacrifices to the *jinn*, or takes an oath by them, and likewise the one who places his trust in a magician or fortune teller.

Thirdly: *Tawḥīd al-Asmā wal-Ṣifāt* (the Oneness of Allāh in His Names and Attributes) - this is to describe Allāh with that which He has described Himself with or His Prophet (ﷺ) has

---

[37] *Ḥāshiyah Kitāb al-Tawḥīd*, Ibn Qāsim, p. 11.

described Him with, from His most beautiful Names and most lofty Attributes, without comparison, distortion or change.[38] Allāh says:

لَيْسَ كَمِثْلِهِۦ شَىْءٌ ۖ وَهُوَ ٱلسَّمِيعُ ٱلْبَصِيرُ ﴿١١﴾

There is nothing like Him; and He is the All-Hearer, the All-Seer.

Sūrah al-Shūrā, verse 11

Hence, if the slave knows the Names and Attributes of his Lord, and their correct meanings, this will bring him closer to Allāh and will make him realise His Greatness. Consequently, this will cause him to humble himself in front of his Lord, to fear Him, to have hope in Him, and to call out to Him using these Names and Attributes. Allāh says:

وَلِلَّهِ ٱلْأَسْمَآءُ ٱلْحُسْنَىٰ فَٱدْعُوهُ بِهَا ۖ

And (all) the Most Beautiful Names belong to Allāh, so call on Him by them.

Sūrah al-A'rāf, verse 180

If one knows that Allāh is *al-Raḥmān* (the Most Gracious) and *al-Raḥīm* (the Oft- Forgiving) he will hope for His mercy and will make *du'ā* to Him just as Ayyūb (عليه السلام) did. Allāh mentions:

وَأَيُّوبَ إِذْ نَادَىٰ رَبَّهُۥٓ أَنِّى مَسَّنِىَ ٱلضُّرُّ
وَأَنتَ أَرْحَمُ ٱلرَّٰحِمِينَ ﴿٨٣﴾

And (remember) Ayyūb, when he cried to his Lord: "Verily, distress has seized me, and You are the Most Merciful of all those who show mercy.

Sūrah al-Anbiyā', verse 83

Attaining and realising the correct *tawḥīd* has a great impact on preventing evil and achieving good. Each of these three categories

---

[38] Ibid.

of *tawḥīd* are related to each other and cannot be separated, indeed the whole Qur'ān itself is *tawḥīd*.

2. Holding fast to the Qur'ān and *Sunnah*:

Allāh says:

وَأَنَّ هَٰذَا صِرَٰطِي مُسْتَقِيمًا فَٱتَّبِعُوهُ ۖ وَلَا تَتَّبِعُوا۟ ٱلسُّبُلَ
فَتَفَرَّقَ بِكُمْ عَن سَبِيلِهِۦ ۚ ذَٰلِكُمْ وَصَّىٰكُم بِهِۦ لَعَلَّكُمْ
تَتَّقُونَ ﴿١٥٣﴾

And verily, this is My Straight Path, so follow it, and follow not (other) paths, for they will separate you away from His Path. This He has ordained for you that you may become pious.
Sūrah al-An'ām, verse 153

Shaykh 'Abdul-Raḥmān al-Sa'dī said: "***(And verily, this is My Straight Path)*** refers to these rulings and their likes from that which Allāh has mentioned in His Book and clarified for His slaves. It is the path of Allāh which leads to Him and to His Paradise; the balanced and easy path, ***(so follow it)*** that you may achieve success and reach happiness. ***(And follow not (other) paths)*** refers to the paths contrary to this path, ***(for they will separate you away from His Path)*** by leading you astray and diverting you. If you stray from the Straight Path, then all other paths lead to the Fire. ***(This He has ordained for you that you may become pious)***, so if you remain firm upon that which Allāh has mentioned to you both in knowledge and action (i.e. in belief and practice), you will become from the pious and successful slaves of Allāh."

The straight path was mentioned in the singular tense and was described as being 'His path' because there is only one path which leads to Him.

3. Fear of Allāh:

Allāh says:

وَمَن يَتَّقِ ٱللَّهَ يَجْعَل لَّهُۥ مَخْرَجًا ﴿٢﴾

And whosoever fears Allāh and keeps his duty to Him, He will make a way for him to get out (from every difficulty).

Sūrah al-Ṭalāq, verse 2

And Allāh says:

وَرَحْمَتِي وَسِعَتْ كُلَّ شَيْءٍ ۚ فَسَأَكْتُبُهَا لِلَّذِينَ
يَتَّقُونَ وَيُؤْتُونَ ٱلزَّكَوٰةَ وَٱلَّذِينَ هُم بِـَٔايَٰتِنَا
يُؤْمِنُونَ ﴿١٥٦﴾

...and My mercy embraces all things. That (mercy) I shall ordain for those who are the pious, and give Zakāt, and those who believe in Our Āyāt (proofs, evidences, signs etc.)

Sūrah al-A'rāf, verse 156

He also says:

وَنَجَّيْنَا ٱلَّذِينَ ءَامَنُوا۟ وَكَانُوا۟ يَتَّقُونَ ﴿١٨﴾

And We saved those who believed and used to fear Allāh, keep their duty to Him and avoid evil.

Sūrah Fuṣṣilat, verse 18

Fearing Allāh then, has a direct impact on solving difficulties and preventing evil. The more the slave fears Allāh and is conscious of Him in open and secret the more likely he is to receive the protection of Allāh in the removal of these evils.

4. Trusting in Allāh and relying upon Him:

Allāh says:

وَمَن يَتَوَكَّلْ عَلَى ٱللَّهِ فَهُوَ حَسْبُهُۥٓ

And whosoever puts his trust in Allāh, then He will suffice him.
Sūrah al-Ṭalāq, verse 3

He also says:

وَأُفَوِّضُ أَمْرِىٓ إِلَى ٱللَّهِ ۚ إِنَّ ٱللَّهَ بَصِيرٌۢ بِٱلْعِبَادِ ﴿٤٤﴾

...and my affair I leave it to Allāh. Verily, Allāh is the All-Seer of (His) slaves.
Sūrah Ghāfir, verse 44

Ibn ʿAbbās (ﷺ) said:

(حَسْبُنَا اللهُ وَنِعْمَ الْوَكِيلُ)

"***'Allāh is sufficient for us, and He is the Best Disposer of affairs'*** was said by Ibrāhīm (ﷺ) when he was thrown in the fire, and it was said by Muḥammad (ﷺ) when it was said to him: ***'Verily the people have gathered against you, therefore, fear them'***"[39]

5. Sincerely turning to Allāh, repenting to Him, leaving all sins and returning the rights and belongings of people back to them:

Allāh says:

وَمَآ أَصَٰبَكُم مِّن مُّصِيبَةٍ فَبِمَا كَسَبَتْ أَيْدِيكُمْ
وَيَعْفُواْ عَن كَثِيرٍ ﴿٣٠﴾

And whatever of misfortune befalls you, it is because of what your hands have earned. And He pardons much.
Sūrah al-Shūrā, verse 30

[39] *Sahih al-Bukhari*, vol. 7, p. 172.

Much of the evil that befalls is as a result of sins and oppressing others, so repenting from one's sins and leaving them, as well as returning people's rights back to them all assist in removing calamities by the will of Allāh. Allāh says:[40]

وَمَن يَتَّقِ ٱللَّهَ يَجۡعَل لَّهُۥ مِنۡ أَمۡرِهِۦ يُسۡرٗا ﴿٤﴾

And whosoever fears Allāh and keeps his duty to Him, He will make his matter easy for him.

Sūrah al-Ṭalāq, verse 4

And He says:

وَمَن يَتَّقِ ٱللَّهَ يَجۡعَل لَّهُۥ مَخۡرَجٗا ﴿٢﴾

And whosoever fears Allāh and keeps his duty to Him, He will make a way for him to get out (from every difficulty).

Sūrah al-Ṭalāq, verse 2

He also says:

وَتُوبُوٓاْ إِلَى ٱللَّهِ جَمِيعًا أَيُّهَ ٱلۡمُؤۡمِنُونَ لَعَلَّكُمۡ
تُفۡلِحُونَ ﴿٣١﴾

And all of you beg Allāh to forgive you all, O believers, that you may be successful.

Sūrah al-Nūr, verse 31

6. Constantly remembering Allāh

This path is the advice of the leader of mankind (ﷺ). Whosoever remembers Allāh, Allāh will protect him from every evil and bad thing; His remembrance is attained by following His orders and refraining from His prohibitions. Allāh is the Creator and He is the One who has the ability to protect, as He says:

[40] This verse was added by Shaykh Ibn Bāz, in support of what we have mentioned.

فَٱللَّهُ خَيْرٌ حَٰفِظًا وَهُوَ أَرْحَمُ ٱلرَّٰحِمِينَ ﴿٦٤﴾

But Allāh is the Best to guard, and He is the Most Merciful of those who show mercy.

Sūrah Yūsuf, verse 64

Ibn 'Abbās (ﷺ) narrated: "*I was behind the Prophet (ﷺ) and he said: 'O boy! Indeed I will teach you some words: preserve Allāh and He will preserve you, preserve Allāh and you will find Him wherever you turn. If you ask then ask of Allāh, and if you seek assistance then seek Allāh's assistance, and know that if the whole of mankind was to gather to benefit you in something, they would not benefit you except in that which has already been written for you, and were they to gather to harm you, they would not harm you except in that which has already been written against you. The pens have been lifted and the pages have dried.*'"[41]

7. Righteous actions and seeking to come closer to Allāh by them (*tawassul*):

Allāh says:

مَنْ عَمِلَ صَٰلِحًا مِّن ذَكَرٍ أَوْ أُنثَىٰ وَهُوَ مُؤْمِنٌ فَلَنُحْيِيَنَّهُۥ حَيَوٰةً طَيِّبَةً وَلَنَجْزِيَنَّهُمْ أَجْرَهُم بِأَحْسَنِ مَا كَانُوا۟ يَعْمَلُونَ ﴿٩٧﴾

Whoever works righteousness –whether male or female- while he (or she) is a true believer verily, to him We will give a good life, and We shall pay them certainly a reward in proportion to the best of what they used to do.

Sūrah al-Naḥl, verse 97

In the story of the three who sought refuge in the cave, there is evidence to show the merit of righteous actions and how one can

---

[41] Authentic, collected by al-Tirmidhī.

seek to come closer to Allāh by them. When the boulder fell onto the mouth of the cave and trapped the three men, they sought to come closer to Allāh using their righteous actions, and each one of them said: "*O Allāh if I performed this action for Your sake then relieve us from our situation.*"[42]

8. Remaining upright upon the religion of Allāh:

Allāh says:

إِنَّ ٱلَّذِينَ قَالُوا۟ رَبُّنَا ٱللَّهُ ثُمَّ ٱسْتَقَـٰمُوا۟ تَتَنَزَّلُ عَلَيْهِمُ
ٱلْمَلَـٰٓئِكَةُ أَلَّا تَخَافُوا۟ وَلَا تَحْزَنُوا۟ وَأَبْشِرُوا۟ بِٱلْجَنَّةِ
ٱلَّتِى كُنتُمْ تُوعَدُونَ ﴿٣٠﴾ نَحْنُ أَوْلِيَآؤُكُمْ فِى ٱلْحَيَوٰةِ
ٱلدُّنْيَا وَفِى ٱلْـَٔاخِرَةِ ۖ وَلَكُمْ فِيهَا مَا تَشْتَهِىٓ أَنفُسُكُمْ
وَلَكُمْ فِيهَا مَا تَدَّعُونَ ﴿٣١﴾ نُزُلًا مِّنْ غَفُورٍ رَّحِيمٍ ﴿٣٢﴾

Verily, those who say: "Our Lord is Allāh (Alone)," and then they stand firm, on them the angels will descend (at the time of their death) (saying): "Fear not, nor grieve! But receive the glad tidings of Paradise which you have been promised! We have been your friends in the life of this world and are (so) in the Hereafter. Therein you shall have (all) that your inner-selves desire, and therein you shall have (all) for which you ask. An entertainment from (Allāh), the Oft-Forgiving, Most Merciful.

Sūrah Fuṣṣilat, verses 30-32

9. Preserving the five daily prayers and especially the *fajr* prayer:

Allāh says:

حَـٰفِظُوا۟ عَلَى ٱلصَّلَوَٰتِ وَٱلصَّلَوٰةِ ٱلْوُسْطَىٰ

Guard strictly the prayers especially the middle ('Asr) prayer.

Sūrah al-Baqarah, verse 238

---

[42] Collected by al-Bukhārī and Muslim, *Sahih Muslim*, no. 2743.

On the authority of Jundub ibn Sufyān (ﷺ) that the Prophet (ﷺ) said: "*Whosoever prays the morning (fajr) prayer then he is in the protection of Allāh. So see O son of Adam, let not anything summon you from the protection of Allāh.*"[43]

10. Spending in charity, doing good and helping others:

It has been reported that the Prophet (ﷺ) said: "*Verily charity in secret extinguishes the anger of Allāh, and prevents an evil death.*"[44] It is also reported that he (ﷺ) said: "*Hasten in giving in charity for indeed calamities do not pass it.*"[45] Furthermore, the Prophet (ﷺ) said: "*Hasten in giving charity for indeed calamities do not pass it, and it seals seventy doors of evil.*"[46]

So, from the means of preventing evil is to give to the poor and needy, for in this there is prevention. This is something which has been tried. However, it is the Muslim's responsibility to make his intention sincere and to ensure that he gives willingly. Also, in charity there is a cure for illnesses, as the Prophet (ﷺ) said: "*Cure your ill with charity.*"[47]

Also, doing good and benefiting others has an impact on preventing the befalling of calamities. It was also the advice of the Prophet (ﷺ): "*Whosoever from amongst you is able to benefit his brother then let him do so.*"[48]

The Prophet (ﷺ) said: "*The most beloved of people to Allāh are the most beneficial of them (to others). The most beloved of actions to Allāh is to make another Muslim happy, or to relieve*

---

[43] *Sahih Muslim*, vol. 1, p. 454.

[44] Authentic, collected by Ṭabarānī.

[45] Weak, collected by Ṭabarānī.

[46] *Majmaʿ al-Zawā'id*, vol. 3, p. 110.

[47] This *ḥadith* is *ḥasan* [sound], collected by Ṭabarānī, see *Ṣaḥīḥ al-Jāmiʿ*, vol. 3, p. 140, no. 3353.

[48] Collected by Muslim.

him of some difficulty, or to repay some debt he owes, or to repel his hunger. Helping my brother in some need of his is more beloved to me than spending a month in a mosque (worshipping). Whosoever withholds his anger, Allāh will screen his faults, and whosoever suppresses his rage whilst having the ability to act upon it, Allāh will fill his heart with pleasure on the Day of Judgement. Whosoever helps his brother in some need of his until it is settled, Allāh will make firm his foot on the Day feet will slip. Indeed evil character spoils actions just as vinegar spoils honey."[49]

Allāh says:

وَافْعَلُوا الْخَيْرَ لَعَلَّكُمْ تُفْلِحُونَ ۩ ﴿٧٧﴾

...and do good that you may be successful.
Sūrah al-Ḥajj, verse 77

11. The removal of pictures and statues from one's house:

Indeed, the angels do not enter a house in which there are pictures and statues, and a house in which there are no angels is a nesting place for the devils. This is mentioned in the *ḥadīth* of Abū Hurairah (رضي الله عنه) in which the Prophet (ﷺ) said: "*The angels do not enter a house in which there are pictures or statues.*"[50]

12. Continuously reciting certain chapters of the Qur'ān, certain verses and certain *du'ās* and *adhkār*:

In the remembrance of Allāh and reciting *adhkār* there is protection from evil by the will of Allāh. Allāh mentions concerning Yūnus (عليه السلام) when he was in the stomach of the whale:

---

[49] This *ḥadīth* is *ḥasan* (sound), as in *Ṣaḥīḥ al-Jāmi'*, vol. 1, p. 97.

[50] *Sahih Muslim*, no. 2112.

فَلَوۡلَآ أَنَّهُۥ كَانَ مِنَ ٱلۡمُسَبِّحِينَ ١٤٣ لَلَبِثَ فِي بَطۡنِهِۦٓ إِلَىٰ
يَوۡمِ يُبۡعَثُونَ ١٤٤

Had he not been of them who glorify Allāh. He would have indeed remained inside its belly (the fish) till the Day of Resurrection.

Sūrah al-Ṣāffāt, verses 143-144

Ibn al-Qayyim mentioned: "...and in the remembrance of Allāh there are some one hundred benefits; from them is that it repels *shayṭān* and represses him."[51] Allāh says:

وَمَن يَعۡشُ عَن ذِكۡرِ ٱلرَّحۡمَٰنِ نُقَيِّضۡ لَهُۥ شَيۡطَٰنٗا
فَهُوَ لَهُۥ قَرِينٞ ٣٦

And whosoever turns away blindly from the remembrance of the Most Gracious (Allāh), We appoint for him shayṭān to be a companion to him.

Sūrah al-Zukhruf, verse 36[52]

And Allāh says:

وَمَنۡ أَعۡرَضَ عَن ذِكۡرِي فَإِنَّ لَهُۥ مَعِيشَةٗ ضَنكٗا

But whosoever turns away from My Reminder verily, for him is a life of hardship.

Sūrah Ṭā-Hā, verse 124

Turning away from the remembrance of Allāh includes turning away from the remembrance which He revealed, i.e. the Qur'ān.[53] Allāh has mentioned in the Qur'ān and *Sunnah adhkār* which protect people not only from the evil of humans and *jinn*, but

---

[51] *Al-Wābil al-Ṣayyib wa Rāfiʿ al-Kalim al-Ṭayyib*, p. 91.

[52] This verse was added here by Shaykh Ibn Bāz, to supplement what we have mentioned.

[53] *Al-Wābil al-Ṣayyib wa Rāfiʿ al-Kalim al-Ṭayyib*, p. 102.

from all the evils of the world. We will now mention some of those *adhkār* which are beneficial *Inshā Allāh*.

CHAPTER 3

Sūrahs, Verses and *Adhkār* which Repel *Shayṭān*

1. *Sūrah al-Baqarah* repels *shayṭān* from the house:

Abū Hurairah (ﷺ) narrated that the Prophet (ﷺ) said: *"Do not turn your houses into graveyards, for verily shayṭān flees from the house in which Sūrah al-Baqarah is recited."*[54]

On the authority of Abū Umāmah (ﷺ), the Prophet (ﷺ) said: *"Recite the Qur'ān for verily it will come on the Day of Judgement as an intercessor for its reciters; recite the two flowers al-Baqarah and Āl-ʿImrān, for they will come on the Day of Judgement as though they are two clouds, or shade or two flocks of birds stretching their wings in the air, pleading for those who recite them. Recite Sūrah al-Baqarah, for to take it is a blessing, and to give it up is a cause of grief, and the magicians cannot confront it."*[55]

---

[54] *Sahih Muslim*, vol. 1, p. 539, no. 780.

[55] Ibid, vol. 1, p. 553, no. 804.

2. The merits of reciting *Āyat al-Kursī* before sleeping:

Abū Hurairah (⬥) said: *"The Prophet (⬥) deputised me in the safeguarding of the charity of Ramaḍān, so someone came to me and continued to urge me for some food, so I took him and said: 'By Allāh, I will hand you over to the Prophet (⬥)'"* ...the story continues... *"until the man who urged me for food said: 'Before you sleep recite Āyat al-Kursī, for if you do so a guardian from Allāh will remain with you until the morning, and no devil will approach you.' The Prophet (⬥) said: 'He has told the truth even though he is a liar.'"*[56]

3. Reciting the last two verses of *Sūrah al-Baqarah* prevents evil and harm:

The Prophet (⬥) said: *"Whosoever recites the last two verses of Sūrah al-Baqarah at night, it will be sufficient for him from the evil of all that harms."*[57]

Shaykh Ibn Bāz said: "And the meaning - and Allāh knows best - is that they protect him from every evil", and Ibn al-Qayyim said: "What is correct is that they protect him from the evil that harms him."[58]

4. Reciting *Sūrah al-Ikhlāṣ* and the last two *Sūrahs* of the Qur'ān prevents evil and harm:

On the authority of 'Abdullāh ibn Khubayb who said: *"We came out on a very dark and rainy night in search of the Prophet (⬥) so he could lead us in prayer. He said: 'Say.' I said nothing, then he said: 'Say He is Allāh the One (Sūrah al-Ikhlāṣ) and the muʿawwidhatayn (Sūrahs al-Falaq and al-Nās) thrice in the*

---

[56] *Fatḥ al-Bārī: Sharḥ Ṣaḥīḥ al-Bukhārī*, vol. 8, p. 672.

[57] *Sahih al-Bukhari*, vol. 9, p. 94 and *Sahih Muslim*, vol. 1, p. 555, no. 255.

[58] We would like to point out that we began with the statement of Shaykh Ibn Bāz only as it is more general, even though the shaykh requested we place Ibn al-Qayyim's statement before his.

morning and evening. It will protect you from everything.'"[59]

Shaykh Ibn Bāz said: "One should recite these three *Sūrahs* three times at the beginning of the day after *Fajr* prayer and at the beginning of the night after *Maghrib* prayer."[60]

5. To read at the beginning and end of each day three times:

بِسْمِ اللهِ الَّذِي لَا يَضُرُّ مَعَ اسْمِهِ شَيْءٌ فِي الْأَرْضِ وَلَا فِي السَّمَاءِ وَهُوَ السَّمِيعُ الْعَلِيمُ

In the Name of Allāh with whose Name nothing harms on the earth or in the heavens, and He is All-Hearing and All-Knowing.

On the authority of 'Uthmān (ؓ), the Prophet (ﷺ) said: "*There is no servant who says 'In the Name of Allāh with whose Name nothing harms on the earth or in the heavens, and He is All-Hearing and All-Knowing' three times at the beginning of every morning and at the end of every evening except that nothing will harm him.*"[61]

6. *Tasmiyah* (saying '*bismillāh*') in everything:

Abū Mulayḥ stated, "*A man informed me that he was riding behind the Prophet (ﷺ) when his camel stumbled so he said: 'May shaytān be cursed.' The Prophet (ﷺ) said, 'Do not say 'may shaytān be cursed' for if you say that he will feel proud until he becomes like a house. He will claim that it was his strength that overpowered it; rather, say 'Bismillāh' (In the name of Allāh), for if you say that he will be humiliated until he becomes like a fly.'*"[62]

---

[59] A *ḥasan* (sound) *ḥadīth*, collected by Abū Dāwūd and al-Tirmidhī, see *Ṣaḥīḥ Sunan Abū Dāwūd*, vol. 3, p. 182.

[60] *Risālah fī Ḥukm al-Siḥr wal-Kahānah*, p. 35.

[61] *Sunan Abu Dawud*, no. 5088, and *Sunan al-Tirmidhi*, no. 3385. Authenticated by Shaykh Ibn Bāz.

[62] *Sunan Abu Dawud*, no. 4982, authenticated by Shaykh Ibn Bāz.

When we recited on people who had been possessed and spoke to the *jinn* and asked the reason for their entering the possessed, they would reply that he threw a stone and did not say '*bismillāh*' or did such and such and did not say '*bismillāh*'. So, the Muslim should be conscious of this and say '*bismillāh*' whenever he does something like opening a door or throwing something and so on.

Specific Ways to Protect Oneself from the *Jinn* and *Shayāṭīn*

1. To seek refuge in Allāh from *shayṭān*:

Allāh says:

وَإِمَّا يَنزَغَنَّكَ مِنَ ٱلشَّيْطَٰنِ نَزْغٌ فَٱسْتَعِذْ بِٱللَّهِ إِنَّهُۥ
هُوَ ٱلسَّمِيعُ ٱلْعَلِيمُ ﴿٣٦﴾

And if an evil whisper from shayṭān tries to turn you away (O Muḥammad) (from doing good), then seek refuge in Allāh. Verily, He is the All-Hearer, the All-Knower.

Sūrah Fuṣṣilat, verse 36

And Allāh says:

فَإِذَا قَرَأْتَ ٱلْقُرْءَانَ فَٱسْتَعِذْ بِٱللَّهِ مِنَ ٱلشَّيْطَٰنِ ٱلرَّجِيمِ ﴿٩٨﴾
إِنَّهُۥ لَيْسَ لَهُۥ سُلْطَٰنٌ عَلَى ٱلَّذِينَ ءَامَنُوا۟ وَعَلَىٰ رَبِّهِمْ
يَتَوَكَّلُونَ ﴿٩٩﴾ إِنَّمَا سُلْطَٰنُهُۥ عَلَى ٱلَّذِينَ يَتَوَلَّوْنَهُۥ
وَٱلَّذِينَ هُم بِهِۦ مُشْرِكُونَ

So when you want to recite the Qur'ān, seek refuge with Allāh from shayṭān the outcast. Verily! He has no power over those who believe and put their trust only in their Lord. His power is only over those who obey and follow him, and those who join partners with Him (Allāh).

Sūrah al-Naḥl, verses 98-100

2. To seek refuge in the complete words of Allāh every time one descends from a place:

Khawlah bint Ḥakīm narrated that she heard the Prophet (ﷺ) say: "*Whoever descends in a place and says:*

أَعُوذُ بِكَلِمَاتِ اللهِ التَّامَّاتِ مِنْ شَرِّ مَا خَلَقَ

I seek refuge in the complete Words of Allāh from the evil of that which He has created

will not be harmed by anything until he leaves that place."[63]

Abū Hurairah (ﷺ) narrated that a man came to the Prophet (ﷺ) and said: "*O Messenger of Allāh, I have suffered greatly from a scorpion which stung me last night, so the Prophet (ﷺ) said: 'You should have said in the evening, I seek refuge in the complete words of Allāh from the evil which He has created.'*"[64]

Shaykh Ibn Bāz said: "'*Bismillāh*' should be said in the day and in the night, when a person enters a place or a building. It should be said in the desert, in the air and on sea."[65] We have already mentioned that the *jinn* dwell in the deserts, wildernesses and in valleys so the Muslim should recite these *duʿās* when he passes by these places.

3. To seek refuge in the Words of Allāh whenever one is frightened:

On the authority of ʿAmr ibn Shuʿayb, on his father, on his grandfather that the Prophet (ﷺ) used to teach them to say when they were frightened:

أَعُوذُ بِكَلِمَاتِ اللهِ التَّامَّةِ مِنْ غَضَبِهِ وَشَرِّ عِبَادِهِ وَمِنْ هَمَزَاتِ الشَّيَاطِينِ وَأَنْ يَحْضُرُونِ

---

[63] *Sahih Muslim*, vol. 4, p. 2080, no. 2728.

[64] *Sahih Muslim*, vol. 3, p. 2081.

[65] *Risālah fī Ḥukm al-Siḥr wal-Kahanah*, pp. 6-8.

"I seek refuge in the complete Words of Allāh from His anger, the evil of His slaves and from the whisperings of the shayāṭīn, and that they should come near me."[66]

Allāh says:

وَقُل رَّبِّ أَعُوذُ بِكَ مِنْ هَمَزَٰتِ ٱلشَّيَٰطِينِ ﴿٩٧﴾ وَأَعُوذُ بِكَ رَبِّ أَن يَحْضُرُونِ ﴿٩٨﴾

And say: "My Lord! I seek refuge with You from the whisperings of the shayāṭīn (devils). And I seek refuge with You, My Lord! Lest they should come near me."
Sūrah al-Mu'minūn, verses 97-98

The reason for this is that when a person is frightened, his heart becomes weak and *shayṭān* gains strength over him and is able to enter him. For this reason, it is recommended to seek refuge from them in this situation.

4. To say a hundred times a day:

لَا إِلَهَ إِلَّا اللهُ وَحْدَهُ لَا شَرِيكَ لَه، لَهُ الْمُلْكُ وَلَهُ الْحَمْدُ وَهُوَ عَلَى كُلِّ شَيْءٍ قَدِيرٌ

None has the right to be worshipped but Allāh Alone, He has no partner, for Him is the dominion and for Him is all Praise, and He is Able to do all things.

It has been authentically reported that the Prophet (ﷺ) said: *"Whoever says 'None has the right to be worshipped but Allāh Alone, He has no partner, for Him is the dominion and for Him is all Praise, and He is Able to do all things', a hundred times, will have the reward of freeing ten slaves, one hundred good deeds will be written for him, and a hundred bad deeds will be wiped away. It will be a protection from shayṭān for that day until the evening, and no-one will have come with better than him except one who does more than this. Whoever says 'Glorified is Allāh,*

[66] *Sunan Abu Dawud*, no. 3893, and *Sunan al-Tirmidhī*, no. 3519.

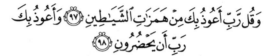

and all Praise be to Him' a hundred times a day will have his sins wiped away, even if they are like the froth of the sea."[67]

5. That which repels *shayṭān* when entering the house:

Jābir (رضي الله عنه) reported that he heard the Prophet (ﷺ) say: *"If a person remembers Allāh when he enters his house and when he eats, shayṭān will say (to the devils), 'There is neither dinner nor a place to sleep for you.' If one enters and does not mention Allāh, shayṭān says: 'You have found a place for the night,' and if one does not mention Allāh when he eats, shayṭān says, 'You have found a place to sleep and dinner.'"*[68]

6. That which repels *shayṭān* when leaving the house:

On the authority of Anas (رضي الله عنه) that the Prophet (ﷺ) said: *"Whoever says – meaning when he leaves his house –*

بِسْمِ اللهِ تَوَكَّلْتُ عَلَى اللهِ وَلَا حَوْلَ وَلَا قُوَّةَ إِلَّا بِاللهِ

'In the name of Allāh, I trust in Allāh, and there is neither power nor might except with Allāh,' It will be said to him: it is sufficient (as protection for you) and you have been guided, and shayṭān will leave him."[69]

7. That which repels *shayṭān* when having marital relations:

Ibn ʿAbbās (رضي الله عنه) narrated that the Prophet (ﷺ) said: *"When one of you approaches his family (for relations), he should say:*

بِسْمِ اللهِ اللَّهُمَّ جَنِّبْنَا الشَّيْطَانَ وَجَنِّبِ الشَّيْطَانَ مَا رَزَقْتَنَا

'In the name of Allāh, O Allāh, keep the devil away from us and keep the devil away from what you have blessed us with.' If a

---

[67] *Sahih al-Bukhari*, vol. 2, p. 442, no. 293, and *Sahih Muslim*, vol. 4, p. 2071, no. 2691.

[68] *Sahih Muslim*, vol. 3, p. 1598, no. 2018.

[69] Authentic, collected by Abū Dāwūd and al-Tirmidhī, see *Ṣaḥīḥ Sunan al-Tirmidhī*, vol. 3, p. 151.

child has been decreed for them shayṭān will never harm it."[70]

8. The supplication for entering the toilet:

Anas (ﷺ) narrated that the Prophet (ﷺ) used to say when entering the toilet:

اَللَّهُمَّ إِنِّي أَعُوذُ بِكَ مِنَ الْخُبُثِ وَالْخَبَائِث

I seek refuge in Allāh from all evil and all evil doers.[71]

It has already been mentioned that the *jinn* dwell and are found in these types of places, so the Muslim should always remember this *duʿā.*[72]

9. Refraining from urinating in crevices, holes and burrows:

It is narrated that the Prophet (ﷺ) said: "*Do not urinate into a burrow*". Qatādah was asked: "Why is it disliked to urinate into a burrow?" He replied: "It is said they are the dwellings of the *jinn.*"[73]

10. That which repels *shayṭān* when angry:

On the authority of Sulaymān ibn Sard who said: "*Two men swore whilst in the presence of the Prophet (ﷺ) and whilst we were with him. One of them was swearing at the other and his face was red, so the Prophet (ﷺ) said: 'Indeed I know a statement, if he were to say it, he would be relieved from his anger. He should say: I seek refuge in Allāh from shayṭān the outcast.' It was said to the man: 'Do you not hear what the Prophet (ﷺ) said.' He replied: 'I am not mad.'*"[74]

---

[70] Collected by Bukhārī and Muslim, see *Sahih Muslim*, vol. 2, p. 1078, no. 1434.

[71] *Sahih al-Bukhari*, vol. 1, p. 67, no. 142.

[72] Shaykh Ibn Bāz added: meaning this *duʿā* should be recited before entering the toilet.

[73] Authentic, collected by al-Nasā'ī.

[74] *Sahih al-Bukhari*, vol. 4, p. 112, no. 6115, *Sahih Muslim*, vol. 4, p. 2015, no. 6210.

CHAPTER 4

Possession (*Al-Mass*)[75]

Definition:

Linguistically: In the Arabic language this is when the *jinn* afflicts and touches a person. It was then more commonly used to mean possession.

In the terminology of the *sharīʿah*, possession is when a person is harmed by a *jinnī* from within his body, or outside of it or both; it is more general than convulsions (*al-ṣarʿ*).

Types of Possession (*al-Mass*):

1. '*Kullī*' - Complete possession: this is when the *jinnī* afflicts the whole body, like those people who have convulsions.

2. '*Juz'ī*' - Partial possession: this is when the *jinnī* afflicts a certain limb or part of the body, such as the leg, shoulder, or tongue.

---

[75] Translator's note: what is being referred to here by 'possession' is that which takes place as a result of the *jinn* touching/possessing a person, which may then causes him to show symptoms of insanity and madness. It should be noted that due to there not being a direct translation for some of the Arabic terminology used, I will mostly suffice with words which are only a rough translation, assuming that the reader now understands what is being referred to.

3. '*Dā'im*' - Continuous possession: this is when the *jinnī* remains in the body for a long period of time.

4. '*Ṭā'if*' - Partial possession: this is when the effects are only felt for a few minutes, like severe nightmares.

Symptoms of Possession *(al-Mass)*:

Before we discuss the symptoms of possession, the following should be noted:

For every illness there are symptoms which usually indicate its presence. We say 'usually' because certain illnesses may share the same symptoms. This is why it is important for the one treating that he checks and verifies the illness in front of him; this does not happen without experience, skill and success granted by Allāh. Since possession is from the illnesses a person is afflicted with, it shares certain symptoms with other illnesses, however, the experienced person who is pious in his sayings and actions will usually be able to diagnose it. In many cases, certain people who recite over the possessed hasten in their judgement, so one person may say: it is possession, whilst another may claim it is magic, and a third person may say it is the evil eye. It is obligatory upon the one who recites [over others] to fear Allāh and to remember His saying:

وَلَا تَقْفُ مَا لَيْسَ لَكَ بِهِۦ عِلْمٌ ۚ
إِنَّ ٱلسَّمْعَ وَٱلْبَصَرَ وَٱلْفُؤَادَ كُلُّ أُو۟لَٰٓئِكَ كَانَ عَنْهُ مَسْـُٔولًا ﴿٣٦﴾

And follow not (O man i.e., say not, or do not or witness not) that of which you have no knowledge. Verily! The hearing, and the sight, and the heart, of each of those one will be questioned (by Allāh).

Sūrah al-Isrā', verse 36

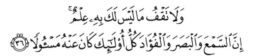

Also, let it be known that speaking without knowledge in these affairs has many evil consequences. We will mention a story that we witnessed when we recited upon somebody. One of us recited upon a girl and on doing so she collapsed and began to scream but the reciter continued to recite over her, and whilst reciting she said: "Do I have possession (*al-mass*)?" He replied: "There is nothing wrong with you," and at this she calmed down and relaxed. After he finished reciting, he asked her brothers about this, and they informed him that someone who had previously recited upon her had told her she was possessed. This psychologically affected her and she started collapsing whenever she was recited upon. After she realised that there was nothing wrong with her, she returned back to normal. So, we advise all those who recite [over others] against making haphazard and random statements.

Let it also be known that this confusion which takes place amongst those who recite, also takes place amongst doctors, especially those who do not believe in the *jinn* and this type of possession. Hence, it may be that the patient is possessed but the doctors consider it to be a mental illness. We once met with a consultant, who informed us that when he receives patients of this nature, some of them leave without any change but after a while they become better and inform him that they went to someone who recited over them; they were cured by the will of Allāh. The situation of the patient must be verified and properly diagnosed.

Reasons behind incorrect diagnosis:

There are many reasons why people are diagnosed incorrectly and without verification. The most prominent of these are:

1. Lack of fear of Allāh; this is the reason for failure in everything.

2. Embarrassment - the correct diagnosis may not always be clear, but because the reciter does not want to seem ignorant in front of the patient and his/her family, he will give any answer rather than state that he does not know. This again comes back to the lack of fear of Allāh.

3. Constant pressure from people on those who cure and recite upon others is another reason. In many instances, these people do not accept 'no' for an answer. This may cause that person to give any answer in order to be left alone; this is not something permissible for those that cure. We advise people not to pressurise the reciter/curer if he does not know the exact cause of the illness.

4. Confusion between illnesses and their symptoms - whether amongst those who cure [others] or amongst doctors. For example, those that recite over others may recite over one who is possessed, but because the *jinnī* does not speak to him for a reason, he says it is "*ayn*' (the evil-eye). This is incorrect; just because the *jinnī* does not speak, it does not mean he is absent. It may be that the *jinnī* fled whilst the recitation took place or that it is mute.

Likewise, a person who is inflicted with the evil-eye, (which is a dangerous condition, as will be explained in the appropriate chapter), may be diagnosed as possessed. Sometimes the symptoms of magic, the evil-eye and possession may be similar to symptoms of physical and psychological illnesses. For example, from the symptoms of possession is anxiety, but this does not mean that every person who has anxiety is possessed (*al-mass*). This is because many psychological illnesses are a cause of anxiety, just as turning away from the remembrance of Allāh is also a cause of anxiety. Allāh says:

وَمَنْ أَعْرَضَ عَن ذِكْرِى فَإِنَّ لَهُۥ مَعِيشَةً ضَنكًا
وَنَحْشُرُهُۥ يَوْمَ ٱلْقِيَٰمَةِ أَعْمَىٰ ﴿١٢٤﴾

But whosoever turns away from My Reminder verily, for him is a life of hardship, and We shall raise him up blind on the Day of Resurrection.

Sūrah Ṭā-Hā, verse 124

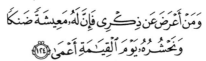

Also, headaches can arise as a result of possession or as a result of physical illnesses. Ibn Ḥajr stated: "The reasons for headaches are many: from them is a tumour in the stomach or its veins, or a harsh trapped wind because it is full. They [i.e. headaches] may be due to violent movement such as sex and vomiting, or lack of sleep, or too much talking. Also from the causes are worry, grief, sadness, hunger and fever. Being struck on the head, having a brain tumour, lifting something heavy on the head, and over-heating or exposing the head to excessive cold can all lead to headaches."[76] So, does each headache necessarily mean there is possession involved?

5. The lack of belief amongst some people that possession (i.e. *jinn* possession) exists, especially amongst psychologists; this causes them to diagnose something which is on the opposite side of the spectrum from possession.

6. Lack of experience and knowledge; this leads to a downfall in everything.

Ibn al-Qayyim mentions that the proficient doctor is the one who pays attention to twenty matters whilst seeking a cure.[77] We will mention the following:

1. To view the illness and correctly identify it.

2. To see what the illness was a result of, and the causes of its appearance.

3. The habits of the patient.

4. To cure the illness in a way that ensures that another more serious illness does not appear in its place.

---

[76] *Fatḥ al-Bārī*, vol. 10, p. 162.

[77] *Zād al-Ma'ād*, pp. 143-144.

5. To look at the illness and decide whether it is curable or not. If it is not curable, he does not give the patient false hope or cure him under false pretences.

6. That he should have experience of the illnesses of the heart and soul and know their cure.

7. To be kind and gentle with the patient, just as one is with a child.

8. That he uses both natural and divine cures.

Symptoms of Possession:[78]

Possession has many symptoms which indicate its presence; these symptoms can be for possession and for other illnesses. From these symptoms are those which take place whilst saying the *adhān* or reciting upon the afflicted, and also from them are those which take place whilst asleep and others which take place whilst awake:

1. Symptoms whilst saying the adhān or reciting:

The one who has been possessed (*al-mass*) will normally faint or collapse when the *adhān* is said in his ear or when he is recited upon. He may also go into convulsions or start to scream or cry whilst collapsing, or he may gaze at the sky or to the right and left. We have personally witnessed all of these symptoms whilst reciting upon people.

2. Symptoms which occur whilst awake:

It should be noted that these symptoms are not specific to possession (*al-mass*), but may also be symptoms for other physical and psychological illnesses. These symptoms are:

---

[78] These symptoms have been identified through experience.

a) Insomnia and anxiety.

b) Preferring to be alone and secluded.

c) Constant headaches for which there are no medical explanation.

d) Laziness and being absentminded.

e) Convulsions and epilepsy.

f) Lack of concern in matters of cleanliness and hygiene.

g) It is possible that none of these symptoms are present, or that there are other symptoms which are present. It should be known that these symptoms also occur in the one afflicted by magic.

3. Symptoms which occur whilst asleep:

Likewise these symptoms are also not specific to possession:

a) Nightmares.

b) Disturbing dreams, such as seeing oneself on a desolate road, or seeing black cats and ghosts/phantoms etc.

c) Excessive laughing, or crying and screaming whilst asleep.

Situations in which a *jinnī* enters a person:

There is a difference between what causes the *jinn* to enter a person and the situation in which this will take place. The first refers to the reasons for which the *jinn* possess, whereas the second refers to the most likely state a person will be in when this possession occurs. In this section we will mention the second issue, as for the first issue then this will be mentioned shortly *Inshā Allāh*.

The situations [and states a person is likely to be in when] a *jinnī* enters a person are:

a) Extreme anger.

b) Extreme fear.

c) Extreme happiness.

d) Extreme forgetfulness and negligence.

e) Drowning in one's desires.

f) When one hurts and harms the *jinn*.

CHAPTER 5

Convulsions & Fits (*Al-Ṣarʿ*)[79]

Definition:

Linguistically, it means to throw on the earth; it is used to refer specifically to humans collapsing in convulsions, referring to this well known illness.[80]

In the terminology of the *sharīʿah*, it is an illness which prevents, but not totally, the physical limbs from moving, sensing and standing.[81]

Convulsions (*al-ṣarʿ*) are a disorder which afflicts a person in the brain, sometimes to the extent that he does not realise what he is saying. He is unable to connect what he has said with what he wishes to say. As a result of these convulsions a person may suffer from memory loss, and accompanying this disorder in the

[79] Translator's note: the term '*al-ṣarʿ*' is likewise a term which has no exact translation in the English language, and what is meant by it is the possession of the body by the *jinn*, to the extent that the *jinn* has the ability to control the thoughts and actions of the possessed.

[80] *Lisān al-ʿArab*, 197.

[81] *Al-Qānūn fī al-Ṭibb*, Ibn Sīnā, vol. 2, p. 76.

brain is a disorder which affects his movements, so he cannot command where he is going. He may even lose the ability to walk straight or at a normal pace.[82]

Types of Convulsions (*al-Ṣarʿ*):

They are of two types:

1. Convulsions caused by the *jinn*.
2. Medical convulsions.

Ibn al-Qayyim said: "Convulsions are of two types: a type that is a result of the mixing of evil spirits, and the other type is that which the doctors discuss and cure."[83] Here we will discuss the first of these two types; the second type can be found in the books of medicine.

Evidences from the Qur'ān and *Sunnah* proving the existence of convulsions:

The existence of convulsions [caused by *jinn*] has been proven by the texts of the Qur'ān and *Sunnah*, as well as by the *ijmāʿ* (consensus) of the scholars, and by intellect (*ʿaql*).

Firstly, from the Qur'ān:

Allāh says:

ٱلَّذِينَ يَأْكُلُونَ ٱلرِّبَوٰا۟ لَا يَقُومُونَ إِلَّا كَمَا يَقُومُ ٱلَّذِى
يَتَخَبَّطُهُ ٱلشَّيْطَٰنُ مِنَ ٱلْمَسِّ

Those who eat ribā (usury) will not stand (on the Day of Resurrection) except like the standing of a person beaten by Shayṭān leading him to insanity.

Sūrah al-Baqarah, verse 275

---

[82] See *ʿĀlam al-Jinn wa al-Malā'ikah*, pp. 76-77.

[83] *Al-Ṭibb al-Nabawī*, pp. 190-191.

Ibn Kathīr said in explanation of this verse: "This means they will stand from their graves on the Day of Judgement, like the one who has had convulsions and then stands from his illness after the striking of *shayṭān*; that is an uneven and imbalanced standing."[84]

Imām al-Qurṭubī said: "In this verse, there is proof against those who deny convulsions from the *jinn*, those who instead claim it is only natural and that *shayṭān* does not possess people nor does he afflict them with possession (*al-mass*)."[85]

Allāh says:

إِنَّ ٱلَّذِينَ ٱتَّقَوْا۟ إِذَا مَسَّهُمْ طَيْفٌ مِّنَ ٱلشَّيْطَٰنِ
تَذَكَّرُوا۟ فَإِذَا هُم مُّبْصِرُونَ ﴿٢٠١﴾

Verily, those who are pious, when an evil thought comes to them from shayṭān, they remember (Allāh), and (indeed) they then see (aright).

Sūrah al-Aʿrāf, verse 201

Ibn Kathīr said in its explanation: "...and from amongst them (i.e. the scholars) are those who explained the above verse as referring to the touch of *shayṭān* which causes convulsions. He then mentioned the story of the woman who had convulsions during the time of the Prophet (ﷺ)."[86]

Secondly, from the Sunnah:

1. On the authority of 'Aṭā' that Ibn 'Abbās (ﷺ) said: "*Shall I not show you a woman from the women of Paradise?' I replied: 'Yes.' He said: This black woman came to the Prophet (ﷺ) and said: 'I get convulsions and thus become unveiled so make duʿā for me.'*

---

[84] *Tafsīr al-Qur'ān al-'Aẓīm*, vol. 1, p. 326.

[85] *Aḥkām al-Qur'ān*, vol. 3, p. 355.

[86] *Tafsīr al-Qur'ān al-'Aẓīm*, vol. 2, p. 279.

He replied: 'If you wish be patient then for you is Paradise, and if you wish I will ask Allāh to cure you.' She said: 'I will be patient, but I become unveiled so ask Allāh to screen me.' He then made duʿā for her."[87]

Similar to this is the following narration: *"A woman came to the Prophet (ﷺ) and said: 'Make duʿā to Allāh [for me].' He replied: 'If you wish I will make duʿā to Allāh to cure you, and if you wish to be patient, then you will not be held to account.' She said: 'I will be patient and not be held to account.'"*[88]

2. The *ḥadīth* of Ṣafiyyah that the Prophet (ﷺ) said: *"Verily shayṭān flows in the son of Adam just as blood flows."*[89]

3. The authentic *ḥadīth* in which the Prophet (ﷺ) said: *"Not a single child is born except that shayṭān touches him, hence, he is born crying. The only exception to this is Maryam and her son (ʿĪsā) due to the saying of her mother: 'I seek refuge in You for her and her offspring from shayṭān the outcast.'"*[90]

4. The *ḥadīth* of Abū Saʿīd al-Khudrī (ؓ) in which the Prophet (ﷺ) said: *"If one of you yawns let him cover his mouth for indeed shayṭān enters."*[91]

Thirdly, sayings of the scholars with regards to convulsions:

Ibn al-Qayyim mentions: "I witnessed our shaykh[92] send someone to speak to the spirit inside a person who had convulsions. He said: 'The shaykh tells you to leave for this is not something *ḥalāl*

---

[87] *Sahih al-Bukhari*, vol. 4, p. 25, no. 5652, *Sahih Muslim*, vol. 4, p. 1994, no. 2576.

[88] *Fatḥ al-Bārī*, vol. 10, p. 115.

[89] *Sahih al-Bukhari*, vol. 2, p. 437, no. 3270, *Sahih Muslim*, vol. 4, p. 1712, no. 2174.

[90] Collected by Muslim.

[91] *Sahih Muslim*, vol. 3, p. 2293.

[92] i.e. Ibn Taymiyyah.

(permissible) for you', so it would leave. Sometimes, he would speak to it himself, and sometimes the spirit would be a '*mārid*' so he would force it to leave by beating it. When it would leave, the afflicted would awake without feeling any pain. We and others have seen him do this many times."[93]

He also mentions: "He (i.e. Ibn Taymiyyah) informed me that he once recited in the ear of a person afflicted with convulsions, and the spirit said: "Yes," in a long and drawn out voice. The *shaykh* said: 'I took a stick and beat it on the neck until my hands were exhausted from beating it. The people witnessing thought he would surely die, and then she (i.e. the spirit) said: 'I love him'. I replied: 'But he does not love you'. She said: 'I wish to make *Ḥajj* with him'. I replied: 'He does not wish to make *Ḥajj* with you;' she then said: 'I will leave out of respect for you.' I replied: 'Rather out of obedience to Allāh and His Messenger.' She then said: 'I will leave.' Then the afflicted sat up looking to his right and left and said: 'What brings the *shaykh* to me?' So they asked him: 'And all these beatings?' He replied: 'Why would the *shaykh* beat me when I have done nothing wrong?' He did not feel that he had been beaten at all.'"[94]

Ibn Taymiyyah said: "The existence of the *jinn* has been established in the Qur'ān and *Sunnah*, and by the agreement of the *salaf* (pious predecessors), and likewise the entering of the *jinn* into a human is also something agreed upon by the scholars of *Ahlus-Sunnah*. It is something common and witnessed; it enters a person and says things which he (the afflicted) is not aware of. Indeed, he is beaten in such way that were a camel to be beaten similar to it, it would die, but that person does not feel it. 'Abdullāh ibn Aḥmad ibn Ḥanbal said: 'I said to my father: 'Indeed a people claim that the *jinn* do not enter into the body of a human.' He replied: 'O my son, they lie for that is it, talking on his tongue.'"[95]

---

[93] *Al-Ṭibb al-Nabawī*, p. 193.

[94] Ibid, p. 194.

[95] *Majmū' Fatāwā*, vol. 24, p. 276.

It has been reported that whilst Imām Aḥmad ibn Ḥanbal was in the *masjid*, a man came to him from the Khalifah Mutawakkil informing him that one of the *khalifah's* slave girls had been afflicted with convulsions. He requested that the Imām make *du'ā* for her. Instead, he took out a wooden shoe and said: "Go to his house and sit at the head of the slave girl and say to it (i.e. the *jinnī*) that Aḥmad says: 'Either you leave her or you will be beaten with this shoe seventy times.' So the man went to the slave girl and did as Imām Aḥmad had ordered him to do. The *jinnī* said: 'I hear and obey; were Aḥmad to request I leave Iraq I would do so, for indeed he is obedient to Allāh, and whosoever is obedient to Allāh everything is obedient to him.' It then left, and the slave girl recovered and had children. After Imām Aḥmad passed away it returned to her, so the *khalifah* sent for Abū Bakr al-Marwazī and explained the situation to him. He took his shoe and came to the slave girl, but the *jinnī* said to him: 'I will not leave her nor will I obey you, for indeed Aḥmad obeyed Allāh so we were ordered to obey him.'"[96]

Reasons which cause the *jinn* to enter a person:

There are many reasons which cause the *jinn* to enter a person:

1. A test and trial from Allāh:

Indeed, Allāh due to His infinite wisdom tests and tries His slaves with many calamities; convulsions are from these calamities. Allāh says:

وَنَبْلُوكُم بِٱلشَّرِّ وَٱلْخَيْرِ فِتْنَةً ۖ وَإِلَيْنَا تُرْجَعُونَ ﴿٣٥﴾

...and we shall make a trial of you with evil and with good. And to Us you will be returned.

Sūrah al-Anbiyā', verse 35

---

[96] *Ākam al-Murjān fī Aḥkām al-Jānn*, pp. 114-115.

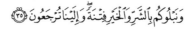

It is incumbent upon the one who has been afflicted to be patient, and to seek the reward of Allāh whilst utilising the permissible means to cure himself.

2. A punishment from Allāh:

This may be as a result of the slave committing sins. Allāh says:

وَمَآ أَصَٰبَكُم مِّن مُّصِيبَةٍ فَبِمَا كَسَبَتْ أَيْدِيكُمْ
وَيَعْفُوا۟ عَن كَثِيرٍ ﴿٣٠﴾

And whatever of misfortune befalls you, it is because of what your hands have earned. And He pardons much.
Sūrah al-Shūrā, verse 30

So as a person becomes more and more distant from his Lord and Creator, *shayṭān* is able to overcome and overpower him. Hence, his life becomes miserable. Allāh mentions:

وَمَن يَعْشُ عَن ذِكْرِ ٱلرَّحْمَٰنِ نُقَيِّضْ لَهُۥ شَيْطَٰنًا
فَهُوَ لَهُۥ قَرِينٌ ﴿٣٦﴾

And whosoever turns away blindly from the remembrance of the Most Gracious (Allāh), We appoint for him shayṭān to be a companion to him.
Sūrah al-Zukhruf, verse 36

Ibn al-Qayyim stated: "The majority of [cases of] possession by these spirits is as a result of the possessed having very little religion and their hearts and tongues being negligent of the remembrance of Allāh, and seeking His protection. Consequently, these evil spirits meet the one who has isolated himself and has no weapon, and is in a sense naked, and thus are able to affect him."[97]

---

[97] *Zād al-Maʿād*, vol. 4, p. 69.

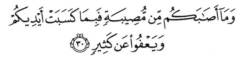

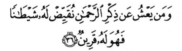

This is something we witnessed commonly in those we recited upon, for many of them had weak faith (*īmān*) and were negligent of their religious duties, whilst others were drowning in their desires. Returning to Allāh and leaving sins is an important way with which one can repel *shayṭān*.

3. Due to desire, passion and love:

A *jinnī* may be attracted to a human, as Ibn Taymiyyah said, "This is from evil which has been made *ḥarām* (unlawful) by Allāh, just as it is for humans even if they agree. So what if it is by force? This is evil coupled with oppression. The *jinnī* should be made aware of the evil and oppression it is committing, and the fact that the law of Allāh and His Messenger is also applicable to it."[98]

4. A means of revenge:

Ibn Taymiyyah affirmed, "And it may occur – and this is the most common reason- out of hatred and revenge. For example, a human may harm one of them by urinating on them, or throwing hot water on them or killing them, (whether knowingly or unknowingly). The *jinn* are ignorant and oppressive by nature so they take revenge with that person with more than he deserves."[99]

So if this is the case and the person did it unknowingly, it should be explained to the *jinn* that a person who does something unintentionally does not deserve to be punished. If the incident took place in the person's own house, the *jinn* are made aware that the person owns the house and thus has the right to do in it as he pleases from the lawful things. Rather it is not allowed for them to be in someone's property without their permission, for they have their own places of dwelling such as ruins and caves etc.[100]

---

[98] *Majmūʿ al- Fatāwā*, vol. 19, p. 40.

[99] Ibid.

[100] Ibid.

5. Foolishness on the part of the jinn:

Just as there are amongst humans those who harm others out of foolishness, then likewise this is also present amongst the *jinn*. Ibn Taymiyyah said: "It may be as a result of frivolity and wickedness; this is the least serious of cases."[101]

6. As a result of magic:

A magician may send a *jinnī* into the person he wishes to place magic upon, so it enters and harms him. We have witnessed this in cases where the *jinn* have mentioned that they possess a person due to magic.

A Doubt and its Clarification:

There is a certain misconception which people hold and ask about: Why do the *jinn* only enter Muslims? Why do they not possess non-Muslims?

Firstly: Who claimed that the *jinn* do not possess non-Muslims? Rather, they enter and harm them; this is something that non-Muslim doctors have accepted, both past and present:

With regard to the past, Ibn al-Qayyim mentions: "As for the convulsions caused by spirits, then their leaders and intellectuals accept this and do not reject it, and they agree that the cure for it is to repel them using good and pious spirits, which nullify the effects of the evil spirits. This is something mentioned by Apocrates in some of his books in which he discusses certain cures for convulsions. He says: 'This is beneficial for the convulsions which are as a result of physical ailments. It does not benefit that which is as a result of spirits.'"[102]

---

[101] Ibid.

[102] *Al-Ṭibb al-Nabawī*, p. 191.

In modern times, there are also doctors who have accepted convulsions caused by spirits. They have carried out studies based upon this, i.e. illnesses that are caused by spirits and not by nerves in the brain as some explain it to be.

Carrington, a member of the American Institute of Psychological Studies said concerning insanity caused by possession: "It is apparent that possession is at the very least real and cannot be ignored, especially since there are many amazing incidents which support this. Since this is the case, then studying it is necessary and compulsory, not only from an academic point of view, but also because hundreds and maybe thousands of people complain of such ailments. Curing these people requires quick diagnosis and immediate medication. If we accept the existence of this type of insanity, it will open up for us a wide area of research, and it will require the attention and skill of modern science and psychological thought."[103]

So, doctors can only accept the existence and effects of these spirits. The effects of these spirits means that there are illnesses which modern medicine cannot cure as successfully as Islām can with help of *du'ās* from the Qur'ān and *Sunnah*. These will be mentioned shortly.

Secondly - People who reject convulsions caused by spirits explain this phenomenon in a number of ways. One of these is to describe the illness as a psychological one. An example of this is when we once recited over an American woman who had accepted Islām and were told by her husband that once, while she was being recited upon, the *jinnī* inside her spoke in English and said that it had possessed her since she was four years old and still a non-Muslim.

Thirdly - The disbelievers have been given the good of this world and will have no portion of the Hereafter. Whereas the believer

[103] *'Ālam al-Jinn wal-Malā'ikah*, p. 83.

is tried and tested during this life as we have already mentioned. This is so that Allāh may examine the level of his *īmān*, or raise his station (in the Hereafter) or remove his sins, or so that he may return to Allāh after he has become distanced from Him. Allāh says:

ظَهَرَ ٱلْفَسَادُ فِى ٱلْبَرِّ وَٱلْبَحْرِ بِمَا كَسَبَتْ
أَيْدِى ٱلنَّاسِ لِيُذِيقَهُم بَعْضَ ٱلَّذِى عَمِلُوا۟ لَعَلَّهُمْ يَرْجِعُونَ ﴿٤١﴾

Evil has appeared on land and sea because of what the hands of men have earned, that He (Allāh) may make them taste a part of that which they have done, in order that they may return.
Sūrah al-Rūm, verse 41

It is reported that the Prophet (ﷺ) said: "*The disbeliever will be brought and dipped into the Fire, and it will be said to him: 'Have you ever seen any good? Have you ever seen a blessing?' He will reply: 'No, O my Lord.' Another person will be brought who was the most miserable in the world and he will be given a taste of Paradise and it will be said to him: 'Have you ever had misery?' He will reply: 'No, by Allāh my Lord.'*"[104]

The final reason is that the disbelievers are helpers of one another. The human Muslim is not allowed to harm others including the Muslim *jinn*, but the disbelieving *jinn* may harm Muslims out of revenge and hatred because of their lack of fear of Allāh and ignorance of Him. This is similar to what some disbelieving humans do.

---

[104] *Sunan Ibn Majah*, vol. 2, p. 1445, no. 4321.

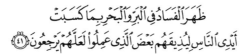

Chapter 6
Seeking Medication

Despite the numerous illnesses and ailments that may afflict a person, it is from the immense mercy of Allāh that he has opened the doors of hope for them, from which they can seek the means to a cure. The believer does not despair from the mercy of Allāh:

إِنَّهُۥ لَا يَاْيْـَٔسُ مِن رَّوْحِ ٱللَّهِ إِلَّا ٱلْقَوْمُ ٱلْكَـٰفِرُونَ

Certainly no one despairs of Allāh's Mercy, except the people who disbelieve.
Sūrah Yūsuf, verse 87

However, we should realise that the mercy of Allāh is only close to those who are believers and do good. Allāh says:

وَرَحْمَتِى وَسِعَتْ كُلَّ شَىْءٍ ۚ فَسَأَكْتُبُهَا لِلَّذِينَ
يَتَّقُونَ وَيُؤْتُونَ ٱلزَّكَوٰةَ وَٱلَّذِينَ هُم بِـَٔايَـٰتِنَا
يُؤْمِنُونَ ﴿١٥٦﴾

...and My mercy embraces all things. That (mercy) I shall ordain for those who are the pious, and give Zakāt, and those

who believe in Our Āyāt (proofs, evidences, signs etc)
Sūrah al-A'rāf, verse 156

In the *ḥadīth* of Jābir (ﷺ), the Prophet (ﷺ) said: "*For every illness there is a cure, so if the cure strikes the illness it will heal [it] by the will of Allāh.*"[105] The Prophet (ﷺ) also said: "*Allāh has not sent an illness without a cure.*"[106]

Shurayk narrated, "*I was once with the Prophet (ﷺ) and some Bedouins came and asked: 'O Messenger of Allāh, shall we cure ourselves?' He replied: 'Yes, O slaves of Allāh, cure yourselves for verily Allāh has not sent an illness except that He has sent a cure for it save one illness.' They asked: 'Which illness?' He replied: 'Death.'*"[107]

Also, Abū Khuzāmah said, "'*O Messenger of Allāh, do you see the incantaions (ruqyah) we use, and the medicine we cure ourselves with, and the preventions we take, do any of them repel the decree of Allāh?' He replied: 'It is all from the decree of Allāh.'*"[108]

The texts that we have just mentioned contain a number of important points. Some of these are:

1. Strengthening the resolve of both the patient and the doctor.

2. The encouragement of seeking a cure.

3. The permissibility of using permissible (*shar'ī*) forms of incantation (*ruqyah*).

4. Everything that takes place is by the decree and will of Allāh.

---

[105] *Sahih Muslim*, vol. 4, p. 1729, no. 2204.

[106] *Sahih al-Bukhari*, vol. 4, p. 32, no. 5678, also collected by Muslim.

[107] Collected by Aḥmad, al-Haythamī said that it is authentic.

[108] *Sunan al-Tirmidhi*, no. 2066, Imām al-Dhahabī stated that it is authentic.

5. Sometimes the cure may not be successful due to a partiular reason.

Ibn al-Qayyim mentioned: "Every illness has its cure which can be used to heal the illness. The Prophet (ﷺ) mentioned that the illness and cure must be compatible, so it is not sufficient just to have a cure; rather it must be the appropriate one. If the dose goes beyond the required amount it will result in another illness, and if it is too weak it will be unsuccessful. When the cure does not strike the illness it will not heal; if it is not the correct time to use the cure it will be unbeneficial. Likewise, if the body is unable to cope with the cure or there is something else present which prevents the cure from having its effects it will not heal. However, if it is correct in every sense it will surely heal, by the will of Allāh."[109]

A cure may not be successful for many reasons. Some of these reasons are that Allāh in His infinite wisdom does not will for a person to be cured in order to test him, or raise his station, or remove his sins, or to punish him:

وَمَا رَبُّكَ بِظَلَّٰمٍ لِّلْعَبِيدِ ﴿٤٦﴾

And your Lord is not an oppressor to the slaves.
Sūrah Fuṣṣilat, verse 46

Another reason is that although a person may take a cure, it may not be the correct cure needed to remove the illness.

Ibn al-Qayyim mentions whilst speaking about the cure for convulsions: "The cure for this is with two things, the first involves the patient and the second involves the one who is administering the cure. As for the patient, a strong resolve is needed. Alongside this, the patient must sincerely turn to the One who has created these spirits, and seek protection from Him with both the heart and tongue conforming in this. For indeed, it is a type of battle;

---

[109] *Zād al-Maʿād.*

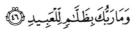

and one can only win a battle if he has a weapon which fulfils the following criteria:

1. That the weapon itself is good and solid.

2. That the arm which yields this weapon is strong.

If one of these two characteristics is missing then the weapon is of no benefit even if it is huge. This is even more so if both of these characteristics are absent, like the person who is devoid of *tawḥīd*, trust in Allāh and fear of Him, and he does not possess a weapon either. These two characteristics should also be possessed by the one who is curing."[110]

---

[110] Ibid, pp. 67-68.

Chapter 7

The Effects of the Qur'ān

Allāh says:

وَنُنَزِّلُ مِنَ ٱلْقُرْءَانِ مَا هُوَ شِفَآءٌ وَرَحْمَةٌ لِّلْمُؤْمِنِينَ
وَلَا يَزِيدُ ٱلظَّـٰلِمِينَ إِلَّا خَسَارًا ﴿٨٢﴾

And We send down of the Qur'ān that which is a healing and a mercy to those who believe, and it increases the Ẓalimūn (polytheists and wrong-doers) nothing but loss.

Sūrah al-Isrā', verse 82

Allāh states that the Qur'ān is a 'cure and mercy for the believers', meaning it dispels the illnesses of the heart such as doubt, hypocrisy, and *shirk*. It is also a mercy which helps to acquire *īmān*, wisdom, and all types of good; this is only for those who believe in it and follow it. As for those who disbelieve and are oppressive, it does not increase them in anything except disbelief; this is as a result of their own faults.[111]

[111] *Tafsīr Ibn Kathīr*, vol. 3, p. 54.

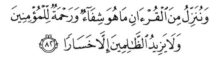

Allāh says:

يَٰٓأَيُّهَا ٱلنَّاسُ قَدۡ جَآءَتۡكُم مَّوۡعِظَةٞ مِّن رَّبِّكُمۡ
وَشِفَآءٞ لِّمَا فِي ٱلصُّدُورِ وَهُدٗى وَرَحۡمَةٞ لِّلۡمُؤۡمِنِينَ ٥٧

O mankind! There has come to you a good advice from your Lord (the Qur'ān), and a healing for that which is in your breasts – a guidance and a mercy for the believers.

Sūrah Yūnus, verse 57

His statement: ***'A cure for that which is in the breasts (i.e. the hearts)'*** refers to the doubts and confusions one may have, and their evils. ***'And a guidance and mercy for the believers'*** means that through it one acquires guidance and mercy from Allāh; again, this is only for those who believe in it and have certainty regarding that which has been mentioned in it.[112]

Allāh says:

قُلۡ هُوَ لِلَّذِينَ ءَامَنُواْ هُدٗى وَشِفَآءٞۖ

Say: it is for those who believe, a guide and a healing.

Sūrah Fuṣṣilat, verse 44

He also says:

أَوَلَمۡ يَكۡفِهِمۡ أَنَّآ أَنزَلۡنَا عَلَيۡكَ ٱلۡكِتَٰبَ يُتۡلَىٰ عَلَيۡهِمۡۚ
إِنَّ فِي ذَٰلِكَ لَرَحۡمَةٗ وَذِكۡرَىٰ لِقَوۡمٖ يُؤۡمِنُونَ

Is it not sufficient for them that We have sent down to you the Book (the Qur'ān) which is recited to them? Verily, herein is mercy and a reminder for a people who believe.

Sūrah al-'Ankabūt, verse 51

---

[112] *Tafsīr Ibn Kathīr*, vol. 2, p. 363.

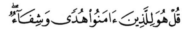

The explanation of all the previously mentioned verses revolves around one main theme; that is the Qur'ān being a cure for the diseases of doubt and a source of mercy for the believers.

There are also many other verses in the Qur'ān which mention the merits of recitation and the merits of the remembrance of Allāh in general. These include the following saying of Allāh:

ٱلَّذِينَ ءَامَنُوا۟ وَتَطْمَئِنُّ قُلُوبُهُم بِذِكْرِ ٱللَّهِ ۗ أَلَا بِذِكْرِ ٱللَّهِ
تَطْمَئِنُّ ٱلْقُلُوبُ ﴿٢٨﴾

Those who believed and whose hearts find rest in the remembrance of Allāh: verily, in the remembrance of Allāh do hearts find rest.

Sūrah al-Ra'd, verse 28

وَٱلذَّٰكِرِينَ ٱللَّهَ كَثِيرًا
وَٱلذَّٰكِرَٰتِ أَعَدَّ ٱللَّهُ لَهُم مَّغْفِرَةً وَأَجْرًا عَظِيمًا ﴿٣٥﴾

...and the men and the women who remember Allāh much with their hearts and tongues, Allāh has prepared for them forgiveness and a great reward (Paradise).

Sūrah al-Aḥzāb, verse 35

The Prophet (ﷺ) said: *"Do not turn your houses into graveyards; verily shayṭān flees from the house in which Sūrah al-Baqarah is recited."*[113]

Also, the authentic *Sunnah* has come with many *ḥadīths* which state the merits of the Qur'ān and its recitation, and seeking a cure with it.

Abū Sa'īd (رضي الله عنه) narrated that a number of the companions of the Prophet (ﷺ) were once travelling. They passed by a village and

[113] *Sahih Muslim*, vol. 1, p. 539, no. 780.

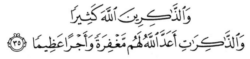

asked its people to host them, but they refused. The companions were then asked: "Is there anybody among you who recites incantations, for our leader has been stung?" So a man replied: "Yes", and recited Sūrah al-Fātiḥah over him thus curing him. He was given a flock of sheep, but he refused to accept it unless the Prophet (ﷺ) allowed him to do so. He mentioned it to the Prophet (ﷺ) and said: "O Messenger of Allāh, by Allāh I only recited Sūrah al-Fātiḥah over him." The Prophet (ﷺ) smiled and said: "How did you know it was a 'ruqyah'?" He then said: "Take from them (i.e. the sheep) and give me a share from it."[114]

The point of benefit from this *ḥadīth* is the saying of the Prophet (ﷺ): *"And how did you know it was a 'ruqyah'?"* Imām al-Nawawī said: "In it is a declaration that the Qur'ān is a *ruqyah* so it is recommended to recite it over the one who has been stung, or is ill or anyone who has any sort of ailment."[115]

'Ā'ishah narrated that: *"During his final illness, the Prophet (ﷺ) would blow over himself after reciting the mu'awwidhāt (Sūrahs al-Falaq and al-Nās). When the illness became worse, I would recite them and then spit lightly into his hands, and wipe them over his body due to the blessings of his hands."*[116]

From this, it can be seen that permissible (*shar'ī*) *ruqyah* is from the most beneficial of cures, by the will of Allāh. Its numerous benefits have been mentioned in the *Sunnah*:

It is reported that 'Abdul-'Azīz said: "I and Thābit entered upon Anas ibn Mālik. Thābit said: 'O Abū Hurairah I am unwell!' Anas replied: 'Shall I recite over you with the ruqyah of the Prophet (ﷺ)?' He replied: 'Yes.' Thābit said: 'O Allāh! Lord of mankind, the One who removes harm, cure, for You are the One

---

[114] *Ṣaḥīḥ Muslim: Sharḥ al-Nawawī*, vol. 14, p. 187.

[115] Ibid, vol. 14, p. 188.

[116] Collected by al-Bukhārī, see *Fatḥ al-Bārī*, vol. 10, p. 205, no. 5735.

who cures, There is none who cures except You; a curing which causes the illness to depart.'"[117]

'Awf ibn Mālik said: "We used to use incantations (*ruqyah*) in the days of '*jāhiliyyah*' (days of ignorance), so we said: 'O Messenger of Allāh! What do you think of this?' He replied: *'Let me hear your incantations, there is no harm in them so long as they do not consist of shirk.'*"[118]

Ibn al-Qayyim stated: "The Qur'ān is a complete cure from all diseases related to the heart and body, and all the ailments of this world and the Hereafter, but, it is not necessarily the case that each and every person is successful in its application. If the one who is ill seeks medication through it in the correct manner with truth, *īmān*, acceptance, strong belief and having fulfilled all the conditions, it is impossible for the disease to withstand it. If the speech of the Lord of the heavens and earth was revealed on a mountain, it would cause the mountain to crumble;[119] how then is it possible for the disease to withstand it? The one who has been granted understanding of the Qur'ān realises that the cure for every single illness of the heart and body has been pointed out in the Qur'ān. The way to protect oneself from these diseases has also been mentioned. Allāh says:

أَوَلَمْ يَكْفِهِمْ أَنَّآ أَنزَلْنَا عَلَيْكَ ٱلْكِتَٰبَ يُتْلَىٰ عَلَيْهِمْ ۚ
إِنَّ فِى ذَٰلِكَ لَرَحْمَةً وَذِكْرَىٰ لِقَوْمٍ يُؤْمِنُونَ

Is it not sufficient for them that We have sent down to you the Book (the Qur'ān) which is recited to them? Verily, herein is mercy and a reminder for a people who believe.

Sūrah al-'Ankabūt, verse 51

[117] *Sahih al-Bukhari*, vol. 10, p. 178.

[118] *Sahih Muslim*, vol. 2, p. 1727.

[119] This refers to the Qur'ānic verse: ***"Had we sent down this Qur'ān on a mountain, you would surely have seen it humbling itself and rent asunder by the fear of Allāh."***

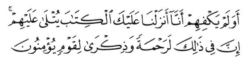

Whosoever is not cured by the Qur'ān then may Allāh not cure him; and whosoever does not find the Qur'ān sufficient, may Allāh make nothing sufficient for him."[120]

[120] *Al-Ṭibb al-Nabawī*, pp. 525-526, with slight changes.

Chapter 8
Types of Medicine

Ibn al-Qayyim said: "The medicine of the Prophet (ﷺ) was of three types:

1. Natural medicine.

2. Divine medicine.

3. A combination of both."[121]

We will start with divine medication; this is the permissible form of incantations (*ruqyah*) which have been mentioned in the Qur'ān and *Sunnah*. It will be discussed in a general manner.

Definition of '*ruqyah*':

'*Ruqyah*' means protection. Ibn al-Athīr said: "*Ruqyah* is protection which is sought by the one who is ill, from ailments such as fever or convulsions etc."[122]

---

[121] *Zād al-Ma'ād*, vol. 4, p. 24.

[122] *Lisān al-'Arab*, vol. 14, p. 332.

Types of '*ruqyah*':

'*Ruqyah*' is of two types: *sharʿī* (permissible) and *shirkī* (one involving *shirk*, i.e. the association of partners with Allāh).[123]

Firstly: Permissible incantations (Ruqyah al-sharʿī):

Its conditions – There are a number of conditions which have been mentioned in the *sharīʿah* in order for incantations to be classified as permissible (*sharʿī*):

1. The '*ruqyah*' should comprise of the speech of Allāh, His names or His attributes.

2. It should be recited to the Arabic language, or its meanings should be translated into another language.

3. To believe that the '*ruqyah*' in and of itself does not help; rather the cure is by the will of Allāh.

Ibn Ḥajr said: "The scholars have agreed that '*ruqyah*' is permissible if it conforms to these conditions."[124]

Therefore it is imperative that the incantation (*ruqyah*) be permissible (*sharʿī*), due to the saying of the Prophet (ﷺ): "*There is nothing wrong with 'ruqyah' as long as it is does not comprise of shirk.*"[125]

However, it is feared that people will fall into practices similar to that of magicians; this is not allowed due to the saying of the Prophet (ﷺ): "*He is not one of us who gives evil omens or asks someone to do it for him, nor the one who fortune tells or the*

---

[123] Translator's note: The second type of *ruqyah* (*shirkī*) will be discussed later. See page 106.

[124] *Fatḥ al-Bārī*, vol. 10, p. 206.

[125] *Sahīh Muslim*, vol. 2, p. 1727.

one who gets his fortune told, nor the one who bewitches or the one who asks to bewitch."[126] Hence, it is not permissible to go to fortune tellers or soothsayers; this will be elaborated upon shortly *Inshā Allāh.*

In addition to the above, the following points should also be noted:

4. The incantation should not be used incorrectly. For example, one may not use it whilst in the toilet or in a graveyard etc. Ibn Taymiyyah said: "It is not permissible to make incantation with something which has no meaning, especially if it comprises of *shirk*, for this is *ḥarām*. The majority of what the deceivers read has *shirk* in it. They may also overtly recite some Qur'ān in order to conceal their statements of *shirk*. Seeking a cure with that which Allāh and His Messenger have ordained should be sufficient; there is no need to recite that which has *shirk* in it."[127]

Important Principles

Indeed, the one who uses '*ruqyah*' is utilising a strong and divine weapon, but a weapon is only as good as the one who uses it, as has been mentioned by Ibn-al-Qayyim. In order for this weapon to have an impact, with the will of Allāh, the following points should be remembered by both the one reciting the incantation and the one it is being recited upon:

Firstly - The one reciting the incantation (*ruqyah*):

1. Correct belief:

This is to have the belief of the pious predecessors of this nation (*Ummah*), and to be aware of falling into *shirk* (association of

[126] *Musnad al-Bazzār*, vol. 4, p. 33.

[127] *Īḍāḥ al-Dilālah*, p. 45.

partners with Allāh) and innovations (*bid'ah*). The Prophet (ﷺ) said: "*Whosoever enters into this affair of ours that which is not from it, will have it rejected.*"[128]

Also, from part of this belief is to sincerely turn to Allāh and trust in Him:

وَعَلَى ٱللَّهِ فَتَوَكَّلُوٓاْ إِن كُنتُم مُّؤْمِنِينَ ﴿٢٣﴾

And put your trust in Allāh if you are believers indeed.
Sūrah al-Mā'idah, verse 23

From this belief is to realise that all benefit and harm is controlled by Allāh, for He is the only One who benefits and harms, as He says:

وَإِن يَمْسَسْكَ ٱللَّهُ بِضُرٍّ فَلَا كَاشِفَ لَهُۥٓ إِلَّا هُوَ ۖ وَإِن
يُرِدْكَ بِخَيْرٍ فَلَا رَآدَّ لِفَضْلِهِۦ ۚ يُصِيبُ بِهِۦ مَن يَشَآءُ مِنْ عِبَادِهِۦ ۚ
وَهُوَ ٱلْغَفُورُ ٱلرَّحِيمُ ﴿١٠٧﴾

And if Allāh touches you with harm, there is none who can remove it but He, and if He intends any good for you, there is none who can repel His favour which He causes it to reach whomsoever of His slaves He wills. And He is the Oft-Forgiving, the Most Merciful.
Sūrah Yūnus, verse 107

2. Sincere Intention:

The intention of a person plays an important role in determining the effect his recitation has. The one reciting incantaions should be mindful of his intention and ensure it is sincere, hence, he should not seek money or fame through his recitation; rather his goal should be the pleasure of Allāh and Paradise. The Prophet (ﷺ) said: "*Whosoever relieves a distress of his brother, Allāh*

[128] Collected by al-Bukāhrī and Muslim.

will relieve a distress for him from the distresses of the Day of Judgement."[129]

Allāh says:

وَمَآ أُمِرُوٓا۟ إِلَّا لِيَعْبُدُوا۟ ٱللَّهَ مُخْلِصِينَ لَهُ ٱلدِّينَ

And they were commanded not, but that they should worship Allāh, and worship none but Him Alone.
Sūrah al-Bayyinah, verse 5

The Prophet (ﷺ) said: "*Verily actions are judged by their intentions, and for everyone is that which they intended.*"[130] He (ﷺ) also said: "*Verily you will not live for a long time and perform an action with which you seek the Face of Allāh, except that you will increase in profit and station.*"[131]

3. Obedience of Allāh and refraining from being disobedient to Him:

The closer the one who recites incantaions is to Allāh, the more of an impact his recitation will have, by the will of Allāh. The same goes for the opposite, for *shayṭān* overcomes a person due to his disobedience and sin. Allāh says:

وَمَن يَعْشُ عَن ذِكْرِ ٱلرَّحْمَٰنِ نُقَيِّضْ لَهُۥ شَيْطَٰنًا
فَهُوَ لَهُۥ قَرِينٌ ﴿٣٦﴾

And whosoever turns away blindly from the remembrance of the Most Gracious (Allāh), We appoint for him shayṭān to be a companion to him.
Sūrah al-Zukhruf, verse 36

---

[129] *Sahih Muslim*, no. 1888.

[130] Collected by al-Bukhārī and Muslim.

[131] Collected by al-Bukhārī and Muslim.

Therefore, the one who recites [upon others] must be a good example by praying the five prayers in congregation, and always being honest, patient and trustworthy.

4. Staying away from ḥarām and doubtful matters:

This includes refraining from being in seclusion with a woman who he is not *maḥram* for, with the excuse of reciting upon her. The Prophet (ﷺ) said: "*'Beware of entering upon women.' A man from the Anṣār said: 'O Messenger of Allāh, how about the in-laws?' He replied: 'That is death.'*"[132] He (ﷺ) also said: "*Let not a man after this day enter upon a woman without having one or two men with him.*"[133]

5. Calling to Allāh:

A common error made by those who recite incantaions upon others is that when they see mistakes and sins in the people they are reciting over, they do not advise them, but just recite upon them. This is wrong, because most of the people who have been afflicted by these types of problems have distanced themselves from Allāh; this may well be the cause of their affliction. Allāh says:

وَمَنْ أَحْسَنُ قَوْلًا مِّمَّن دَعَآ إِلَى ٱللَّهِ وَعَمِلَ صَٰلِحًا وَقَالَ
إِنَّنِى مِنَ ٱلْمُسْلِمِينَ ﴿٣٣﴾

And who is better in speech than he who [says: "My Lord is Allāh" and then stands firm and] invites (men) to Allāh, and does righteous deeds, and says: "I am one of the Muslims."
Sūrah Fuṣṣilat, verse 33

So, it is incumbent upon those who recite to give *da'wah* (call to Allāh), order the good and forbid the evil. This can be done by

---

[132] *Sahīh Muslim: Sharḥ al-Nawawī*, vol. 4, p. 153.

[133] Ibid, vol. 4, p. 155.

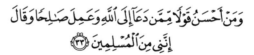

advising the one who is ill and his family to fear Allāh, pray the five daily prayers, make *du'ā* and *dhikr* (remembrance of Allāh), be patient upon Allāh's decrees, and to refrain from sins.

6. To screen those afflicted and to protect their secrets:

This constitutes not revealing the identity of those who have been afflicted by these illnesses, nor spreading their secrets, for people dislike that their personal affairs be known. The Prophet (ﷺ) said: *"The one whose advice is sought is entrusted."*[134]

He (ﷺ) also said: *"Whosoever screens a Muslim, Allāh will screen him on the Day of Judgement."*[135]

7. Knowledge of the condition of the afflicted:

We have already mentioned that diagnosing the illness correctly is half the cure, so knowledge of the status and condition of the afflicted is very important. This can be achieved in a number of ways:

a) Acumen and insight - This means as al-Rāzī said: "Using the apparent signs to learn about the hidden affairs."[136] Allāh says:

إِنَّ فِي ذَٰلِكَ لَآيَاتٍ لِّلْمُتَوَسِّمِينَ ﴿٧٥﴾

Surely! In this are signs for those who see.
Sūrah al-Ḥijr, verse 75

This can also be proven from the *ḥadīth* of Umm Salamah when the Prophet (ﷺ) saw in her house a girl who had a burn on her face. He said: *"Make ruqyah for indeed she has the evil-eye."*[137]

---

134 Collected by al-Tirmidhī and Ibn Mājah.

135 *Sahih Muslim*, vol. 4, p. 1996, no. 2580.

136 *Al-Farāsah*.

137 Collected by al-Bukhārī.

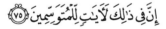

b) Similarly, to ask the afflicted and his/her family about things which may be considered to be a sign in uncovering the reality of the illness, which can then assist the reciter in helping to learn about the condition of the ill person.

c) Likewise, experience and practice have a role in learning about the illnesses of people.

8. Knowledge of the jinn and their conditions and states:

This includes not being afraid of them or their threats. Allāh says:

وَأَنَّهُۥ كَانَ رِجَالٌ مِّنَ ٱلْإِنسِ يَعُوذُونَ بِرِجَالٍ مِّنَ ٱلْجِنِّ
فَزَادُوهُمْ رَهَقًا ﴿٦﴾

And verily, there were men among mankind who took shelter with the males among the jinn, but they (jinn) increased them (mankind) in sin and transgression.

Sūrah Jinn, verse 6

Likewise, one should know that *shayṭān* is weak, as Allāh says:

إِنَّ كَيْدَ ٱلشَّيْطَٰنِ كَانَ ضَعِيفًا ﴿٧٦﴾

Ever feeble indeed is the plot of shayṭān.

Sūrah al-Nisā', verse 76

Ibn al-Qayyim said: "It is important for both the one who is reciting incantations and the one being recited upon to know that the plots of *shayṭān* are weak. Despite the unnatural strength the *jinn* possess in various things they are sometimes very weak as mentioned by Allāh in the above verse."[138]

Also, one should know that the *jinn* are compulsive liars, so not everything they say should be believed, as the Prophet (ﷺ) said

[138] *Al-Ṭibb al-Nabawī*, p. 192.

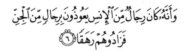

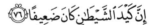

to Abū Hurairah: *"He has told you the truth even though he is a liar."*[139]

9. Making the one afflicted and his family feel good and positive:

Indeed, all illnesses have certain negative effects upon those afflicted by them; sometimes one may even have doubts concerning the cure and whether it will be successful or not. Therefore, the one who is reciting incantations should help the afflicted person feel positive and at ease, and not worse. How many ill people have lost their will to get better due to the negativity of those who are curing them? And how many have been cured, by the will of Allāh due to them being stronger than their illness.

It is reported that the Prophet (ﷺ) said: *"When you enter upon one who is ill, make him feel better with regards to his life, for indeed that will not repel anything but will make him feel positive."*[140]

Secondly - the one being recited upon:

There are many things that the one being recited upon should bear in mind. Some of the things mentioned above are also applicable to the afflicted person. These include correct belief, sincere intention, obedience to Allāh, refraining from His disobedience and keeping away from *ḥarām*.

Ibn al-Qayyim stated: "The cure for this is with two things; the first involves the patient and the second involves the curer. The patient must have a strong resolve and sincerely turn to the One who has created these spirits, and to seek protection from Him ... and the one who is curing, must also possess both these characteristics."[141]

---

[139] Collected by al-Bukhārī.

[140] Collected by al-Tirmidhī, but weak in its narration due to the presence of Mūsā ibn Muḥammad al-Taymī, whose *ḥadīths* are rejected.

[141] *Al-Ṭibb al-Nabawī*, p. 192.

As well as these above points, there are others which should also be remembered:

1. To firmly believe that all benefit and harm is from Allāh alone:

Allāh says:

وَإِن يَمْسَسْكَ ٱللَّهُ بِضُرٍّ فَلَا كَاشِفَ لَهُۥٓ إِلَّا هُوَ ۖ وَإِن يُرِدْكَ بِخَيْرٍ فَلَا رَآدَّ لِفَضْلِهِۦ ۚ يُصِيبُ بِهِۦ مَن يَشَآءُ مِنْ عِبَادِهِۦ ۚ وَهُوَ ٱلْغَفُورُ ٱلرَّحِيمُ ﴿١٠٧﴾

And if Allāh touches you with harm, there is none who can remove it but He, and if He intends any good for you, there is none who can repel His favour which He causes it to reach whomsoever of His slaves He wills. And He is the Oft-Forgiving, the Most Merciful.

Sūrah Yūnus, verse 107

Some afflicted people attach themselves to the person reciting incantations more than they attach themselves to Allāh. This is why you find them saying: so and so is better than so and so; this can lead to *shirk*.

2. Patience:

It is very important for the ill person to be patient, to have a strong resolve and not to be hasty in seeking a cure.

Does Using '*Ruqyah*' Disavow a Person's Trust (*Tawakkul*) in Allāh?

Some of the scholars disliked the use of medication. Imām al-Bukhārī has mentioned this in his *Ṣaḥīḥ* in the chapter heading 'Those who do not use '*ruqyah*'.

In this chapter, he mentions the *ḥadīth* of Ibn ʿAbbās (ﷺ): *"The Prophet (ﷺ) came out to us one day and said: 'The nations were displayed before me; a Prophet would pass by with just one man, and another with two men, and another with a group, and a Prophet who would have no-one. Then I saw a vast amount of people filling the horizon and I hoped that it would be my nation. Instead, it was said: 'This is Mūsā and his people'. Then it was said to me: 'Wait'. I then saw a vast amount of people and it was said: 'This is your nation and among them are seventy thousand who will enter Paradise without any reckoning.' So the people dispersed without knowing (who they would be). The companions spoke amongst themselves and said: 'As for us, we were born upon shirk, but we believed in Allāh and His Messenger, and these are our children.' When this reached the Prophet (ﷺ) he said: 'They are those who do not use evil omens, nor do they cauterise, nor do they make 'ruqyah'; rather they trust in their Lord.' 'Ukāshah stood up and said: 'Am I from them, O Messenger of Allāh?' He replied: 'Yes.' So another man stood and said: 'And me?' He replied: "Ukāshah has preceded you in it.'"*[142]

The author of *Taysīr al-ʿAzīz al-Ḥamīd* said:

> Know that this *ḥadīth* does not mean that they never used to take the necessary means in order to achieve something, as some ignorant people think. Indeed, using the necessary means is something natural and necessary which no-one can leave, not even the animals; rather trust in Allāh (*tawakkul*) is in itself a means, as Allāh says,

وَمَن يَتَوَكَّلْ عَلَى ٱللَّهِ فَهُوَ حَسْبُهُۥٓ

And whosoever puts his trust in Allāh, then He will suffice him.

> This means that Allāh is sufficient for a person. What is meant in the *ḥadīth* [mentioned above] is that they leave

[142] Collected by al-Bukhārī and Muslim. See *Sahih al-Bukhari*, vol. 10, p. 279.

those matters which are disliked even though they are in need of them. Instead they entrust their affairs to Allāh. They are leaving these things not because they are a means, but because they are a means which are disliked, because in many cases, the one who is ill becomes attached to the means to a cure, even if it is a spider's web.

Taking the necessary means and medication which do not contain any elements of doubt does not disavow ones trust in Allāh. Thus, leaving it is not from the *sharī'ah* as can be seen from the following *ḥadīth*: *"Allāh has not sent down an illness except that He has sent for it a cure."* Also, the *ḥadīth* of Shurayk mentions: *"I was and some Bedouins came and (ﷺ) once with the Prophet asked: 'O Messenger of Allāh, shall we cure ourselves?' He replied: 'Yes, O slaves of Allāh, cure yourselves for verily Allāh has not sent an illness except that He has sent a cure for it save one illness.' They asked: 'Which illness?' He replied: 'Death.'"*[143]

Ibn al-Qayyim said: "These *ḥadīths* affirm both the causes (responsible for illnesses etc.) and the means (which help to cure). They refute those that have denied the permissibility of seeking a cure, and affirm that seeking a cure does not disavow trusting in Allāh, just as one does not disavow his trust in Allāh by repelling hunger with food, thirst with drink and hot and cold with their opposites. Rather, the essence of *tawḥīd* is not attained until one utilises the means which Allāh has placed, which bring about the results for which they are used.

To leave these means is itself a vilification of *tawakkul.* Such a person believes that leaving cures is stronger than *tawakkul*, rather leaving them disavows *tawakkul*, the essence of which is to rely upon Allāh in all that benefits

---

[143] Authentic, collected by Aḥmad.

> the slave in this world and the Hereafter. It is also essential that *tawakkul* is coupled with the correct and appropriate means used in order to achieve something, or else it is a vilification of the *sharīʿah*, so the slave does not call his helplessness *tawakkul*, nor his *tawakkul* helplessness."[144]

Shaykh Ibn ʿUthaymīn was asked: Does '*ruqyah*' disavow one's trust in Allāh (*tawakkul*)?

He replied: "*Tawakkul* is to truly rely upon Allāh in the attainment of good and prevention of evil whilst taking the necessary means which Allāh has laid down. *Tawakkul* is not from the one who relies upon Allāh without taking these necesssary means, for verily this is speaking ill of Allāh and His wisdom, for Allāh has connected the causes and their means.

An important question arises here: Who had the most trust in Allāh?

The answer: It was the Prophet (ﷺ).

Would he take the necessary means in order to prevent evil? The answer is yes, for when he (ﷺ) used to leave for battle he would wear armour in order to protect himself from arrows. In the battle of Uḥud, he wore two shields; all in preparation for what may happen. So, taking the necessary means does not disavow *tawakkul* if a person believes that these means have no effect except by the will and power of Allāh. As such, a person reciting upon himself or his ill brothers does not disavow *tawakkul*, for it has been established that the Prophet (ﷺ) would recite upon himself with the *muʿawwidhatayn* (*Sūrahs al-Falaq* and *al-Nās*) and that he would recite upon his companions when they fell ill, and Allāh knows best."[145]

---

[144] *Taysīr al-ʿAzīz al-Ḥamīd*, pp. 110-111.

[145] *Majmūʿ Fatāwā Ibn ʿUthaymīn*, vol. 1, p. 66.

Charging a Fee for Reciting Incantations (*Ruqyah*)

Abū Saʿīd (ﷺ) narrated that once a number of the companions of the Prophet (ﷺ) were travelling. They passed by a village, and asked its people to host them, but they refused. The companions were asked: "Is there anyone among you one who recites (incantations), for our leader has been stung?" A man replied: "Yes", and recited over him Sūrah al-Fātiḥah thus curing him. He was given a flock of sheep, but he refused to accept it unless the Prophet (ﷺ) allowed him to do so. He mentioned it to the Prophet (ﷺ) and said: "O Messenger of Allāh, by Allāh I only recited Sūrah al-Fātiḥah over him." He smiled and said: "And how did you know it was a 'ruqyah'?" He then said: "Take (the sheep) from them and give me a share from it."[146]

The saying of the Prophet (ﷺ): *"Take from them and give me a share from it,"* clearly indicates the permissibility of taking a fee for '*ruqyah*' with *Sūrah al-Fātiḥah*; this is completely *ḥalāl*. This statement also shows that the Prophet (ﷺ) wished to encourage them, and clarify the fact that what they did was permissible.

The *ḥadīth* of Yaʿlā ibn Murrah also indicates this: *"A woman came to the Prophet (ﷺ) with her son who had been afflicted with an illness. The Prophet (ﷺ) said: 'Leave O enemy of Allāh for I am the Messenger of Allāh,' so it left, and the woman gave him two rams and some dried yoghurt and ghee. The Prophet (ﷺ) said: 'O Yaʿlā, take the dried yoghurt and ghee and one of the rams and return the other to her.'"*[147]

However, today, many of those who recite incantations upon others have taken this to an extreme and ask for too much money. This has become their primary objective leading to their intentions becoming distorted; consequently, their recitation is devoid of blessing.

---

[146] *Ṣaḥīḥ Muslim: Sharḥ al-Nawawī*, vol. 14, p. 187.

[147] Authentic, collected by Aḥmad.

It is obligatory upon those who recite upon others to fear Allāh and not to make wealth their main aim. They should not ask for excessive amounts; rather, they should take into consideration the situation of those who are in need.

Also, a very real danger is that magicians and impostors, who deceive people, will use recitation as a means to exploit them. Thus, they mix good with evil, and consume people's money; this is a common occurrence today.

If the recitation of the one who recites incantations upon others bears fruit, he should seek the reward from Allāh, and if he is given something he accepts it. But, if he is able to refuse, this is better for him and his reward will be greater, and his recitation will be more beneficial by the will of Allāh.

Certain matters to be cautious of

1. The presence of many people around a certain individual who recites incantations upon others may be taken as a sign that he has certain special qualities, and his importance may be considered greater than that which he is reciting i.e., the Qur'ān. This is wrong and something dangerous so be aware!

2. When *shayṭān* sees people clinging to a certain person who recites incantations upon others, he may help that person without him realising. He may even announce his fear of that person so people trust in him more than in what he is reciting. Thus, they believe he possesses a special quality which then causes people who have even the slightest of doubts to go to him, so he can inform them whether they are possessed or not.

3. People who recite incantations upon others should be aware of the dangers of pride and vanity, especially when they see many people coming to them and how they have been cured by the permission of Allāh through their recitation.

4. Taking too much money from people as fees; this has already been discussed.

5. Failure or being prevented from diagnosing people's illnesses; this has also been mentioned.

Secondly: *Ruqyah al-shirkī* (involving *shirk* i.e. the association of partners with Allāh)

In this type of *ruqyah*, assistance is sought from other than Allāh. This includes making *du'ā* to other than Allāh, asking for help from other than Allāh, and seeking refuge in other than Allāh by the names of the *jinn*, angels, prophets and the righteous; this is all from major *shirk*.

Likewise, making *ruqyah* with something which has no meaning neither in Arabic or another language is impermissible, becuase one cannot be sure as to what is being said.

Chapter 9
Amulets and Charms (*Tamā'im*)

The singular term is '*tamīmah*'; they are beads which the Arabs used to place on their children claiming that they repelled the evil-eye and spirits. When Islām came, it revoked it.[148]

Ibn Ḥajr said: "*Tamā'im* is the plural of '*tamīmah*', and it is beads or something hung around the neck. In *Jāhiliyyah* (pre-Islām), people used to believe it would repel harm."[149]

Its Types

Firstly – this involves that which is from the Qur'ān, such as writing a verse from it, or a name from the Names of Allāh or His Attributes, and then to hang it on a part of the body. The scholars have differed regarding the permissibility of this:

---

[148] *Lisān al-'Arab*, vol. 12, p. 70.

[149] *Fatḥ al-Bārī*, vol. 10, p. 206.

The First opinion:
It is permissible - this is the saying of some of the companions, including ʿAbdullāh ibn ʿAmr ibn al-ʿĀṣ. It is also mentioned in the narration of ʿĀ'ishah, the saying of Abū Jaʿfar al-Bāqir, and in a narration from Imām Aḥmad. The *ḥadīths* which forbid amulets are considered by these scholars to refer only to those which have *shirk* in them.

The Second opinion:
It is impermissible - this is the saying of a number of the companions including Ibn Masʿūd and Ibn ʿAbbās. It is mentioned in the narrations of Ḥudhayfah, ʿUqbah ibn ʿĀmir and Ibn ʿAkīm, and also in the sayings of a number of the *tābiʿūn* (students of the companions) including the students of Ibn Masʿūd. It is a narration from Imām Aḥmad which has been chosen by many of his followers especially the latter ones.

Their evidence can be found in the following *ḥadīth*: "*Verily, 'ruqyahs', amulets and 'tiwalah' [what is used to gain the love of one's spouse] are all shirk.*"[150]

The correct opinion [out of the two] is the second one. This is due to the following reasons:

1. The general texts which have been reported regarding this. There are no other texts contrary to these, nor any texts which specify the ruling mentioned in these *ḥadīths*.

2. In order to prevent people from using it as a means or a reason to wear that which is not allowed.

3. Anything which is hung from the Qur'ān will be disrespected whilst relieving oneself, or whilst in a state of impurity etc.[151]

---

[150] Collected by Abū Dāwūd, Ibn Mājah and Aḥmad.

[151] *Fatḥ al-Majīd*, p. 136.

Secondly - that which does not consist of Qur'ānic verses, but consists of beads or threads or the names of the *jinn* etc. This is *ḥarām* and is from *shirk* (associating partners with Allāh). People hang these amulets on themselves or their cars or on the doors of their houses, claiming that they repel evil; this is all impermissible.

The Permanent Committee of Scholars in Saudi Arabia has been asked about this:

Q: What is the ruling of carrying pocket sized Qur'āns in one's pocket for protection against the evil-eye and all evils, whilst believing they are Allāh's holy verses and having the sincere belief in Allāh, and likewise placing them in cars or someplace else?

Q: What is the ruling of carrying charms written from the Qur'ān, in order to protect oneself or for other reasons, such as to help one to pass (an exam) or to be cured from an illness or magic?

Q: What is the ruling of hanging Qur'ānic verses in golden chains etc in order to protect oneself from evil?

> A: Allāh revealed the Qur'ān in order for people to worship Him by reciting it, and to contemplate over its meanings, so they may know His rulings and act according to them. This will be a sermon to them and will cause their hearts to soften, and their limbs to tremble. It will cure their hearts from ignorance and misguidance and act as purification for their souls from *shirk* and sins. Allāh has made the Qur'ān a source of guidance and mercy for the one who opens up his heart and pays heed to it. Allāh says:
>
> يَٰٓأَيُّهَا ٱلنَّاسُ قَدْ جَآءَتْكُم مَّوْعِظَةٌ مِّن رَّبِّكُمْ وَشِفَآءٌ لِّمَا فِى ٱلصُّدُورِ وَهُدًى وَرَحْمَةٌ لِّلْمُؤْمِنِينَ ﴿٥٧﴾

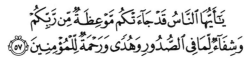

O mankind! There has come to you a good advice from your Lord (the Qur'ān), and a healing for that which is in your breasts, - a guidance and a mercy for the believers.
Sūrah Yūnus, verse 57

He mentions:

ٱللَّهُ نَزَّلَ أَحْسَنَ ٱلْحَدِيثِ كِتَٰبًا مُّتَشَٰبِهًا مَّثَانِىَ تَقْشَعِرُّ مِنْهُ جُلُودُ ٱلَّذِينَ يَخْشَوْنَ رَبَّهُمْ ثُمَّ تَلِينُ جُلُودُهُمْ وَقُلُوبُهُمْ إِلَىٰ ذِكْرِ ٱللَّهِ ذَٰلِكَ هُدَى ٱللَّهِ يَهْدِى بِهِۦ مَن يَشَآءُ

Allāh has sent down the Best Statement, a Book (this Qur'ān), its parts resembling each other (in goodness and truth) (and) oft-repeated. The skins of those who fear their Lord shiver from it (when they recite it or hear it). Then their skin and their heart soften to the remembrance of Allāh. He Guides therewith whom He wills;
Sūrah al-Zumar, verse 23

Allāh also says:

إِنَّ فِى ذَٰلِكَ لَذِكْرَىٰ لِمَن كَانَ لَهُۥ قَلْبٌ أَوْ أَلْقَى ٱلسَّمْعَ وَهُوَ شَهِيدٌ ﴿٣٧﴾

Verily, therein is indeed a reminder for him who has a heart or gives ear while he is heedful.
Sūrah Qāf, verse 37

Allāh made the Qur'ān a miracle for His Prophet (ﷺ) and a clear sign to all of mankind. It was a miracle that showed that he is the Messenger of Allāh, so that he may convey the message to people. It was revealed as a mercy to the people, and a proof against them (if they are heedless). Allāh says:

وَقَالُواْ لَوْلَآ أُنزِلَ عَلَيْهِ ءَايَٰتٌ مِّن رَّبِّهِۦ قُلْ إِنَّمَا ٱلْءَايَٰتُ
عِندَ ٱللَّهِ وَإِنَّمَآ أَنَا۠ نَذِيرٌ مُّبِينٌ ﴿٥٠﴾ أَوَلَمْ يَكْفِهِمْ أَنَّآ أَنزَلْنَا
عَلَيْكَ ٱلْكِتَٰبَ يُتْلَىٰ عَلَيْهِمْ إِنَّ فِى ذَٰلِكَ لَرَحْمَةً
وَذِكْرَىٰ لِقَوْمٍ يُؤْمِنُونَ ﴿٥١﴾

And they say: "Why are not signs sent down to him from his Lord? Say: "The signs are only with Allāh, and I am only a plain warner." Is it not sufficient for them that We have sent down to you the Book (the Qur'ān) which is recited to them? Verily, herein is mercy and a reminder for people who believe.

Sūrah al-'Ankabūt, verses 50-51

He says:

تِلْكَ ءَايَٰتُ ٱلْكِتَٰبِ ٱلْمُبِينِ ﴿٢﴾

These are the Verses of the Manifest Book.

Sūrah al-Qaṣaṣ, verse 2

Allāh also says:

تِلْكَ ءَايَٰتُ ٱلْكِتَٰبِ ٱلْحَكِيمِ ﴿٢﴾

These are the Verses of the Wise Book (the Qur'ān).

Sūrah Luqmān, verse 2

The Qur'ān is principally a Book of laws and rulings, a clear sign, an amazing miracle and powerful proof which Allāh revealed to assist His Messenger (ﷺ). However, it has also been established that the Prophet (ﷺ) would make incantation (*ruqyah*) on himself using the Qur'ān, by reciting *Sūrahs Ikhlāṣ*, *Falaq* and *Nās*. Likewise, it has been established that he allowed incantation to be made with that which had no *shirk* in it. He approved of his companions doing this, and allowed them to accept fees for this. 'Awf ibn Mālik narrated: "*We used to use incantations in the days of ignorance (jāhiliyyah), so we said: 'O Messenger of Allāh! What do you think of this?'*

He replied: 'Let me hear your incantations; there is no harm in them so long as they do not consist of shirk.'" Collected by Muslim.

The *ḥadīth* of Abū Sa'īd (ﷺ) also supports this: *"A number of the companions of the Prophet (ﷺ) were travelling. They passed by a village, and asked its people to host them, but they refused. The companions were asked: 'Is there anyone among you one who recites (over others), for our leader has been stung?' A man replied: 'Yes', and recited over him Sūrah al-Fātiḥah thus curing him. He was given a flock of sheep, but he refused to accept it unless the Prophet (ﷺ) allowed him to do so. He mentioned it to the Prophet (ﷺ) and said: 'O Messenger of Allāh, by Allāh I only recited Sūrah al-Fātiḥah over him.' He smiled and said: 'And how did you know it was a 'ruqyah'?' He then said: 'Take (the sheep) from them and give me a share from it.'"* Collected by Bukhārī and Muslim.

Also, on the authority of 'Ā'ishah who said: *"Before sleeping, the Prophet (ﷺ) would spit lightly into his hands after reciting Sūrahs Ikhlāṣ, Falaq and Nās, then he would wipe over his face and what he was able to of his body. 'Ā'ishah said: So when he became ill he would order me to do this for him."* Collected by Bukhārī.

On the authority of 'Ā'ishah: *"The Prophet (ﷺ) would recite over some of his family members; he would wipe the body with his right hand and say "O Allāh! Lord of mankind, remove all harm, cure, for You are the One who cures, there is none who cures except You, a curing which causes the illness to depart."* Collected by Bukhārī.

The Prophet (ﷺ) had the Qur'ān revealed to him; he was the most knowledgeable regarding its rulings and status; yet, it has not been established anywhere that he ever hung upon himself or anyone else an amulet, whether from the Qur'ān or other than it. Neither did he ever use a charm to protect himself or anyone else from evil. He never carried it with him on his clothes or possessions in order to achieve success and victory or to remove any harm. If it was allowed, he would have done it and conveyed its permissibility to his nation (*Ummah*) and explained it to them because the saying of Allāh states:

يَٰٓأَيُّهَا ٱلرَّسُولُ بَلِّغْ مَآ أُنزِلَ إِلَيْكَ مِن رَّبِّكَ ۖ وَإِن لَّمْ تَفْعَلْ
فَمَا بَلَّغْتَ رِسَالَتَهُۥ

O Messenger (Muḥammad)! Proclaim (the Message) which has been sent down to you from your Lord. And if you do not, then you have not conveyed His Message.

Sūrah al-Mā'idah, verse 67

Were he to have practiced this, then the companions would have narrated it, and acted upon it, for they are the most eager of people in preaching the message. They are the most eager of those who preserve the *sharī'ah* in saying and action; they are the closest of those who strictly adhere to the teachings of the Prophet (ﷺ), but, it has not been established from any of them. This shows that carrying the Qur'ān or placing it in a car or in a house, solely for the purposes of attaining good or repelling evil is impermissible.

Likewise, using it as a charm or writing it in a golden chain in order to hang around ones neck etc. is impermissible. This contradicts the way of the Prophet (ﷺ) and his companions, because the following *ḥadīth* states: "*Whosoever hangs an amulet then may Allāh not fulfil it (i.e. his wants from it).*" Another narration states: "*Whosoever hangs an amulet has committed shirk.*" Collected by Aḥmad.

The Prophet (ﷺ) said: *"Verily 'ruqyah', amulets and tiwalah (that which causes the husband to love his wife) are shirk."* The only exception to this is those incantations which do not contain *shirk*. However, he did not include any form of amulets in this, therefore showing that they are impermissible. This is the opinion of Ibn Mas'ūd, Ibn 'Abbās, and a number of companions and *tābi'ūn* such as al-Nakha'ī.

A number of scholars have allowed the hanging of amulets if they are from the Qur'ān, or from the Names of Allāh or His Attributes in order to protect oneself etc. They excluded this type of amulet from the *ḥadīth* which forbids them just as certain incantations have been excluded from the general impermissibility (i.e. those which do not contan *shirk*). This is because the Qur'ān is the speech of Allāh and one of His Attributes which does not consist of any *shirk*, therefore, it is permissible to use and hang them. It is said this is the saying of some of the companions, such as 'Abdullāh ibn 'Amr ibn al-'Āṣ, but this narration is weak due to the presence of Muḥammad ibn Isḥāq who is a '*mudallis*' [one who causes confusion because he concealed the identity of the one he narrated from]. Even if the *ḥadīth's* authenticity was established, there is no proof in the content of it because the narration states that he used to teach the Qur'ān to the older children, and write it for the younger ones and place it around their necks. It is most likely that he did this in order to assist them in the memorisation of the Qur'ān by repeating that which was written, and not to protect them from evil and harm. Therefore, this is not from the amulets we are discussing.

Shaykh 'Abdul-Raḥmān ibn Ḥasan in his book '*Fatḥ al-Majīd*' chose the opinion of Ibn Mas'ūd and his companions, i.e. the impermissibility of all types of amulets. He said: "It is the correct opinion for three reasons; firstly, because of the general prohibition. Secondly, in order to prevent people from using it as a means to hang that which is impermissible, i.e. that which is not from the Qur'ān, and thirdly, because anything which is hung from the Qur'ān may be disrespected whilst relieving oneself etc, and Allāh knows best."[152]

Tiwalah

This is a type of bead or charm from magic with which the wife gains the love of her husband.[153] Ibn Ḥajr said: "*Tiwalah* was something a woman would use in order to gain the love of her husband; it is a type of magic."

Tiwalah is impermissible and is from *shirk*; this is because of the saying of the Prophet (ﷺ): "*Verily ruqyah, amulets and tiwalah are shirk.*"

[152] *Fatāwā al-Lajnah al-Dā'imah*, vol. 1, pp. 197-201.

[153] *Lisān al-ʿArab*, vol. 11, p. 81.

Chapter 10

Fortune Tellers and Soothsayers

Fortune tellers

Ibn Manẓūr said: "A fortune teller is the one who receives news of the future and claims to know the unseen."

Al-Azharī said: "Fortune telling was present before the coming of the Prophet (ﷺ). When he was sent, the heavens were guarded with shooting stars, and the *jinn* and *shayaṭīn* were prevented from stealing news from the heavens and passing it to the fortune tellers. It became obsolete, and Allāh destroyed the falsities of the fortune tellers with the Qur'ān which differentiates between truth and falsehood."[154]

---

[154] *Lisān al-ʿArab*, vol. 13, p. 363.

Soothsayers

Ibn Manẓūr said: "Linguistically, it refers to a fortune teller. In the *ḥadīth*: "*Whosoever approaches a soothsayer,*" 'soothsayer', refers to a person who claims to know the knowledge of the unseen which is only known to Allāh."[155]

In '*Kitāb al-Tawḥīd*', Imām al-Baghawī said: "The soothsayer is the one who claims to know affairs using signs to point him to something which has been stolen for example."

Ibn Qāsim said: "The soothsayer is the one who provides detail about a burglary and the culprit, or the location of something that someone has lost etc. using certain signs he claims to see. It is probable that the *shayaṭīn* descend upon him and mix with his spirit."[156]

The ruling of seeking help from fortune tellers, soothsayers, and magicians etc.

Indeed, good health is something which every person wishes for; it is a crown upon the heads of those who possess it. However, it can only be seen by those who have lost it, as the Prophet (ﷺ) said: *"The majority of people are negligent of two blessings: good health and free time."*[157]

However, does a person seek a cure through unlawful (*ḥarām*) means by using that which involves illusions and lies? Does a person seek assistance from the magicians, soothsayers and fortune tellers? The answer is never. The Prophet (ﷺ) has warned us against seeking a cure in an unlawful manner: *"Verily Allāh has sent the illness and its cure, so seek the cures but do not cure with that which is ḥarām."*[158]

---

[155] *Lisān al-ʿArab*, vol. 9, p. 238.

[156] *Ḥāshiyah Kitāb al-Tawḥīd*, p. 206.

[157] *Sahih al-Bukhari*, vol. 4, p. 175, no. 6412.

[158] *Sunan Abu Dawud*, vol. 4, p. 7, no. 3874.

Seeking a cure in that which involves lies has evil outcomes. Indeed, many people chase these false illusions and may even feel content with them, especially if that illusionist and impostor is good at deceiving and cheating others. Shaykh Ibn Bāz said:

> It is forbidden to go to soothsayers and magicians and their likes from those who claim the knowledge of the unseen. To believe them is worse; indeed, it is a type of disbelief said: "*Whosoever approaches* (ﷺ) (*kufr*) as the Prophet *a fortune teller and believes him, his prayer will not be accepted for forty days.*" Collected by Muslim.[159] Imām Muslim also narrates on the authority of Muʿāwiyah ibn forbade approaching the (ﷺ) that the Prophet (ؓ) Ḥakm fortune tellers and asking them.
>
> He (ﷺ) also said: "*Whosoever goes to a fortune teller and believes in what he says, he has disbelieved in that which* Collected by "*.(ﷺ) has been revealed upon Muḥammad* Tirmidhī and Nasā'ī.[160]
>
> *Ḥadīths* of this kind are many in number, hence, it is incumbent upon the Muslim to be aware of asking fortune tellers, soothsayers, and all those who claim to have news of the unseen. These people wish to confuse the Muslims by referring to it as medicine or something similar.
>
> Some people inform others of the unseen by smelling the scarf or clothes of those who are ill; they claim it is a form of medicine. These people have done something from the affairs of the unseen and have not obtained this information simply by smelling clothes. This is only to confuse people so that they consider it to be a form of medicine. These people may even give the ill person some medicine which may heal him by the decree of

---

[159] *Ṣaḥīḥ Muslim: Sharḥ al-Nawawī*, vol. 14, p. 227.

[160] Collected by al-Tirmidhī, al-Nasā'ī and Aḥmad, see *Musnad Aḥmad*, vol. 2, p. 429.

> Allāh. People then consider the medicine to be the reason behind the cure. However, the illness may have been as a result of some of the *jinn* who cooperate with these people and inform him of the illness. These people then please the *jinn* with some sort of worship, and thus they leave the ill person. This is something that is well-known about the *jinn* and *shayaṭīn* and those who cooperate with them.[161]

Imām al-Nawawī said: "Know that fortune telling, going to fortune tellers, blowing in the sand and pebbles etc, and learning about these things is unlawful (*ḥarām*). Taking a fee for any of the above is also unlawful as has been mentioned in authentic texts."[162]

Warning

Today, the circle of magicians and fortune tellers is increasing, as it has done throughout time. These people seek to destroy people's belief and turn them away from the true *tawḥīd* of Allāh, so that people rely on them instead of Allāh.

Also, these people are well aware that deception and cheating is the easiest and fastest way to consume people's money. One of these fortune tellers was once asked: "What caused you to turn to this?" He replied: "I used to be a taxi driver, then I realised that fortune telling was the easiest way to take people's money."

To become a fortune-teller, all that is required is knowledge of how to deceive and cheat, and to memorise certain phrases, writings, and deceptive mutterings.

---

[161] *Iqāmat al-Barāhīn 'alā man Istaghātha bighayr Illāh aw Ṣaddaqa al-Kahanah wal-'Arrāfīn*, pp. 34-35.

[162] *Rawḍah al-Ṭālibīn*, vol. 9, p. 346.

Differentiating between the good and the bad

There are certain signs by which one can recognise magicians, soothsayers and fortune tellers and those similar to them. In order for the Muslims to avoid becoming sacrificial lambs to these people, hence destroying their beliefs and religion, here are some of the signs by which these people can be recognised:

1. Asking for the name of one's mother and possibly father as well; this is the most common sign. We say concerning this: Why ask about the names of one's parents? Whenever you see one of them ask about this, flee from them just as you would flee from a lion.

2. Asking to see one's scarf, hat or clothes etc. When you see this, flee from him as you fled from the first.

3. Mutterings which have no meaning in any language. It may be he recites a verse from the Qur'ān every so often to deceive people. It has already been mentioned that one of the conditions of the permissible incantation is that it must be in the Arabic language or that its meanings be translated into another.

4. Amulets and charms which consist of broken words, charts and diagrams – the person may even write something from the Qur'ān as deception. These amulets are most likely to be closed; the person will be severely warned against opening them. This creates fear which causes that person not to open them. Once, when we tried to open one to show someone what it consisted of, he became frightened as if it was a bomb waiting to explode.

5. Asking a person to do something which contradicts the *sharī'ah*, such as not using water and not bathing. This will mean a person cannot make *wuḍu* or pray. Also, some people are advised not to shake people's hands. Once, when I went to visit someone, I shook his hand and then went to shake the hand of his brother who was with him, but he refused. When I asked about this, I was told that he had visited one of these people who had advised

him not to shake hands with anyone. Or, he may be asked to seclude himself for a certain period of time.

6. Giving something to the ill, and asking them to bury it in a certain place, or to sacrifice an animal and bury it in a certain place, and such similar acts.

CHAPTER 11

How to Make Incantations (*Ruqyah*) Upon the One who is Possessed

It is recommended for the one making incantations to be close to Allāh (by obeying Him) and to refrain from being disobedient to Him. The closer one is to his Lord, the more fear Allāh will place in his enemy.

Likewise, he should be prepared and mentally strong; it is also better if he has someone with him in case he requires assistance.

Before beginning, he should make the *adhān* in the ear of the afflicted, for the Prophet (ﷺ) said: "*When the adhān is called shayṭān flees and passes wind so that he will not hear the adhān...*"[163]

After this, he should place his hand on the forehead of the possessed, and recite *Sūrah al-Fātiḥah*, the first five verses of

[163] *Sahih al-Bukhari*, vol. 1, p. 307, no. 574.

Sūrah al-Baqarah, and the following, beginning with *Āyah al-Kursī* and then the last three verses of *Sūrah al-Baqarah*:

ٱللَّهُ لَآ إِلَٰهَ إِلَّا هُوَ ٱلْحَيُّ ٱلْقَيُّومُ ۚ لَا تَأْخُذُهُۥ سِنَةٌ وَلَا نَوْمٌ ۚ
لَّهُۥ مَا فِى ٱلسَّمَٰوَٰتِ وَمَا فِى ٱلْأَرْضِ ۗ مَن ذَا ٱلَّذِى يَشْفَعُ عِندَهُۥٓ
إِلَّا بِإِذْنِهِۦ ۚ يَعْلَمُ مَا بَيْنَ أَيْدِيهِمْ وَمَا خَلْفَهُمْ ۖ وَلَا يُحِيطُونَ
بِشَىْءٍ مِّنْ عِلْمِهِۦٓ إِلَّا بِمَا شَآءَ ۚ وَسِعَ كُرْسِيُّهُ ٱلسَّمَٰوَٰتِ
وَٱلْأَرْضَ ۖ وَلَا يَـُٔودُهُۥ حِفْظُهُمَا ۚ وَهُوَ ٱلْعَلِىُّ ٱلْعَظِيمُ ﴿٢٥٥﴾

Allāh! None has the right to be worshipped but He, Al-Ḥayyul-Qayyūm (the Ever Living, the One Who sustains and protects all that exists). Neither slumber nor sleep overtakes Him. To Him belongs whatever is in the heavens and whatever is on the earth. Who is he that can intercede with Him except with His Permission? He knows what happens to them (His creatures) in this world, and what will happen to them in the Hereafter. And they will never compass anything of His Knowledge except that which He wills. His kursī (footstool) extends over the heavens and the earth, and He feels no fatigue in guarding and preserving them. And He is the Most High, the Most Great.

Sūrah al-Baqarah, verse 255

لِلَّهِ مَا فِي ٱلسَّمَٰوَٰتِ
وَمَا فِي ٱلْأَرْضِ ۗ وَإِن تُبْدُوا۟ مَا فِىٓ أَنفُسِكُمْ أَوْ تُخْفُوهُ
يُحَاسِبْكُم بِهِ ٱللَّهُ ۖ فَيَغْفِرُ لِمَن يَشَآءُ وَيُعَذِّبُ مَن يَشَآءُ ۗ
وَٱللَّهُ عَلَىٰ كُلِّ شَىْءٍ قَدِيرٌ ﴿٢٨٤﴾ ءَامَنَ ٱلرَّسُولُ بِمَآ أُنزِلَ
إِلَيْهِ مِن رَّبِّهِۦ وَٱلْمُؤْمِنُونَ ۚ كُلٌّ ءَامَنَ بِٱللَّهِ وَمَلَٰٓئِكَتِهِۦ وَكُتُبِهِۦ
وَرُسُلِهِۦ لَا نُفَرِّقُ بَيْنَ أَحَدٍ مِّن رُّسُلِهِۦ ۚ وَقَالُوا۟ سَمِعْنَا
وَأَطَعْنَا ۖ غُفْرَانَكَ رَبَّنَا وَإِلَيْكَ ٱلْمَصِيرُ ﴿٢٨٥﴾ لَا يُكَلِّفُ
ٱللَّهُ نَفْسًا إِلَّا وُسْعَهَا ۚ لَهَا مَا كَسَبَتْ وَعَلَيْهَا مَا ٱكْتَسَبَتْ ۗ
رَبَّنَا لَا تُؤَاخِذْنَآ إِن نَّسِينَآ أَوْ أَخْطَأْنَا ۚ رَبَّنَا وَلَا تَحْمِلْ
عَلَيْنَآ إِصْرًا كَمَا حَمَلْتَهُۥ عَلَى ٱلَّذِينَ مِن قَبْلِنَا ۚ رَبَّنَا وَلَا
تُحَمِّلْنَا مَا لَا طَاقَةَ لَنَا بِهِۦ ۖ وَٱعْفُ عَنَّا وَٱغْفِرْ لَنَا وَٱرْحَمْنَآ ۚ
أَنتَ مَوْلَىٰنَا فَٱنصُرْنَا عَلَى ٱلْقَوْمِ ٱلْكَٰفِرِينَ ﴿٢٨٦﴾

To Allāh belongs all that is in the heavens and all that is on the earth, and whether you disclose what is in your own selves or conceal it, Allāh will call you to account for it. Then He forgives whom He wills and punishes whom He wills. And Allāh is Able to do all things. The Messenger (Muḥammad) believes in what has been sent down to him from his Lord, and (so do) the believers. Each one believes in Allāh, His Angels, His Books, His Messengers. (They say), "We make no distinction between one another of His Messengers" - and they say, "We hear, and we obey. (We seek) Your Forgiveness our Lord, and to You is the return (of all). Allāh burdens not a person beyond his scope. He gets reward for that (good) which he has earned, and he is punished for that (evil) which he has earned. "Our Lord! Punish us not if we forget or fall into error, our Lord! Lay not on us a burden like that which You did lay on those before us (Jews and Christians); our Lord! Put not on us a burden greater than we have strength to bear. Pardon us and grant us Forgiveness. Have mercy on us. You are our Maula

(Patron, Supporter and Protector etc.) and give us victory over the disbelieving people."
Sūrah al-Baqarah, verses 284-286

After this, the following verses and incantations are recited:
1)

بِسۡمِ ٱللَّهِ ٱلرَّحۡمَٰنِ ٱلرَّحِيمِ

الٓمٓ ﴿١﴾ ٱللَّهُ لَآ إِلَٰهَ إِلَّا هُوَ ٱلۡحَيُّ ٱلۡقَيُّومُ ﴿٢﴾ نَزَّلَ عَلَيۡكَ ٱلۡكِتَٰبَ
بِٱلۡحَقِّ مُصَدِّقٗا لِّمَا بَيۡنَ يَدَيۡهِ وَأَنزَلَ ٱلتَّوۡرَىٰةَ وَٱلۡإِنجِيلَ ﴿٣﴾ مِن
قَبۡلُ هُدٗى لِّلنَّاسِ وَأَنزَلَ ٱلۡفُرۡقَانَۗ إِنَّ ٱلَّذِينَ كَفَرُواْ بِـَٔايَٰتِ ٱللَّهِ لَهُمۡ
عَذَابٞ شَدِيدٞۗ وَٱللَّهُ عَزِيزٞ ذُو ٱنتِقَامٍ ﴿٤﴾ إِنَّ ٱللَّهَ لَا يَخۡفَىٰ عَلَيۡهِ
شَيۡءٞ فِي ٱلۡأَرۡضِ وَلَا فِي ٱلسَّمَآءِ ﴿٥﴾ هُوَ ٱلَّذِي يُصَوِّرُكُمۡ
فِي ٱلۡأَرۡحَامِ كَيۡفَ يَشَآءُۚ لَآ إِلَٰهَ إِلَّا هُوَ ٱلۡعَزِيزُ ٱلۡحَكِيمُ ﴿٦﴾ هُوَ
ٱلَّذِيٓ أَنزَلَ عَلَيۡكَ ٱلۡكِتَٰبَ مِنۡهُ ءَايَٰتٞ مُّحۡكَمَٰتٌ هُنَّ أُمُّ ٱلۡكِتَٰبِ
وَأُخَرُ مُتَشَٰبِهَٰتٞۖ فَأَمَّا ٱلَّذِينَ فِي قُلُوبِهِمۡ زَيۡغٞ فَيَتَّبِعُونَ مَا تَشَٰبَهَ
مِنۡهُ ٱبۡتِغَآءَ ٱلۡفِتۡنَةِ وَٱبۡتِغَآءَ تَأۡوِيلِهِۦۖ وَمَا يَعۡلَمُ تَأۡوِيلَهُۥٓ إِلَّا ٱللَّهُۗ
وَٱلرَّٰسِخُونَ فِي ٱلۡعِلۡمِ يَقُولُونَ ءَامَنَّا بِهِۦ كُلّٞ مِّنۡ عِندِ رَبِّنَاۗ وَمَا يَذَّكَّرُ
إِلَّآ أُوْلُواْ ٱلۡأَلۡبَٰبِ ﴿٧﴾ رَبَّنَا لَا تُزِغۡ قُلُوبَنَا بَعۡدَ إِذۡ هَدَيۡتَنَا وَهَبۡ
لَنَا مِن لَّدُنكَ رَحۡمَةًۚ إِنَّكَ أَنتَ ٱلۡوَهَّابُ ﴿٨﴾ رَبَّنَآ إِنَّكَ جَامِعُ
ٱلنَّاسِ لِيَوۡمٖ لَّا رَيۡبَ فِيهِۚ إِنَّ ٱللَّهَ لَا يُخۡلِفُ ٱلۡمِيعَادَ ﴿٩﴾
إِنَّ ٱلَّذِينَ كَفَرُواْ لَن تُغۡنِيَ عَنۡهُمۡ أَمۡوَٰلُهُمۡ وَلَآ أَوۡلَٰدُهُم
مِّنَ ٱللَّهِ شَيۡـٔٗاۖ وَأُوْلَٰٓئِكَ هُمۡ وَقُودُ ٱلنَّارِ ﴿١٠﴾

Alif Lām Mīm. Allāh! None has the right to be worshipped but He, Al-Ḥayyul-Qayyūm (the Ever Living, the One Who sustains and protects all that exists). It is He Who has sent down the Book (the Qur'ān) to you (Muḥammad) with truth, confirming what came before it. And He sent down the Torah and the Injīl (Gospel). Aforetime, as a guidance to mankind. And He sent down the criterion (this Qur'ān). Truly, those who disbelieve in the Āyat (proofs, evidences, verses, lessons etc.) of Allāh, for them there is a severe torment; and Allāh is All-Mighty, All-

Able of Retribution. Truly, nothing is hidden from Allāh, in the heavens or in the earth. He it is Who shapes you in the wombs as He wills. None has the right to be worshipped but He, the All-Mighty, the All-Wise. It is He Who has sent down to you (Muḥammad) the Book. In it are Verses that are entirely clear, they are the foundations of the Book and others not entirely clear. So as for those in whose hearts there is a deviation (from the truth) they follow that which is not entirely clear thereof, seeking Al-Fitnah (polytheism and trials), and seeking for its hidden meanings, but none knows its hidden meanings save Allāh. And those who are firmly grounded in knowledge say: "We believe in it, the whole of it (clear and unclear Verses) are from our Lord." And none receive admonition except men of understanding. (They say): "Our Lord! Let not our hearts deviate (from the truth) after You have guided us, and grant us mercy from You. Truly, You are the Bestower. Our Lord! Verily, it is You Who will gather mankind together on the Day about which there is no doubt. Verily, Allāh never breaks His Promise." Verily, those who disbelieve, neither their properties nor their offspring will avail them whatsoever against Allāh; and it is they who will be fuel of the Fire.

Sūrah Āl-ʿImrān, verses 1-10

2)

إِنَّ رَبَّكُمُ ٱللَّهُ ٱلَّذِى خَلَقَ ٱلسَّمَٰوَٰتِ وَٱلْأَرْضَ فِى سِتَّةِ
أَيَّامٍ ثُمَّ ٱسْتَوَىٰ عَلَى ٱلْعَرْشِ يُغْشِى ٱلَّيْلَ ٱلنَّهَارَ يَطْلُبُهُۥ حَثِيثًا
وَٱلشَّمْسَ وَٱلْقَمَرَ وَٱلنُّجُومَ مُسَخَّرَٰتٍۭ بِأَمْرِهِۦٓ ۗ أَلَا لَهُ ٱلْخَلْقُ
وَٱلْأَمْرُ ۗ تَبَارَكَ ٱللَّهُ رَبُّ ٱلْعَٰلَمِينَ ﴿٥٤﴾ ٱدْعُوا۟ رَبَّكُمْ تَضَرُّعًا
وَخُفْيَةً ۚ إِنَّهُۥ لَا يُحِبُّ ٱلْمُعْتَدِينَ ﴿٥٥﴾ وَلَا تُفْسِدُوا۟ فِى
ٱلْأَرْضِ بَعْدَ إِصْلَٰحِهَا وَٱدْعُوهُ خَوْفًا وَطَمَعًا ۚ إِنَّ رَحْمَتَ
ٱللَّهِ قَرِيبٌ مِّنَ ٱلْمُحْسِنِينَ ﴿٥٦﴾ وَهُوَ ٱلَّذِى يُرْسِلُ
ٱلرِّيَٰحَ بُشْرًۢا بَيْنَ يَدَىْ رَحْمَتِهِۦ ۖ حَتَّىٰٓ إِذَآ أَقَلَّتْ سَحَابًا
ثِقَالًا سُقْنَٰهُ لِبَلَدٍ مَّيِّتٍ فَأَنزَلْنَا بِهِ ٱلْمَآءَ فَأَخْرَجْنَا بِهِۦ مِن كُلِّ
ٱلثَّمَرَٰتِ ۚ كَذَٰلِكَ نُخْرِجُ ٱلْمَوْتَىٰ لَعَلَّكُمْ تَذَكَّرُونَ ﴿٥٧﴾

Indeed your Lord is Allāh, Who created the heavens and the earth in Six Days, and then He rose over (Istawa) the Throne (really in a manner that suits His Majesty). He brings the night as a cover over the day, seeking it rapidly, and (He created) the sun, the moon, the stars subjected to His Command. Surely, His is the Creation and Commandment. Blessed is Allāh, the Lord of the ʿĀlamīn (mankind, jinn and all that exists)! Invoke your Lord with humility and in secret. He likes not the aggressors. And do not do mischief on the earth, after it has been set in order, and invoke Him with fear and hope. Surely, Allāh's Mercy is (ever) near unto the good-doers. And it is He Who sends the winds as heralds of glad tidings, going before His Mercy (rain). Till when they have carried a heavy-laden cloud, We drive it to a land that is dead, then We cause water (rain) to descend thereon. Then We produce every kind of fruit therewith. Similarly, We shall raise up the dead, so that you may remember or take heed.

Sūrah al-Aʿrāf, verses 54-57

3)

وَإِذَا قَرَأْتَ
ٱلْقُرْءَانَ جَعَلْنَا بَيْنَكَ وَبَيْنَ ٱلَّذِينَ لَا يُؤْمِنُونَ بِٱلْءَاخِرَةِ حِجَابًا
مَّسْتُورًا ﴿٤٥﴾ وَجَعَلْنَا عَلَىٰ قُلُوبِهِمْ أَكِنَّةً أَن يَفْقَهُوهُ وَفِىٓ ءَاذَانِهِمْ
وَقْرًا ۚ وَإِذَا ذَكَرْتَ رَبَّكَ فِى ٱلْقُرْءَانِ وَحْدَهُۥ وَلَّوْا۟ عَلَىٰٓ أَدْبَٰرِهِمْ نُفُورًا
﴿٤٦﴾ نَّحْنُ أَعْلَمُ بِمَا يَسْتَمِعُونَ بِهِۦٓ إِذْ يَسْتَمِعُونَ إِلَيْكَ وَإِذْ هُمْ نَجْوَىٰٓ
إِذْ يَقُولُ ٱلظَّٰلِمُونَ إِن تَتَّبِعُونَ إِلَّا رَجُلًا مَّسْحُورًا ﴿٤٧﴾ ٱنظُرْ
كَيْفَ ضَرَبُوا۟ لَكَ ٱلْأَمْثَالَ فَضَلُّوا۟ فَلَا يَسْتَطِيعُونَ سَبِيلًا ﴿٤٨﴾
وَقَالُوٓا۟ أَءِذَا كُنَّا عِظَٰمًا وَرُفَٰتًا أَءِنَّا لَمَبْعُوثُونَ خَلْقًا جَدِيدًا ﴿٤٩﴾
۞ قُلْ كُونُوا۟ حِجَارَةً أَوْ حَدِيدًا ﴿٥٠﴾ أَوْ خَلْقًا مِّمَّا يَكْبُرُ فِى
صُدُورِكُمْ ۚ فَسَيَقُولُونَ مَن يُعِيدُنَا ۖ قُلِ ٱلَّذِى فَطَرَكُمْ أَوَّلَ مَرَّةٍ ۚ
فَسَيُنْغِضُونَ إِلَيْكَ رُءُوسَهُمْ وَيَقُولُونَ مَتَىٰ هُوَ ۖ قُلْ عَسَىٰٓ أَن
يَكُونَ قَرِيبًا ﴿٥١﴾

And when you (Muḥammad) recite the Qur'ān, we put between you and those who believe not in the Hereafter, an invisible veil (or screen their hearts, so they hear or understand it not). And We have put coverings over their hearts lest they should understand it (the Qur'ān), and in their ears deafness. And when you make mention of your Lord Alone in the Qur'ān, they turn on their backs, fleeing in extreme dislike. We know best of what they listen to, when they listen to you. And when they take secret counsel, then the Ẓalimūn (polytheists and wrong-doers) say: "you follow none but a bewitched man." See what examples they have put forward for you. So they have gone astray, and never can they find a way. And they say: "When we are bones and fragments (destroyed), shall we really be resurrected (to be) a new creation?" Say (O Muḥammad) "Be you stones or iron. Or some created thing that is yet greater (or harder) in your breasts (thoughts to be resurrected, even then you shall be resurrected)." Then they will say: "Who shall bring us back (to life)?" Say: "He who created you first!" Then they will shake their heads at you and say: "When will that be?" Say: "Perhaps it is near!"

Sūrah al-Isrā', verses 45-51

4)

۞ وَأَوْحَيْنَآ إِلَىٰ مُوسَىٰٓ أَنْ أَلْقِ عَصَاكَ ۖ فَإِذَا هِىَ تَلْقَفُ مَا
يَأْفِكُونَ ﴿١١٧﴾ فَوَقَعَ ٱلْحَقُّ وَبَطَلَ مَا كَانُوا۟ يَعْمَلُونَ ﴿١١٨﴾ فَغُلِبُوا۟
هُنَالِكَ وَٱنقَلَبُوا۟ صَٰغِرِينَ ﴿١١٩﴾

And we revealed to Mūsā (saying): "Throw your stick," and behold! It swallowed up straight away all the falsehood which they showed. Thus truth was confirmed, and all that they did was made of no effect. So they were defeated there and returned disgraced.

Sūrah al-A'rāf, verses 117-119

5)

وَقَالَ فِرْعَوْنُ ٱئْتُونِى بِكُلِّ سَٰحِرٍ عَلِيمٍ ﴿٧٩﴾ فَلَمَّا جَآءَ ٱلسَّحَرَةُ
قَالَ لَهُم مُّوسَىٰٓ أَلْقُوا۟ مَآ أَنتُم مُّلْقُونَ ﴿٨٠﴾ فَلَمَّآ أَلْقَوْا۟ قَالَ
مُوسَىٰ مَا جِئْتُم بِهِ ٱلسِّحْرُ ۖ إِنَّ ٱللَّهَ سَيُبْطِلُهُۥٓ ۖ إِنَّ ٱللَّهَ لَا يُصْلِحُ
عَمَلَ ٱلْمُفْسِدِينَ ﴿٨١﴾ وَيُحِقُّ ٱللَّهُ ٱلْحَقَّ بِكَلِمَٰتِهِۦ وَلَوْ كَرِهَ
ٱلْمُجْرِمُونَ ﴿٨٢﴾

And Pharaoh said: "Bring me every well-versed sorcerer." And when the sorcerers came, Mūsā said to them: "Cast down what you want to cast!" Then when they had cast down, Mūsā said: "What you have brought is sorcery; Allāh will surely make it of no effect. Verily, Allāh does not set right the work of the evil-doers. And Allāh will establish and make apparent the truth by His Words, however much the Mujrimūn (polytheists, criminals, sinners etc.) may hate it."

Sūrah Yūnus, verses 79-82

6)

قَالُوا۟ يَـٰمُوسَىٰٓ إِمَّآ أَن تُلْقِىَ وَإِمَّآ أَن نَّكُونَ أَوَّلَ مَنْ أَلْقَىٰ ﴿٦٥﴾ قَالَ
بَلْ أَلْقُوا۟ ۖ فَإِذَا حِبَالُهُمْ وَعِصِيُّهُمْ يُخَيَّلُ إِلَيْهِ مِن سِحْرِهِمْ أَنَّهَا تَسْعَىٰ
﴿٦٦﴾ فَأَوْجَسَ فِى نَفْسِهِۦ خِيفَةً مُّوسَىٰ ﴿٦٧﴾ قُلْنَا لَا تَخَفْ إِنَّكَ
أَنتَ ٱلْأَعْلَىٰ ﴿٦٨﴾ وَأَلْقِ مَا فِى يَمِينِكَ تَلْقَفْ مَا صَنَعُوٓا۟ ۖ إِنَّمَا صَنَعُوا۟
كَيْدُ سَـٰحِرٍ ۖ وَلَا يُفْلِحُ ٱلسَّاحِرُ حَيْثُ أَتَىٰ ﴿٦٩﴾

They said: "O Mūsā! Either you throw first or we be the first to throw?" [Mūsā] said: "Nay, throw you (first)!" Then behold! Their ropes and their sticks, by their magic, appeared to him as though they moved fast. So Mūsā conceived fear in himself. We (Allāh) said: "Fear not! Surely, you will have the upper hand. And throw that which is in your right hand! It will swallow up that which they have made. That which they have made is only a magician's trick, and the magician will never be successful, to whatever amount (of skill) he may attain.

Sūrah Ṭa-Ha, verses 65-69

7)

أَفَحَسِبْتُمْ أَنَّمَا خَلَقْنَـٰكُمْ عَبَثًا وَأَنَّكُمْ
إِلَيْنَا لَا تُرْجَعُونَ ﴿١١٥﴾ فَتَعَـٰلَى ٱللَّهُ ٱلْمَلِكُ ٱلْحَقُّ ۖ لَآ إِلَـٰهَ إِلَّا
هُوَ رَبُّ ٱلْعَرْشِ ٱلْكَرِيمِ ﴿١١٦﴾ وَمَن يَدْعُ مَعَ ٱللَّهِ إِلَـٰهًا
ءَاخَرَ لَا بُرْهَـٰنَ لَهُۥ بِهِۦ فَإِنَّمَا حِسَابُهُۥ عِندَ رَبِّهِۦٓ ۚ إِنَّهُۥ لَا يُفْلِحُ
ٱلْكَـٰفِرُونَ ﴿١١٧﴾ وَقُل رَّبِّ ٱغْفِرْ وَٱرْحَمْ وَأَنتَ خَيْرُ ٱلرَّٰحِمِينَ ﴿١١٨﴾

"Did you think We had created you in play (without any purpose), and that you would not be brought back to Us?" So Exalted be Allāh, the True King: none has the right to be worshipped but He, the Lord of the Supreme Throne! And whoever invokes (or worships), besides Allāh, any other god, of whom he has no proof; then his reckoning is only with his Lord. Surely, the disbelievers will not be successful. And say (O

Muḥammad): "My Lord! Forgive and have mercy, for You are the Best of those who show mercy!"

Sūrah al-Mu'minūn, verses 114-118

8)

بِسۡمِ ٱللَّهِ ٱلرَّحۡمَٰنِ ٱلرَّحِيمِ

وَٱلصَّٰٓفَّٰتِ صَفّٗا ﴿١﴾ فَٱلزَّٰجِرَٰتِ زَجۡرٗا ﴿٢﴾ فَٱلتَّٰلِيَٰتِ ذِكۡرًا ﴿٣﴾
إِنَّ إِلَٰهَكُمۡ لَوَٰحِدٞ ﴿٤﴾ رَّبُّ ٱلسَّمَٰوَٰتِ وَٱلۡأَرۡضِ وَمَا بَيۡنَهُمَا وَرَبُّ
ٱلۡمَشَٰرِقِ ﴿٥﴾ إِنَّا زَيَّنَّا ٱلسَّمَآءَ ٱلدُّنۡيَا بِزِينَةٍ ٱلۡكَوَاكِبِ ﴿٦﴾ وَحِفۡظٗا
مِّن كُلِّ شَيۡطَٰنٖ مَّارِدٖ ﴿٧﴾ لَّا يَسَّمَّعُونَ إِلَى ٱلۡمَلَإِ ٱلۡأَعۡلَىٰ وَيُقۡذَفُونَ
مِن كُلِّ جَانِبٖ ﴿٨﴾ دُحُورٗاۖ وَلَهُمۡ عَذَابٞ وَاصِبٌ ﴿٩﴾ إِلَّا مَنۡ خَطِفَ
ٱلۡخَطۡفَةَ فَأَتۡبَعَهُۥ شِهَابٞ ثَاقِبٞ ﴿١٠﴾ فَٱسۡتَفۡتِهِمۡ أَهُمۡ أَشَدُّ خَلۡقًا
أَم مَّنۡ خَلَقۡنَآۚ إِنَّا خَلَقۡنَٰهُم مِّن طِينٖ لَّازِبِۭ ﴿١١﴾ بَلۡ عَجِبۡتَ
وَيَسۡخَرُونَ ﴿١٢﴾ وَإِذَا ذُكِّرُواْ لَا يَذۡكُرُونَ ﴿١٣﴾ وَإِذَا رَأَوۡاْ ءَايَةٗ يَسۡتَسۡخِرُونَ
﴿١٤﴾ وَقَالُوٓاْ إِنۡ هَٰذَآ إِلَّا سِحۡرٞ مُّبِينٌ ﴿١٥﴾ أَءِذَا مِتۡنَا وَكُنَّا تُرَابٗا وَعِظَٰمًا
أَءِنَّا لَمَبۡعُوثُونَ ﴿١٦﴾ أَوَءَابَآؤُنَا ٱلۡأَوَّلُونَ ﴿١٧﴾ قُلۡ نَعَمۡ وَأَنتُمۡ دَٰخِرُونَ

By those (angels) ranked in ranks (or rows). By those (angels) who drive the clouds in a good way. By those (angels) who bring the Book and the Qur'ān from Allāh to mankind. Verily your God is indeed One (Allāh). Lord of the heavens and of the earth, and all that is between them, and Lord of every point of the sun's risings. Verily We have adorned the near heaven with the stars (for beauty). And to guard against every rebellious devil. They cannot listen to the higher group (angels) for they are pelted from every side. Outcast, and theirs is a constant (or painful) torment. Except such as snatch away something by stealing, and they are pursued by a flaming fire of piercing brightness. Then ask them (these polytheists): "are they stronger as creation or those (others like the heavens and the earth and the mountains) whom We have created?" Verily, We created them of a sticky clay. Nay, you (O Muḥammad) wondered (at their insolence) while they mock (at you and the Qur'ān). And when they are reminded, they pay no attention. And when they see an Āyah (a sign or an evidence) from Allāh, they mock at it. And they say: "This is nothing but evident magic!" "When we are dead and have become dust and bones, shall we (then) verily be resurrected? And also our fathers of old?" Say (O Muḥammad): "Yes, and you shall then be humiliated."

Sūrah al-Ṣāffāt, verses 1-18

9)

فَبِأَيِّ ءَالَآءِ رَبِّكُمَا تُكَذِّبَانِ
﴿٢٨﴾ يَسْـَٔلُهُۥ مَن فِي ٱلسَّمَٰوَٰتِ وَٱلْأَرْضِ ۚ كُلَّ يَوْمٍ هُوَ فِي شَأْنٍ ﴿٢٩﴾ فَبِأَيِّ
ءَالَآءِ رَبِّكُمَا تُكَذِّبَانِ ﴿٣٠﴾ سَنَفْرُغُ لَكُمْ أَيُّهَ ٱلثَّقَلَانِ ﴿٣١﴾ فَبِأَيِّ
ءَالَآءِ رَبِّكُمَا تُكَذِّبَانِ ﴿٣٢﴾ يَٰمَعْشَرَ ٱلْجِنِّ وَٱلْإِنسِ إِنِ ٱسْتَطَعْتُمْ
أَن تَنفُذُوا۟ مِنْ أَقْطَارِ ٱلسَّمَٰوَٰتِ وَٱلْأَرْضِ فَٱنفُذُوا۟ ۚ لَا تَنفُذُونَ
إِلَّا بِسُلْطَٰنٍ ﴿٣٣﴾ فَبِأَيِّ ءَالَآءِ رَبِّكُمَا تُكَذِّبَانِ ﴿٣٤﴾

Then which of the Blessings of your Lord will you both (jinn and men) deny? Whosoever is in the heavens and on the earth begs of Him (its needs from Him). Every day He is (engaged) in some affair (such as giving honour or disgrace to some, life or death to some, etc.)! Then which of the Blessings of your Lord will you both (jinn and men) deny? We shall attend to you, O you two classes (jinn and men)! Then which of the Blessings of your Lord will you both (jinn and men) deny? O assembly of jinn and men! If you have power to pass beyond the zones of the heavens and the earth, then pass beyond (them)! But you will never be able to pass them, except with authority (from Allāh)! Then which of the Blessings of your Lord will you both (jinn and men) deny?

Sūrah al-Raḥmān, verses 28-34

10)

لَوْ أَنزَلْنَا هَٰذَا
ٱلْقُرْءَانَ عَلَىٰ جَبَلٍ لَّرَأَيْتَهُۥ خَٰشِعًا مُّتَصَدِّعًا مِّنْ خَشْيَةِ
ٱللَّهِ ۚ وَتِلْكَ ٱلْأَمْثَٰلُ نَضْرِبُهَا لِلنَّاسِ لَعَلَّهُمْ يَتَفَكَّرُونَ
﴿٢١﴾ هُوَ ٱللَّهُ ٱلَّذِى لَآ إِلَٰهَ إِلَّا هُوَ ۖ عَٰلِمُ ٱلْغَيْبِ وَٱلشَّهَٰدَةِ ۖ
هُوَ ٱلرَّحْمَٰنُ ٱلرَّحِيمُ ﴿٢٢﴾ هُوَ ٱللَّهُ ٱلَّذِى لَآ إِلَٰهَ إِلَّا هُوَ
ٱلْمَلِكُ ٱلْقُدُّوسُ ٱلسَّلَٰمُ ٱلْمُؤْمِنُ ٱلْمُهَيْمِنُ ٱلْعَزِيزُ
ٱلْجَبَّارُ ٱلْمُتَكَبِّرُ ۚ سُبْحَٰنَ ٱللَّهِ عَمَّا يُشْرِكُونَ
﴿٢٣﴾ هُوَ ٱللَّهُ ٱلْخَٰلِقُ ٱلْبَارِئُ ٱلْمُصَوِّرُ ۖ لَهُ ٱلْأَسْمَآءُ ٱلْحُسْنَىٰ ۚ
يُسَبِّحُ لَهُۥ مَا فِى ٱلسَّمَٰوَٰتِ وَٱلْأَرْضِ ۖ وَهُوَ ٱلْعَزِيزُ ٱلْحَكِيمُ ﴿٢٤﴾

Had We sent down this Qur'ān on a mountain, you would surely have seen it humbling itself and rent asunder by the fear of Allāh. Such are the parables which We put forward to mankind that they may reflect. He is Allāh, besides Whom none has the right to be worshipped but He, the All-Knower of the unseen and the seen. He is the Most Gracious, the Most Merciful. He is Allāh besides Whom none has the right to be worshipped but He, the King, the Holy, the One Free from all defects, the Giver of security, the Watcher over His creatures, the All-Mighty, the Compeller, the Supreme. Glory be to Allāh! (High is He) above all that they associate as partners with Him. He is Allāh, the Creator, the Inventor of all things, the Bestower of forms. To Him belong the Best Names, all that is in the heavens and the earth glorify Him. And He is the All-Mighty, the All-Wise.

Sūrah al-Ḥashr, verses 21-24

11)

بِسْمِ ٱللَّهِ ٱلرَّحْمَٰنِ ٱلرَّحِيمِ

تَبَٰرَكَ ٱلَّذِى بِيَدِهِ ٱلْمُلْكُ وَهُوَ عَلَىٰ كُلِّ شَىْءٍ قَدِيرٌ ﴿١﴾ ٱلَّذِى خَلَقَ
ٱلْمَوْتَ وَٱلْحَيَوٰةَ لِيَبْلُوَكُمْ أَيُّكُمْ أَحْسَنُ عَمَلًا ۚ وَهُوَ ٱلْعَزِيزُ ٱلْغَفُورُ ﴿٢﴾
ٱلَّذِى خَلَقَ سَبْعَ سَمَٰوَٰتٍ طِبَاقًا ۖ مَّا تَرَىٰ فِى خَلْقِ ٱلرَّحْمَٰنِ مِن
تَفَٰوُتٍ ۖ فَٱرْجِعِ ٱلْبَصَرَ هَلْ تَرَىٰ مِن فُطُورٍ ﴿٣﴾ ثُمَّ ٱرْجِعِ ٱلْبَصَرَ كَرَّتَيْنِ
يَنقَلِبْ إِلَيْكَ ٱلْبَصَرُ خَاسِئًا وَهُوَ حَسِيرٌ ﴿٤﴾

Blessed be He in Whose Hand is the dominion; and He is Able to do all things. Who has created death and life that He may test you which of you is best in deed. And He is the All-Mighty, the Oft-Forgiving. Who has created the seven heavens one above another; you can see no fault in the creation of the Most Gracious. Then look again: "Can you see any rifts?" Then look again and yet again: your sight will return to you in a state of humiliation and worn out.

Sūrah al-Mulk, verses 1-4

12)

وَإِن يَكَادُ ٱلَّذِينَ كَفَرُوا۟ لَيُزْلِقُونَكَ بِأَبْصَٰرِهِمْ
لَمَّا سَمِعُوا۟ ٱلذِّكْرَ وَيَقُولُونَ إِنَّهُۥ لَمَجْنُونٌ ﴿٥١﴾ وَمَا هُوَ إِلَّا ذِكْرٌ لِّلْعَٰلَمِينَ ﴿٥٢﴾

And verily, those who disbelieve would almost make you slip with their eyes (through hatred) when they hear the Reminder (the Qur'ān), and they say: Verily, he (Muḥammad) is a madman. But it is nothing else than a Reminder to all the 'Ālamīn (mankind and jinn).

Sūrah al-Qalam, verses 51-52

13)

بِسْمِ ٱللَّهِ ٱلرَّحْمَٰنِ ٱلرَّحِيمِ

قُلْ يَٰٓأَيُّهَا ٱلْكَٰفِرُونَ ﴿١﴾ لَآ أَعْبُدُ مَا تَعْبُدُونَ ﴿٢﴾
وَلَآ أَنتُمْ عَٰبِدُونَ مَآ أَعْبُدُ ﴿٣﴾ وَلَآ أَنَا۠ عَابِدٌ مَّا عَبَدتُّمْ ﴿٤﴾
وَلَآ أَنتُمْ عَٰبِدُونَ مَآ أَعْبُدُ ﴿٥﴾ لَكُمْ دِينُكُمْ وَلِىَ دِينِ ﴿٦﴾

Say (O Muḥammad): "O disbelievers! I worship not that which you worship. Nor will you worship that which I worship. And I shall not worship that which you are worshipping. Nor will you worship that which I worship. To you be your religion, and to me my religion."

Sūrah al-Kāfirūn

14)

بِسْمِ ٱللَّهِ ٱلرَّحْمَٰنِ ٱلرَّحِيمِ

قُلْ هُوَ ٱللَّهُ أَحَدٌ ﴿١﴾ ٱللَّهُ ٱلصَّمَدُ ﴿٢﴾ لَمْ يَلِدْ
وَلَمْ يُولَدْ ﴿٣﴾ وَلَمْ يَكُن لَّهُۥ كُفُوًا أَحَدٌۢ ﴿٤﴾

Say (O Muḥammad): He is Allāh, the One. Allāh the Self-Sufficient Master, Whom all creatures need, (He neither eats nor drinks). He begets not, nor was He begotten. And there is none co-equal or comparable unto Him."

Sūrah al-Ikhlāṣ

15)

بِسْمِ ٱللَّهِ ٱلرَّحْمَٰنِ ٱلرَّحِيمِ

قُلْ أَعُوذُ بِرَبِّ ٱلْفَلَقِ ﴿١﴾ مِن شَرِّ مَا خَلَقَ ﴿٢﴾ وَمِن
شَرِّ غَاسِقٍ إِذَا وَقَبَ ﴿٣﴾ وَمِن شَرِّ ٱلنَّفَّٰثَٰتِ فِى
ٱلْعُقَدِ ﴿٤﴾ وَمِن شَرِّ حَاسِدٍ إِذَا حَسَدَ ﴿٥﴾

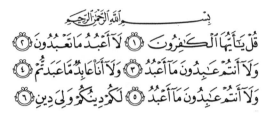

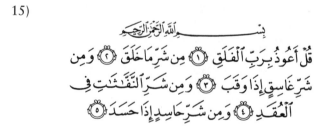

Say: "I seek refuge with (Allāh), the Lord of the daybreak. From the evil of what He has created. And from the evil of the

darkening (night) as it comes with its darkness. And from the evil of those who practise witchcraft when they blow in the knots. And from the evil of the envier when he envies."

Sūrah al-Falaq

16)

بِسْمِ ٱللَّهِ ٱلرَّحْمَٰنِ ٱلرَّحِيمِ

قُلْ أَعُوذُ بِرَبِّ ٱلنَّاسِ ﴿١﴾ مَلِكِ ٱلنَّاسِ ﴿٢﴾ إِلَٰهِ ٱلنَّاسِ ﴿٣﴾ مِن شَرِّ ٱلْوَسْوَاسِ ٱلْخَنَّاسِ ﴿٤﴾ ٱلَّذِى يُوَسْوِسُ فِى صُدُورِ ٱلنَّاسِ ﴿٥﴾ مِنَ ٱلْجِنَّةِ وَٱلنَّاسِ ﴿٦﴾

Say: "I seek refuge with (Allāh) the Lord of mankind. The King of mankind. The God of mankind. From the evil of the whisperer (devil who whispers evil in the hearts of men) who withdraws (from his whispering in one's heart after one remembers Allāh). Of jinn and men."

Sūrah al-Nās[164]

The following incantations should also be recited after the completion of the above verses:

1)

اللَّهُمَّ رَبَّ النَّاسِ مُذْهِبَ البَاسِ ، اشْفِ أَنْتَ الشَّافِي ، لَا شَافِيَ إِلَّا أَنْتَ شِفَاءً لَا يُغَادِرُ سَقَمًا ، أَنْزِلْ رَحْمَةً مِنْ رَحْمَتِكَ ، وَشِفَاءً مِنْ شِفَائِكَ عَلَى هَذَا الوَجَعِ

Allāhuma rabb an-nās, mudh-hib il-bās, ishfi ant ash-shāfī, la shāfī illa anta, shifā'an la yughādiru saqamā, anzil raḥmatan min raḥmatik, wa shifā'an min shifā'ika 'alā hādha al-waja'.

O Allāh! Lord of mankind, the One who removes harm, cure for You are the One who cures. There is none who cures except You, a curing which causes the illness to depart. Send down a mercy from Your mercy, and a cure from Your cure upon this harm.

[164] Footnote from Shaykh Ibn Bāz: It is recommended to recite *Sūrahs Ikhlāṣ*, *Falaq* and *Nās* three times.

2)

بِسْمِ اللهِ، آمَنَّا بِاللهِ الَّذِي لَيْسَ مِنْهُ شَيْءٌ مُمْتَنِع، وَبِعِزَّةِ اللهِ الَّتِي لَا تُرَامُ وَلَا تُضَامُ، وَبِسُلْطَانِ اللهِ
الْمَنِيعِ، نَحْتَجِبُ بِأَسْمَاءِ اللهِ الْحُسْنَى كُلِّهَا عَائِذِينَ بِاللهِ مِنَ الْأَبَالِسَةِ، وَمِنْ شَرِّ كُلِّ مُسِرٍّ وَمُعْلِنٍ، وَمِنْ
شَرِّ مَا يَكِنُّ بِالنَّهَارِ وَيَخْرُجُ بِاللَّيْلِ، وَمِنْ شَرِّ مَا يَكِنُّ بِاللَّيْلِ وَيَخْرُجُ بِالنَّهَارِ، وَمِنْ شَرِّ مَا خَلَقَ وَذَرَأَ
وَبَرَأَ، وَمِنْ شَرِّ طَوَارِقِ اللَّيْلِ وَالنَّهَارِ، وَمِنْ شَرِّ كُلِّ دَابَّةٍ رَبِّي آخِذٌ بِنَاصِيَتِهَا إِنَّ رَبِّي عَلَى صِرَاطٍ
مُسْتَقِيمٍ

Bismillāh, āmannā billāh aladhī laysa minhu shay'un mumtaniʿ, wa biʿizzat illāhi al-latī lā turām wa lā tuḍām, wa bi-sulṭān illāhi al-munīʿ, naḥtajib bi asmā' illāhi al-ḥusnā kulliha āʿidhīn billāhi min al-abālisah, wa min sharri kulli musirr wa muʿlin, wa min sharri ma yakun bin-nahār wa yakhruju bil-layl, wa min sharri ma yakun bil-layl wa yakhtuju bin-nahār, wa min sharri ma khalaqa wa dhara'a wa bara'a, wa min sharri ṭawāriq il-layli wan-nahār, wa min sharri kulli dābbatin rabbī ākhidhun bināṣiyatihā, inna rabbī ʿalā ṣirāṭin mustaqīm.

In the name of Allāh, we believe in Allāh who is able to do anything, and by the Might of Allāh which is not oppressed nor desired against, and by the invincible power of Allāh, we seek protection in all the beautiful Names of Allāh and we seek refuge in Allāh from the devils, and from the evil of all which is hidden and apparent, and from the evil of that which conceals during the day and appears at night, and from the evil of that which conceals during the night and appears during the day, and from the evil of that which He has created, made and originated, and from the evil of those who visit by night and day, and from the evil of every creature which requires its provision from Allāh. Verily, my Lord is on the Straight Path.

3)

بِسْمِ اللهِ، آمَنْتُ بِاللهِ الْعَظِيمِ، وَكَفَرْتُ بِالْجِبْتِ وَالطَّاغُوتِ وَاسْتَمْسَكْتُ بِالْعُرْوَةِ الْوُثْقَى لَا انْفِصَامَ
لَهَا، وَاللهُ سَمِيعٌ عَلِيمٌ، حَسْبِيَ اللهُ وَكَفَى، سَمِعَ اللهُ لِمَنْ دَعَا، لَيْسَ وَرَاءَ اللهِ مُنْتَهَى، رَضِيتُ بِاللهِ رَبًّا
وَبِالْإِسْلَامِ دِينًا وَبِمُحَمَّدٍ صَلَّى اللهُ عَلَيْهِ وَسَلَّمَ نَبِيًّا وَرَسُولًا

Bismillāh, āmantu billāh al-ʿaẓīm, wa kafartu bil-jibti wat-ṭāghūti wastamsaktu bil-ʿurwatil wuthqā lan-fiṣāma lahā, wallāhu samīʿun ʿalīm, hasbiy Allāhu wa kafā, samiʿ Allāhu liman daʿā, laysa warā Allāhi muntahā, raḍītu billāhi rabbā, wa bil-islāmi dīnā, wa bi muḥammadin ṣallalāhu ʿalayhi wa salam nabiyyan wa rasūlā.

In the name of Allāh, I have believed in Allāh, the Great, and have disbelieved in all false deities, and I have grasped the most trustworthy handhold that will never break, and Allāh is All-Hearer, All-Knower. Allāh is sufficient for me, Allāh hears those who invoke Him, there is nothing beyond Allāh. I am pleased with Allāh as my Lord, Islām as my religion, and Muḥammad (ﷺ) as my Prophet and Messenger.

4)

بِسْمِ اللهِ الَّذِي لَا يَضُرُّ مَعَ اسْمِهِ شَيْءٌ فِي الْأَرْضِ وَلَا فِي السَّمَاءِ وَهُوَ السَّمِيعُ الْعَلِيمُ

Bismillāh aladhī la yaḍuru maʿ ismihi shay'un fil arḍi wa lā fis-samā'i wa huwwas samīʿ al-ʿalīm.

In the name of Allāh with whose Name nothing harms in the earth or the heavens, and He is the All-Hearer, the All-Knower.

5)

أَعُوذُ بِكَلِمَاتِ اللهِ التَّامَّاتِ مِنْ شَرِّ مَا خَلَقَ

Aʿūdhu bikallimāt illāhi at-tāmmāt min sharri mā khalaq.

I seek refuge in the complete and perfect Words of Allāh from the evil of what He has created.

6)

أَعُوذُ بِكَلِمَاتِ اللهِ التَّامَّاتِ الَّتِي لَا يُجَاوِزُهُنَّ بَرٌّ وَلَا فَاجِرٌ وَمِنْ شَرِّ مَا خَلَقَ وَذَرَأَ وَبَرَأَ وَمِنْ شَرِّ مَا ذَرَأَ فِي الْأَرْضِ وَمِنْ شَرِّ مَا يَخْرُجُ مِنْهَا وَمِنْ شَرِّ فِتَنِ اللَّيْلِ وَالنَّهَارِ وَمِنْ شَرِّ طَوَارِقِ اللَّيْلِ وَالنَّهَارِ إِلَّا طَارِقٌ يَطْرُقُ بِخَيْرٍ يَا رَحْمٰن

Aʿūdhu bikallimāt illāhi at-tāmmāt allatī lā yujāwizuhunna barrun wa lā fājir, wa min sharri mā khalaqa wa bara'a wa min sharri mā dhara'a fil arḍ, wa min sharri mā yakhruju minhā, wa

min sharri fitan al-layli wan-nahār, wa min sharri ṭawāriq al-layli wan-nahār, illā ṭāriqun yaṭruqu bikhayrin yā raḥmān.
I seek refuge in the complete and perfect Words of Allāh which cannot be passed by any pious or impious, from the evil of what He has created, made and originated, and from the evil of what He has sowed in the earth and the evil of what sprouts from it, and from the evil trials of the night and day, and from the evil of those who visit by night and day except the one who visits with good, O the Most Gracious.

7)

أَعُوْذُ بِكَلِمَاتِ اللهِ التَّامَّةِ مِنْ كُلِّ شَيْطَانٍ وَهَامَّةٍ وَمِنْ كُلِّ عَيْنٍ لَامَّةٍ

Aʿūdhu bikallimāt illāhi at-tāmmah min kulli shayṭānin wa hāmmah wa min kulli ʿaynin lāmmah.
I seek refuge in the complete and perfect Words of Allāh from every *shayṭān* and every vermin, and from the evil-eye which harms.

8)

أَعُوْذُ بِكَلِمَاتِ اللهِ التَّامَّاتِ مِنْ غَضَبِهِ وَعِقَابِهِ وَمِنْ شَرِّ عِبَادِهِ وَمِنْ هَمَزَاتِ الشَّيَاطِيْنِ وَأَنْ يَحْضُرُوْنِ

Aʿūdhu bikallimāt illāhi at-tāmmāt min ghaḍabihi wa ʿiqābihi, wa min sharri ʿibādihi, wa min hamazāt ash-shayāṭīn wa an yahḍarūn.
I seek refuge in the complete and perfect Words of Allāh from His anger, His punishment, and from the evil of His slaves, and from the whisperings of the *shayāṭīn* and that they should come near me.

9)

اللَّهُمَّ إِنِّي أَعُوْذُ بِوَجْهِكَ الْكَرِيْمِ وَكَلِمَاتِكَ التَّامَّاتِ مِنْ شَرِّ مَا أَنْتَ آخِذٌ بِنَاصِيَتِهِ، اللَّهُمَّ أَنْتَ تَكْشِفُ الْمَأْثَمَ وَالْمَغْرَمَ، اللَّهُمَّ لَا يُهْزَمُ جُنْدُكَ وَلَا يُخْلَفُ وَعْدُكَ سُبْحَانَكَ وَبِحَمْدِكَ

Allāhumma innī aʿūdhu bi-wajhikal karīm wa kallimātika at-tāmmāt min sharri mā anta ākhidhun bi-nāṣiyatih, allāuhamma anta takshifu al-ma'tham wal-maghram, Allāhumma la yahzumu junduka wa lā yukhlafu waʿduka, subḥānaka wa biḥamdik.

O Allāh! I seek refuge in Your Noble Face and Your complete and perfect Words from the evil of that which requires Your provision, O Allāh You uncover sin and debt. O Allāh Your army is not defeated, and Your promise is not broken, Glory be to You and be You Praised.

10)

أَعُوْذُ بِوَجْهِ اللهِ العَظِيْمِ الَّذِي لاَ شَيْءَ أَعْظَمُ مِنْهُ وَبِكَلِمَاتِهِ التَّامَّاتِ الَّتِي لاَ يُجَاوِزُهُنَّ بَرٌّ وَلاَ فَاجِرٌ، وَ
بِأَسْمَاءِ اللهِ الحُسْنَى مَا عَلِمْتُ مِنْهَا وَمَا لاَ أَعْلَم، وَمِنْ شَرِّ مَا أَنْتَ آخِذٌ بِنَاصِيَتِهِ إِنَّ رَبِّي عَلَى
صِرَاطٍ مُّسْتَقِيْمٍ

A'ūdhu biwajh illāhi al-aẓīm aladhī lā shay'a a'ẓamu minhu, wa bikalimātihi at-tāmmāt allatī lā yujāwizuhunna barrun wa lā fājir, wa bi asmā' illāhi al-ḥusnā mā 'alimtu minhā wa mā lā a'lam, wa min sharri mā anta ākhidhun bināṣiyatih, inna rabbī 'alā ṣirāṭin mustaqīm.
I seek refuge in the Great Face of Allāh which there is nothing greater than, and in His complete and perfect Words which cannot be passed by the pious or impious, and in the beautiful Names of Allāh, those which I know and those which I do not know, and from the evil of that which requires Your provision. Verily, my Lord is on the Straight Path.

11)

اللَّهُمَّ أَنْتَ رَبِّي لاَ إِلَهَ إِلاَّ أَنْتَ عَلَيْكَ تَوَكَّلْتُ وَأَنْتَ رَبُّ العَرْشِ العَظِيْمِ، مَا شَاءَ اللهُ كَانَ وَمَا لَمْ يَشَأْ لَمْ
يَكُنْ، وَلاَ حَوْلَ وَلاَ قُوَّةَ إِلاَّ بِاللهِ، أَعْلَمُ أَنَّ اللهَ عَلَى كُلِّ شَيْءٍ قَدِيْرٌ، وَأَنَّ اللهَ قَدْ أَحَاطَ بِكُلِّ شَيْءٍ
عِلْمًا وَأَحْصَى كُلَّ شَيْءٍ عَدَدًا

Allāhumma anta rabbī lā ilāha illā anta, 'alayka tawakkaltu, wa anta rabb ul-'arsh al-'aẓīm, mā shā Allāhu kān, wa mā lam yasha' lam yakun, wa lā ḥawla wa lā quwwata illā billāh, a'lamu anna Allāha 'alā kulli shay'in qadīr, wa anna Allāha qad aḥāṭa bi-kulli shay'in 'ilmā, wa aḥṣā kulla shay'in 'adadā.
O Allāh, You are my Lord, none has the right to be worshipped but You, in You I trust, and You are the Lord of the exalted Throne. That which Allāh wills happens, and that which He does

not will does not happen, and there is no power nor might except by Allāh. I know that Allāh is able to do all things, and that Allāh surrounds all things in (His) knowledge, and that He has enumerated everything.

12)

تَحَصَّنْتُ بِالإِلَهِ الَّذِي لَا إِلَهَ إِلَّا هُوَ وَإِلَيْهِ كُلُّ شَيْءٍ وَاعْتَصَمْتُ بِرَبِّي وَرَبِّ كُلِّ شَيْءٍ ، وَتَوَكَّلْتُ عَلَى
الحَيِّ الَّذِي لَا يَمُوتُ ، وَاسْتَدْفَعْتُ الشَّرَّ بِلَا حَوْلَ وَلَا قُوَّةَ إِلَّا بِاللهِ ، حَسْبِيَ اللهُ وَنِعْمَ الوَكِيلُ ، حَسْبِيَ
الرَّبُّ مِنَ العِبَادِ ، حَسْبِيَ الخَالِقُ مِنَ المَخْلُوقِ ، حَسْبِيَ الرَّازِقُ مِنَ المَرْزُوقِ ، حَسْبِيَ اللهُ هُوَ حَسْبِي ،
الَّذِي بِيَدِهِ مَلَكُوتُ كُلِّ شَيْءٍ ، وَهُوَ يُجِيرُ وَلَا يُجَارُ عَلَيْهِ ، حَسْبِيَ اللهُ وَكَفَى ، سَمِعَ اللهُ لِمَنْ دَعَا ، وَ
لَيْسَ وَرَاءَ اللهِ مَرْمَى ، وَصَلَّى اللهُ وَسَلَّمَ عَلَى سَيِّدِنَا مُحَمَّد

Taḥaṣṣantu bil-ilāh aladhī lā ilāha illā huwa, wa ilayhi kullu shay', wa'-taṣamtu bi-rabbī wa rabbu kulli shay', wa tawakkultu 'ala al-ḥayy aladhī lā yamūt, wastadfa'tu ash-sharr bi-lā ḥawla wa lā quwwata illā billāh, ḥasbiy Allāh wa ni'ma al-wakīl, ḥasbiy ar-rabb min al-'ibād, ḥasbiy al-khāliq min al-makhlūq, ḥasbiy ar-rāziq min al-marzūq, ḥasbiy Allāh huwa ḥasbiy, aladhī biyadihi malakūtu kulli shay', wa huwa yujīru wa lā yujūru 'alayh, ḥasbiy Allāh wa kafā, sami' Allāh liman da'ā, wa laysa warā Allāhi muntahā, wa ṣallalāhu wa sallam 'ala sayyidinā Muḥammad.

I seek strength from the true God, none has the right to be worshipped but Him, to Him belongs everything. I rely upon my Lord and the Lord of everything, and I trust in the Ever-Living who will never die, and I seek to repel evil by the power and might which is not except for Allāh. Allāh is sufficient for me, and He is the Best Disposer of affairs. The Lord suffices me from the slaves, the Creator suffices me from the creation, the Provider suffices me from the provided. Allāh is sufficient for me, in whose Hand is the sovereignty of everything, and He protects (all) and there is none to protect from Him, Sufficient is Allāh for me. Allāh hears the one who invokes Him, there is nothing beyond Allāh, and may the peace and blessings of Allāh be upon our Prophet Muḥammad.

Striking and repremanding the *jinn* whilst it is in the afflicted

It has been reported that the Prophet (ﷺ) reprimanded the *jinn*. This can be seen from the *ḥadīth* of Abū Dardā' (ؓ): "*Once whilst the Prophet (ﷺ) was praying, we heard him say: 'I seek refuge in Allāh from you.' Then he said: 'I curse you with the curse of Allāh.' He said this three times. He then outstretched his hand as if he was reaching out for something. When he finished his prayer we asked: 'O Messenger of Allāh, you said something we have never heard you say before in the prayer, and you outstretched your hand.' He replied: 'Indeed, the enemy of Allāh, Iblīs came to me with a coal of fire in order to place it in my face, so I said: 'I seek refuge in Allāh from you three times,' then I said: 'I curse you with the complete curse of Allāh.' He retreated three times, then I wanted to grab him, and by Allāh were it not for the du'ā of my brother Sulaymān, he would have awoken tied up, and the children of Madīnah would have played with him.'*"[165]

He (ﷺ) would also say to the *jinn*: "*Leave O enemy of Allāh for I am the Messenger of Allāh.*"[166]

Ibn al-Qayyim mentions: "I witnessed our shaykh[167] send someone to speak to the spirit inside a person who had convulsions. He said: "The shaykh tells you to leave for this is not something permissible (*ḥalāl*) for you, so it would leave. Sometimes he would speak to them himself, and sometimes the spirit would be a '*mārid*' so he would force it to leave by beating it. When the *jinn* would leave, the afflicted would awake without feeling any pain. We have seen him do this many times."[168]

He also mentions: "He (Ibn Taymiyyah) informed me that he once recited in the ear of a person afflicted with convulsions, and

[165] Collected by Muslim.

[166] *Musnad Aḥmad*, vol. 4, p. 170.

[167] i.e. Ibn Taymiyyah.

[168] *Al-Ṭibb al-Nabawī*, p. 193.

the spirit said: 'Yes,' in a drawn out voice. The shaykh said: I took a stick and beat it on the neck until my hands were exhausted from beating it. The people witnessing thought he would surely die, and then she (i.e. the spirit) said: 'I love him'. I replied: 'But he does not love you'. She said: 'I wish to make *Ḥajj* with him'. I replied: 'He does not wish to make *Ḥajj* with you'; she then said: 'I will leave out of respect for you'. I replied: 'Rather out of obedience to Allāh and His Messenger'. She then said: 'I will leave'. Then the afflicted sat up looking to his right and left and said: 'What brings the shaykh to me?' So they asked him: 'And all these beatings?' He replied: 'Why would the shaykh beat me when I have done nothing wrong?' He did not feel that he had been beaten at all."[169]

Ibn Taymiyyah said: "The existence of the *jinn* has been established in the Qur'ān and *Sunnah*, and by the agreement of the *salaf* (pious predecessors). Likewise, the entering of the *jinn* into the human is something also agreed upon by the scholars; it is something common and witnessed. It enters into a person and says things which the afflicted is not aware of. He is beaten in such a way that if a camel was beaten in a similar way, it would die, but the person does not feel this."[170]

Warning:

People should beware of striking and reprimanding the *jinn*, for it is a dangerous issue which can lead to dangerous consequences, especially if the one using it is not aware of the correct method.

A person may strike someone believing he is possessed when he is not; this may result in great harm, or he may strike him in a sensitive part of the body. Some people go to extremes and use electric shocks; this is wrong.

---

[169] Ibid, p. 194.

[170] *Majmūʿ al-Fatāwā*, vol. 24, p. 276.

The point being made here is that striking someone who is possessed requires knowledge and experience. A person should know when, where and how to strike, and whether or not it is even needed etc.

Shaykh Ibn ʿUthaymīn was asked: "Is it allowed for the one who recites upon people to strike them and speak to the *jinn*?"

He replied: "This is something some of the scholars of the past would do, such as Ibn Taymiyyah. He used speak to them and strike them until they left. But the excessiveness we see today is incorrect."[171]

Striking the *jinn* until it dies:

> An Egyptian family who was trying to cure a member of the family, who was possessed, became despaired after many doctors were unable to help; the oldest son took his father to five soothsayers who claimed to possess the cure.
> The soothsayers agreed that the cause was an evil spirit which had possessed the body and refused to leave of its own free will, therefore force was necessary. They each began to beat it with a stick until it died.[172]

Questions to ask the *jinn* if it speaks:

1. What is your name? What is your religion?

2. Why have you possessed this person?

3. Are you alone in the possessed or are there others? How many? What are their religions?

---

[171] *Ad-Daʿwah* magazine, issue (1456), Thursday, 25 Rabi al-Awwal, 1415 AH.

[172] '*Al-Yawm*' newspaper, 14/12/1413 AH.

How to engage in dialogue with the *jinn*?

There is no specific dialogue one must follow; each person who recites incantations has his own way. What you say to a Muslim *jinnī* will be different from what you to say to a non-Muslim *jinnī*. Similarly, that which you say to the pious Muslim *jinnī* is different from what you say to the disobedient one, etc.

So, if it is a Muslim *jinnī*, remind him of Allāh and that what he is doing is unlawful. Tell him it is an oppression which he will have to answer for on the Day of Judgement. If he mentions a reason for his actions, answer him with wisdom. For example, if the *jinnī* wants revenge because the person unintentionally harmed him, then explain to him that it was an accident, and that anything which is a mistake does not deserve punishment. If the incident happened in the person's house, the *jinnī* is told that a person has the right to do as he pleases in his own property etc.

If the reason is love and desire or foolishness on the part of the *jinn*, it should be told that this is also unlawful. Likewise, if the possession is due to magic, it should be explained to the *jinn* that this is impermissible. The *jinn* may even reveal the place of magic.

If the *jinnī* is a non-Muslim, then it is called to Islām but without force. Allāh says:

لَآ إِكۡرَاهَ فِي ٱلدِّينِۖ

There is no compulsion in religion.
Sūrah al-Baqarah, verse 256[173]

[173] Footnote from Shaykh Ibn Bāz: The non-Muslim *jinnī* must be told that it is obligatory upon it to enter into Islām, and that it is not allowed for it to continue on disbelief, due to the verse: ***"And whosoever chooses a religion other than Islām then it will not be accepted from him, and he will be in the Hereafter from the losers."*** Also, it should be mentioned to them that their possession of this person is oppression. 17/2/1413.

So, if it accepts Islām, then it is taught what the religion comprises of and what it needs to know out of necessity; it then takes the *shahādah* (statement of faith). However, if it refuses, then it is ordered to leave, and if it still refuses then the one reciting continues to recite.

Taking a vow or pledge from the *jinn*:

Certain people who recite upon others take a pledge from the *jinn* that they will leave and never return to that person; it is common for the *jinn* to make such vows by Allāh. However, these *jinn* take pledges and then break them; for this reason, the one who recites should refrain from requesting this.

It is reported in a *ḥadīth* that when the Prophet (ﷺ) would send an army, he would tell its general: *"If you surround a people and they wish you to give them the protection of Allāh and His Prophet, do not give it to them; instead, give them your protection and that of your companions, for breaking your own protection is easier than breaking the protection of Allāh and His Messenger."*[174]

Imam al-Nawawī said: "The scholars have said: 'Protection' here is referring to a pledge, and to break it means to annul and violate it. This means that the the protection of Allāh should not be given to them for it may be broken by those who are ignorant of its status, and annulled by the Bedouins and their likes."[175]

The Permanent Committee of Scholars in Saudi Arabia was asked:
Q: What is the ruling concerning those people who recite upon others using the Qur'ān, and some of these *jinn* present themselves to those present, and when they speak to the *jinn* they take a pledge, insisting they never return to that person?

---

[174] *Sahih Muslim*, vol. 3, p. 1357, no. 1731.

[175] *Ṣaḥīḥ Muslim: Sharḥ al-Nawawī*, vol. 12, p. 39.

A: To recite upon someone is permissible; the Prophet (ﷺ) allowed it as long as it did not involve *shirk*. It is impermissible for a person who witnesses the *jinn* to take a pledge from them that they will not name the person who was afflicted or harm him. May the peace and blessings of Allāh be upon our Prophet Muḥammad, his family and companions.

The Permanent Committee
Head of the Committee: ʿAbdul-ʿAzīz ibn ʿAbdullāh ibn Bāz
Deputy Head: ʿAbdul-Razzāq ʿAfīfī
Member: ʿAbdullāh ibn Ghudayyān
Member: ʿAbdullah ibn Quʿūd[176]

The Second Type of Medicine: Natural

There are some natural medicines which are beneficial, by the will of Allāh, which have been mentioned in the Holy Qur'ān and *Sunnah*. If a person takes them whilst having true and certain belief that all benefit is from Allāh, the medicine will be beneficial, *inshā' Allāh*.

There are also certain medicines which are made from a mixture of herbs. From experience, these are beneficial for certain people, so such medicines may also be used as long as they are not unlawful (*ḥarām*).

Shaykh Ibn ʿUthaymīn said: "Know that medicines are a means which assist one in attaining cure, and the one that causes these medicines to be a successful means is Allāh, so only that which He causes to be successful is so, and these means which Allāh has placed are of two types:

Firstly: One can utilise divine (*sharʿī*) means, such as the Qur'ān and making *duʿā*, for the Prophet (ﷺ) said concerning *Sūrah*

---

[176] *Fatwā* number: 7804.

Fātiḥah: "And how did you know it was a cure?" He (ﷺ) would make *du'ā* for the ill, and those that Allāh wished to cure by his *du'ā* would be cured.

Secondly: Natural means, such as medicines which have been mentioned in the religion like honey or medicines that are known to be beneficial from experience. These medicines must have a real effect and not just an imaginary one. If its effects are known and established then it is allowed, and it will be beneficial *inshā' Allāh*.

However, if the medicine has imaginary effects, it is impermissible, even if it gives the one who is ill peace of mind, and thus inadvertently helps him to overcome his illness. It is impermissible to rely upon such forms of medicine and to even name them as medicines because a person should not chase things which are imaginary. This is why it is forbidden to wear threads and rings believing they will cure illnesses, because they are not from the divine or natural means. That which is neither of the two is impermissible because it is a form of disputing Allāh in His kingdom. This is because a person is placing as a cure other than that which has been placed by Allāh; this is why Shaykh Muḥammad ibn 'Abdul Wahhāb used the following as one of his chapter headings: '*Wearing threads and rings in order to prevent a calamity from befalling is from shirk.*'"[177]

The following are from the beneficial natural medicines, *Insha Allāh*:

1. Honey
2. Black seed
3. Olive oil
4. Zamzam water and rain water
5. Bathing, cleanliness, and perfume

---

[177] *Majmū' Fatāwā Ibn 'Uthaymīn*, vol. 1, pp. 66-69, question no. 33.

Firstly: Honey

Allāh says:

وَأَوْحَىٰ رَبُّكَ إِلَى ٱلنَّحْلِ
أَنِ ٱتَّخِذِى مِنَ ٱلْجِبَالِ بُيُوتًا وَمِنَ ٱلشَّجَرِ وَمِمَّا يَعْرِشُونَ ﴿٦٨﴾ ثُمَّ كُلِى
مِن كُلِّ ٱلثَّمَرَٰتِ فَٱسْلُكِى سُبُلَ رَبِّكِ ذُلُلًا ۚ يَخْرُجُ مِنۢ بُطُونِهَا
شَرَابٌ مُّخْتَلِفٌ أَلْوَٰنُهُۥ فِيهِ شِفَآءٌ لِّلنَّاسِ ۗ إِنَّ فِى ذَٰلِكَ لَءَايَةً لِّقَوْمٍ
يَتَفَكَّرُونَ ﴿٦٩﴾

And your Lord inspired the bees, saying: "Take you habitations in the mountains and in the trees and in what they erect. Then, eat of all fruits, and follow the ways of your Lord made easy (for you)." There comes forth from their bellies, a drink of varying colour wherein is healing for men. Verily, in this is indeed a sign for people who think.

Sūrah al-Naḥl, verses 68-69

On the authority of Ibn Abbas(رضي الله عنه), the Prophet (ﷺ) said: "*Cure is in three: a drink of honey, cupping and cauterisation; I forbid my nation from cauterisation.*"[178]

The cure for convulsions: "Every morning and evening, a cup of honey should be taken, and *Sūrah Jinn* should be recited over a cup of warm water mixed with honey and then drunk. The patient should then go straight to sleep. This should be continued for a week; the patient will be cured by the power of Allāh."[179]

---

[178] *Sahih al-Bukhari*, vol. 4, p. 432.

[179] *Mu'jizāt al-Shifā'*, p. 32.

Secondly: Black seed

The Prophet (ﷺ) said: "*Take this black seed, for verily in it is a cure from every illness except death.*"[180]

Thirdly: Olive oil

The olive tree is a blessed tree whose fruit are also blessed. It has been mentioned a number of times in the Qur'ān:

وَٱلتِّينِ وَٱلزَّيْتُونِ ﴿١﴾ وَطُورِ سِينِينَ ﴿٢﴾

By the fig and the olive. By Mount Sinai.
Sūrah al-Tīn, verses 1-2

Allāh also says:

فَأَنۢبَتْنَا فِيهَا حَبًّا ﴿٢٧﴾ وَعِنَبًا وَقَضْبًا ﴿٢٨﴾ وَزَيْتُونًا وَنَخْلًا ﴿٢٩﴾
وَحَدَآئِقَ غُلْبًا ﴿٣٠﴾ وَفَٰكِهَةً وَأَبًّا ﴿٣١﴾ مَّتَٰعًا لَّكُمْ وَلِأَنْعَٰمِكُمْ ﴿٣٢﴾

And We cause therein the grain to grow. And grapes and clover plants (i.e. green fodder for the cattle). And olives and date-palms. And gardens dense with many trees. And fruits and herbage. (To be) a provision and benefit for you and your cattle.
Sūrah 'Abasa, verses 27-32

He says:

وَشَجَرَةً تَخْرُجُ مِن طُورِ سَيْنَآءَ تَنۢبُتُ بِٱلدُّهْنِ وَصِبْغٍ
لِّلْآكِلِينَ ﴿٢٠﴾

And a tree (olive) that springs forth from Mount Sinai, that grows (produces) oil, and (it is a) relish for the eaters.
Sūrah al-Mu'minūn, verse 20

---

[180] *Ṣaḥīḥ al-Bukhārī: Fatḥ al-Bārī*, vol. 10, p. 150, no. 5687.

And He says:

هُوَ ٱلَّذِىٓ أَنزَلَ مِنَ ٱلسَّمَآءِ مَآءً لَّكُم مِّنْهُ شَرَابٌ وَمِنْهُ
شَجَرٌ فِيهِ تُسِيمُونَ ۝١٠ يُنۢبِتُ لَكُم بِهِ ٱلزَّرْعَ
وَٱلزَّيْتُونَ وَٱلنَّخِيلَ وَٱلْأَعْنَٰبَ

He it is Who sends down water (rain) from the sky; from it you drink and from it (grows) the vegetation on which you send your cattle to pasture. With it He causes to grow for you the crops, the olives, the date-palms, the grapes...

Sūrah aln-Naḥl, verses 10-11

Ibn Kathīr said in its explanation - "Ka'b, Qatādah and Ibn Zayd said: 'It is the tree of Masjid Aqṣā.'"[181] From this we see that the best olives are those from the holy land (Aqṣā). Allāh says:

سُبْحَٰنَ ٱلَّذِىٓ أَسْرَىٰ بِعَبْدِهِۦ لَيْلًا مِّنَ ٱلْمَسْجِدِ ٱلْحَرَامِ
إِلَى ٱلْمَسْجِدِ ٱلْأَقْصَا ٱلَّذِى بَٰرَكْنَا حَوْلَهُۥ

Glorified (and Exalted) be He (Allāh) Who took His slave (Muḥammad) for a journey by night from al-Masjid al-Ḥarām (at Makkah) to al-Masjid al-Aqṣā (in Jerusalem), the neighbourhood whereof We have blessed

Sūrah al-Isrā', verse 1

We have also experienced it to be the best type of olive oil.

The *Sunnah* states:

The Prophet (ﷺ) said: "*Eat olives and use its oil, for indeed it is from a blessed tree.*"[182] He (ﷺ) said: "*Use olives as a food and use its oil, for indeed it is from a blessed tree.*"[183]

---

[181] *Tafsīr al-Qur'ān al-'Aẓīm*, vol. 4, p. 526.

[182] Collected by Ḥākim. However, it is weak due to the presence of 'Abdullāh ibn Sa'īd al-Maqbarī.

[183] Collected by al-Tirmidhī and Ibn Mājah, declared authentic by al-Albānī in *Ṣaḥīḥ al-Jāmi'*, vol. 1, p. 18.

The *ḥadīth* of ʿUqbah ibn ʿĀmir (ﷺ) states that the Prophet (ﷺ) said: *"Use olive oil, eat from it and use its oil, for it is beneficial against piles."* In a narration: *"Whoever uses olive oil will not be approached by shayṭān."*[184] On the authority of ʿUmar (ﷺ), the Prophet (ﷺ) said: *"Eat olives and use its oil, for indeed it is from a blessed tree."*[185]

Benefits of olive oil:[186]

Olives are warm and moist by nature. This is beneficial against poisons. Olives also expand the stomach, expel worms, slow down ageing, strengthen gums, hair and limbs, and all oils weaken the stomach except olive oil.

Fourthly: Zamzam water and rain water

Zamzam water is the best water upon the face of the earth; it is also the holiest. It has been established that the Prophet (ﷺ) said to Abū Dharr (ﷺ) who had stayed next to the Kaʿbah for thirty days, only drinking Zamzam water: *"Verily it is a source of food."*[187]

He (ﷺ) said in another *ḥadīth*: *"The best of water is the water of Zamzam. It is a source of food and a cure for illnesses. The worst water is the water of Barhūt- ruins near Haḍramūt. It gushes in the morning and by evening it has no moisture left in it."*[188]

Ibn al-Qayyim said: "I have personally used Zamzam water as a cure, and it cured me from a number of illnesses, by the will of Allāh."

---

[184] Mentioned by Muḥammad ibn Tūlūn in *al-Manhal al-Rawiyy fī al-Ṭibb al-Nabawī*, p. 224.

[185] Collected by Tirmidhī, see *Ṣaḥīḥ Sunan al-Tirmidhī*, vol. 2, p. 166, no. 1508.

[186] *Al-Aṭʿimah al-Qur'āniyyah Ghadhāun wa dawā'*, vol. 7, p. 225.

[187] *Sahih Muslim*, vol. 4, p. 1922, no. 2473.

[188] Collected by Ṭabarānī, *Ṣaḥīḥ al-Jāmiʿ*, no. 3.

Allāh says concerning rain water:

وَنَزَّلْنَا مِنَ ٱلسَّمَآءِ مَآءً مُّبَٰرَكًا

And We send down blessed water (rain) from the sky
Sūrah Qāf, verse 9

Fifthly: Bathing, cleanliness and perfume

This is something the *Sunnah* has called to, as the Prophet (ﷺ) said: *"Indeed from the rights of Allāh upon the Muslim is that he bathes once every seven days, and if he has any perfume he wears it."*[189]

Perfume:

The Prophet (ﷺ) said: *"Women and perfume have been made beloved to me from the things of this world; the coolness of my eyes has been placed in the prayer."* He (ﷺ) would never refuse perfume.[190] He (ﷺ) also said: *"Whosoever is offered perfume let him not refuse for it is pleasant smelling and light to wear."*[191]

Ibn al-Qayyim stated: "Chapter: The guidance of the Prophet (ﷺ) in preserving ones health with perfume. A nice scent is food for the soul, and the soul is a mount for ones strength, and one increases in strength with perfume. This is because it benefits the brain, heart and all the internal limbs. It also enters happiness into the heart and soul, and it is the most truthful and suitable thing for the soul. Between them is a close connection. It was one of the two most beloved of things to the Prophet (ﷺ) from this world."

---

[189] Ibn Khuzaymah.

[190] *Sahih al-Bukhari*, vol. 4, p. 78.

[191] Collected by Muslim.

He also said: "From the qualities of perfume, is that the angels like it, and the *shayāṭīn* flee from it. The most beloved thing to the *shayāṭīn* is an unpleasant smell. The good souls like pleasant smells, and the evils souls like unpleasant smells, and each soul inclines to that which is most suitable for it....."[192]

Imam al-Shāfiʿī said: "Four things strengthen the body: eating meat, smelling perfume, bathing often and wearing linen."

From the most beneficial type of perfume, *inshā' Allāh*, is ʿOud. It is reported that Ibn ʿUmar (⬥) would use aloeswood and camphor in his censers and say: "*This is what the Prophet (⬥) would use.*"[193] Also, the Prophet (⬥) said, whilst describing the blessings of the people of Paradise: "*...and the fuel used in their censers will be aloeswood.*"[194]

The best type of ʿoud is the black one, then the dark blue one. Both of these should be thick in texture, and the least of them in quality is that which is light and floats in water.

It is said that ʿoud is a type of tree which is cut and buried in the ground for a year. During this time the ground removes that which is unbeneficial. The good ʿoud remains whilst the rest decays. This ʿoud opens blockages, removes trapped wind and excess moist, strengthens the intestines and the heart, pleases the heart, benefits the brain, strengthens the senses, withholds the stomach, and helps to cure urine incontinence which is caused by a weak bladder.

It is also important to note that there is a difference between using ʿoud as an incense, and using certain other herbs, which soothsayers commonly use as incense. The Permanent Committee was asked concerning this:

---

[192] *Al-Ṭibb al-Nabawī*, p. 437.

[193] Collected by Muslim.

[194] Collected by al-Bukhārī.

Q: Is it allowed to use herbs and paper as incense to cure the evil eye?
A: It is not allowed to cure the evil eye with that which has been mentioned, for it is not from the common ways of curing this illness. It is possible that some people use it to attain the pleasure of the *shayāṭīn*, and their assistance in seeking a cure. Such things are cured using permissible forms of incantation (*ruqyah*) which have been mentioned in the authentic *Sunnah*.

Head of theCommittee: ʿAbdul-ʿAzīz ibn ʿAbdullāh ibn Bāz
Deputy Head: ʿAbdul-Razzāq ʿAfīfī
Member: ʿAbdullāh ibn Ghudayyān
Member: ʿAbdullāh ibn Quʿūd

The third type of medicine: Combining the two

It has been reported that the Prophet (ﷺ) said: "*Take the two cures: honey and the Qur'ān.*"[195]

Ibn Ṭūlūn said: "Here, the Prophet (ﷺ) combined natural and divine medicine; medication for both the body and the heart, and the means from the heavens and the earth. There is an added secret in the statement *'Take the two cures'* because a person is being told not just to rely on divine means, but to also take other necessary steps, as well as asking Allāh for His assistance and success."

Important points:

We have already discussed seeking a cure using the Qur'ān, natural medicine which has been mentioned in the Qur'ān and *Sunnah*, and a combination of both. Now, we will mention some important points which a person must adhere to:

---

[195] Collected by Ibn Mājah, but weak in its chain of narration, see *Ḍaʿīf al-Jāmiʿ al-Ṣaghīr*, vol. 3, p. 45.

1. Preserving the five daily prayers.

2. Making *du'ā* to Allāh.

3. Patience.

4. Visiting the ill and making *du'ā* for them.

5. Giving in charity and being good to people.

Firstly: Preserving the five daily prayers

When certain people are ill, they become lax in offering their daily prayers; they may even excuse themselves completely - this is wrong. In fact, it is obligatory to preserve the daily prayers, for they have a great effect in removing calamities. Allāh says:

وَٱسْتَعِينُوا۟ بِٱلصَّبْرِ وَٱلصَّلَوٰةِ ۚ وَإِنَّهَا لَكَبِيرَةٌ إِلَّا عَلَى ٱلْخَـٰشِعِينَ

And seek help in patience and the prayer, and truly it is extremely heavy and hard except for Al-Khāshi'ūn (true believers in Allāh).

Sūrah al-Baqarah, verse 45

He also says:

وَأْمُرْ أَهْلَكَ بِٱلصَّلَوٰةِ وَٱصْطَبِرْ عَلَيْهَا ۖ لَا نَسْـَٔلُكَ رِزْقًا ۖ
نَّحْنُ نَرْزُقُكَ ۗ وَٱلْعَـٰقِبَةُ لِلتَّقْوَىٰ

And enjoin the prayer on your family, and be patient in offering them (the prayers). We ask not of you a provision: We provide for you. And the good end is for the pious.

Sūrah Ṭa-Ha, verse 132

The *Sunnah* mentions: *"If something grieved the Prophet (ﷺ) he would hasten to the prayer."*[196]

---

[196] Collected by Abū Dāwūd and Aḥmad, see *Zād al-Ma'ād*, vol. 4, p. 331.

Ibn al-Qayyim said: "The prayer brings provision, protects health, prevents harm, expels illnesses, strengthens the heart, whitens the face, rejoices the soul, drives away laziness, energises the limbs, increases strength, expands the chest, nurtures the soul, enlightens the heart, preserves blessings, prevents misfortune, brings blessing, distances from *shayṭān*, and brings a person closer to Allāh.

The prayer has an amazing effect in repelling the evils of this world and the Hereafter, especially if it is performed completely inwardly and outwardly. There is nothing like the prayer to repel evil and bring blessings; the secret is that the prayer is a connection to Allāh. The strength of this connection determines whether the doors to good open, whether the ways to evil close, and whether one attains success, health, profit, wealth, comfort, blessings, and happiness. All can be achieved via prayer."[197]

Secondly: *Du'ā*

Allāh says:

وَإِذَا سَأَلَكَ
عِبَادِي عَنِّي فَإِنِّي قَرِيبٌ ۖ أُجِيبُ دَعْوَةَ الدَّاعِ إِذَا دَعَانِ ۖ
فَلْيَسْتَجِيبُوا لِي وَلْيُؤْمِنُوا بِي لَعَلَّهُمْ يَرْشُدُونَ ﴿١٨٦﴾

And when My slaves ask you (O Muḥammad) concerning Me, then (answer them), I am indeed near (to them by My Knowledge). I respond to the invocations of the supplicant when he calls on Me. So let them obey Me and believe in Me, so that they may be led aright.

Sūrah al-Baqarah, verse 186

So, *du'ā* can have a great impact in repelling evil, for Allāh is the One who cures and gives health. He says:

---

[197] *Al-Ṭibb al-Nabawī*, pp. 503-504.

وَإِذَا مَرِضْتُ فَهُوَ يَشْفِينِ ﴿٨٠﴾

And when I am ill, it is He who cures me
Sūrah al-Shuʿarā', verse 80

However, one must make *duʿā* to Allāh sincerely, and turn to him with certainty.

Certain beneficial duʿās:

It is reported that the Prophet (ﷺ) would say in times of hardship:

لا إِلَهَ إِلّا اللهُ العَظِيْمُ الحَلِيْم، لا إِلَهَ إِلّا اللهُ رَبُّ العَرْشِ العَظِيْم، لا إِلَهَ إِلّا اللهُ رَبُّ السَّمَوَاتِ السَّبْعِ وَرَبُّ الأَرْضِ رَبُّ العَرْشِ الكَرِيْم

La ilāha illa Allāh al-ʿAẓīm al-Ḥalīm, la ilāha ilal Allāh rabb al-ʿarsh al-ʿaẓīm, la ilāha ilal Allāh rabb as-samāwāt as-sabʿ wa rabb al-arḍ rabb al-ʿarsh al-karīm.
None has the right to be worshipped except Allāh the Most Great, the Most Forbearing. None has the right to be worshipped except Allāh, Lord of the Magnificent Throne. None has the right to be worshipped except Allāh, Lord of the seven heavens, and Lord of the earth, and Lord of the Noble Throne.[198]

He (ﷺ) would say when something grieved him:

يا حَيُّ يا قَيُّوْمُ بِرَحْمَتِكَ أَسْتَغِيْث

Yā Ḥayyu yā Qayyūm, bi-raḥmatika astaghīth.
O the Ever Living, the One who sustains all, by Your Mercy I seek help and assistance.[199]

---

[198] *Sahih al-Bukhari*, vol. 11, p. 112, also collected by Muslim.

[199] Collected by al-Tirmidhī.

And he (ﷺ) said: "*A slave is not afflicted by sadness and then says:*

اللَّهُمَّ إِنِّي عَبْدُكَ ، ابْنُ عَبْدِكَ ، ابْنُ أَمَتِكَ ، نَاصِيَتِي بِيَدِكَ ، مَاضٍ فِيَّ حُكْمُكَ ، عَدْلٌ فِيَّ قَضَاؤُكَ ، أَسْأَلُكَ بِكُلِّ اسْمٍ هُوَ لَكَ سَمَّيْتَ بِهِ نَفْسَكَ أَوْ أَنْزَلْتَهُ فِي كِتَابِكَ أَوْ عَلَّمْتَهُ أَحَداً مِنْ خَلْقِكَ أَوِ اسْتَأْثَرْتَ بِهِ فِي عِلْمِ الْغَيْبِ عِنْدَكَ أَنْ تَجْعَلَ الْقُرْآنَ الْعَظِيمَ رَبِيعَ قَلْبِي ، وَنُورَ صَدْرِي ، وَجَلاءَ حُزْنِي ، وَذَهَابَ هَمِّي

Allāhuma innī 'abduk, ibn 'abdik, ibn amatik, nāṣiyatī biyadik, māḍin fiyya ḥukmuk, 'adlun fiyya qaḍā'uk, asaluka bi-kulli ismin huwa lak, sammayta bihi nafsak, aw anzaltahu fī kitābik, aw 'allamtahu aḥadan min khalqik, aw-ista'tharta bihi fī 'ilm il-ghaybi 'indak, an taj'al al-Qur'ān al-'aẓīm rabī'a qalbī, wa nūra ṣadrī, wa jalā'ā' ḥuznī, wa dhahāba hammī.
O Allāh, I am Your servant, son of Your servant, son of Your female servant, my forehead is in Your Hand, Your command is executed over me, Your decree over me is just, I ask You by each name which belongs to You which You named Yourself with, or revealed in Your Book, or have taught to any of Your creation, or have preserved in the knowledge of the unseen with You, that You make the Qur'ān the life of my heart, the light of my chest, a departure for my sorrow, and a removal of my worries.
...except that Allāh will cause his grief and sadness to disappear and in its place will come happiness."[200]

He (ﷺ) said: "*The du'ā of Dhin-Nūn which he made whilst in the belly of the fish is not made by a single Muslim in a du'ā except that the du'ā will be answered:*

لَّآ إِلَٰهَ إِلَّآ أَنتَ سُبْحَٰنَكَ إِنِّي كُنتُ مِنَ ٱلظَّٰلِمِينَ

None has the right to be worshipped except You, Glorified are You, Truly, I have been of the wrong-doers."[201]

---

[200] Collected by Aḥmad, see *Musnad Aḥmad*, vol. 1, p. 394, authenticated by Ibn Ḥibbān.

[201] *Sunan al-Tirmidhī*, no. 3500, authenticated by al-Ḥākim and al-Dhahabī.

Thirdly: Patience

Indeed, Allāh has created this world and placed in it calamities and ordeals; thus, it is full of pain and hurt so much so that for every day you laugh, you will cry a number of days. A world like this needs to be faced head-on, and none can do this except the true believer who is immersed in the *īmān* of Allāh. This person fights with the strongest of weapons, i.e. faith in Allāh and patience in the face of such calamities, whilst being pleased with the decree of Allāh. Patience is to faith (*īmān*) what the head is to the body.

Allāh says:

وَلَنَبْلُوَنَّكُم بِشَيْءٍ مِّنَ ٱلْخَوْفِ وَٱلْجُوعِ
وَنَقْصٍ مِّنَ ٱلْأَمْوَٰلِ وَٱلْأَنفُسِ وَٱلثَّمَرَٰتِ ۗ وَبَشِّرِ ٱلصَّٰبِرِينَ
﴿١٥٥﴾ ٱلَّذِينَ إِذَآ أَصَٰبَتْهُم مُّصِيبَةٌ قَالُوٓا۟ إِنَّا لِلَّهِ وَإِنَّآ إِلَيْهِ رَٰجِعُونَ
﴿١٥٦﴾ أُو۟لَٰٓئِكَ عَلَيْهِمْ صَلَوَٰتٌ مِّن رَّبِّهِمْ وَرَحْمَةٌ ۖ وَأُو۟لَٰٓئِكَ
هُمُ ٱلْمُهْتَدُونَ ﴿١٥٧﴾

And certainly, we shall test you with something of fear, hunger, loss of wealth, lives and fruits, but give glad tidings to the patient. Who, when afflicted with calamity, say: "Truly to Allāh we belong and truly, to Him we shall return. They are those on whom the ṣalawāt (i.e. who are blessed and will be forgiven) from their Lord, and (they are those who) receive His Mercy, and it is they who are the guided ones.

Sūrah al-Baqarah, verse 155-157

He says:

وَلَئِن صَبَرْتُمْ لَهُوَ خَيْرٌ لِّلصَّٰبِرِينَ ﴿١٢٦﴾

But if you endure patiently, verily, it is better for the patient.

Sūrah al-Naḥl, verse 126

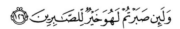

The Prophet (ﷺ) said: "*There is not a single slave who is befallen by a calamity and says: 'To Allāh we belong, and to Him we shall return. O Allāh, reward me in my calamity and replace it with something better,' except that Allāh will reward him in his calamity and replace it with something better.*"[202]

Ibn al-Qayyim said: "This statement is from the greatest cures for the patient, and the most beneficial in this life and the next, for it includes two great principles, which if they are realised will weaken the calamity:

1. That the slave, his family and wealth all belong to Allāh.

2. That the slave's destination is to his Lord, hence, he must at some time leave this world behind, and stand in front of his Lord alone. If this is the beginning and end of the slave, then how can he become overly happy due to the presence of something, or overly sad due to the absence of something else? To reflect upon ones beginning and end is from the greatest cures of an illness."[203]

That which helps one to attain patience

Firstly: To know with certainty, that what has befallen would not have passed, and what has passed would not have befallen. Allāh says:

مَآ أَصَابَ مِن مُّصِيبَةٍ فِي ٱلْأَرْضِ وَلَا فِيٓ أَنفُسِكُمْ إِلَّا فِي
كِتَٰبٍ مِّن قَبْلِ أَن نَّبْرَأَهَآۚ إِنَّ ذَٰلِكَ عَلَى ٱللَّهِ
يَسِيرٌ ﴿٢٢﴾ لِّكَيْلَا تَأْسَوْاْ عَلَىٰ مَا فَاتَكُمْ وَلَا تَفْرَحُواْ
بِمَآ ءَاتَىٰكُمْۗ وَٱللَّهُ لَا يُحِبُّ كُلَّ مُخْتَالٍ فَخُورٍ ﴿٢٣﴾

---

202 *Sahih Muslim*, vol. 2, p. 633.

203 *Al-Ṭibb al-Nabawī*, p. 338.

No calamity befalls on the earth or in yourselves but it is inscribed in the Book of Decrees before We bring it into existence, verily, that is easy for Allāh. In order that you may not grieve at the things which you fail to get, nor rejoice over that which has been given to you. And Allāh likes not prideful boasters.

Sūrah al-Ḥadīd, verse 22-23

Secondly: To look at one's calamity, and realise that his Lord has left for him something similar or better than it. Also, a person should know that by being patient and content, Allāh has promised that he will have that which is better than the calamity. This was the case with the woman who had convulsions during the time of the Prophet (ﷺ), and the Prophet (ﷺ) gave her the choice between asking Allāh to cure her, or Paradise if she was patient; she chose the latter.

Thirdly: To ease one's calamity by realising that there are many people who are afflicted with a similar trial. When one looks to his right, does he see anything except trials? Similarly, when he looks to the left, does he see anything except pain? Furthermore, if one was to look at the inhabitants of the earth, he would only see those who had lost loved ones, or those who were suffering from some misfortune. The happiness of this world is like a dream, or a shade which disappears. If you laugh a little in this world, you will cry much; if one day is pleasant, it will be followed by a period of hardship; if you enjoy some of it, you will be prevented from much of it, and for every day of happiness there is a month of sadness.

Ibn Masʿūd (رضي الله عنه) said: "For every joy, there is sorrow, and a house is not filled with joy except that it is also filled with sorrow."

Hind bint al-Nuʿmān was asked to describe her situation after some calamity befell her family, she replied: "We awoke that morning amongst the most envied of families among the Arabs, but by nightfall there was not a single family except that it took pity on us."

Fourthly: To know that worry does not help; it only makes matters worse. Hence, it is incumbent upon the slave to be pleased with that which Allāh has given, to look at those who are worse off than him and those who have been afflicted with a calamity which is much greater. If he does this, he will become content and pleased with his situation.

Fourthly: Visiting the ill and making *du'ā* for them

It has been reported that the Prophet (ﷺ) said: "*When you enter upon the one who is ill, give him hope, for although that does not repel anything, it makes him happy.*"[204]

Ibn al-Qayyim said: "Easing and comforting the soul of the one who is ill, as well as being pleasant to him and making him feel happy, has an amazing effect on lightening and curing an illness. This is because one's strength and soul become stronger and it helps a person to repel harm. It has often been witnessed that a person becomes rejuvenated when he is visited by those whom he loves and respects, because he sees and speaks to them."[205]

The Prophet (ﷺ) would visit the ill and ask them about what was harming them. He would make *du'ā* for them as well as mentioning what would benefit them. He would say: "*Do not worry, may it [the illness] be a [means of] purification, if Allāh wills.*"[206] He (ﷺ) would say: "*Feed the hungry, visit the ill and relieve the suffering of people.*"[207]

---

[204] Weak, collected by al-Tirmidhī.

[205] *Zād al-Ma'ād*, vol. 4, p. 116.

[206] *Sahih al-Bukhari*, vol. 1, p. 103.

[207] *Fatḥ al-Bārī*, vol. 10, p. 117, no. 5649.

Fifthly: Giving in charity and being good to people

We have already mentioned the benefits of giving charity and doing good, and its effects in repelling evil.[208] The Prophet (ﷺ) said: "*Cure your ill with charity.*"[209]

---

[208] See under the heading: Ways of repelling evil before it befalls, and driving it away after it befalls.

[209] *Ṣaḥīḥ al-Jāmiʿ*, vol. 3, p. 140, no. 3353.

CHAPTER 12
Magic

Definition

Linguistically, it means that which has a hidden cause. From it is the saying of Allāh:

سَحَرُوٓاْ أَعۡيُنَ ٱلنَّاسِ

They bewitched the eyes of the people
Sūrah al-Aʿrāf, verse 116

Likewise, the saying of the Prophet (ﷺ) also mentions this: "*Verily in eloquence there is a form of magic.*"[210]

The Arabs also use the word '*siḥr*' (magic) for deception, because deception is normally something hidden. Magic is a technique which requires experience and skill. It is a science which is based upon principles and rules; these rules are secret. This is why many of those who claim to be big magicians are impostors who just know how to cheat and deceive.[211]

---

[210] *Sahih al-Bukhari*, vol. 4, p. 49, no. 5767.

[211] *Al-Insān wa al-Siḥr*, p. 28.

In the *sharī'ah*, the word for magic (*siḥr*) refers to knots and phrases which have an effect upon the hearts and bodies, and cause illness, death and separation between a husband and wife. Allāh says:

فَيَتَعَلَّمُونَ مِنْهُمَا مَا يُفَرِّقُونَ بِهِۦ بَيْنَ ٱلْمَرْءِ وَزَوْجِهِۦ ۚ
وَمَا هُم بِضَآرِّينَ بِهِۦ مِنْ أَحَدٍ إِلَّا بِإِذْنِ ٱللَّهِ ۚ

And from these (angels) people learn that by which they cause separation between man and his wife, but they could not thus harm anyone except by Allāh's Leave.

Sūrah al-Baqarah, verse 102

He also says:

وَمِن شَرِّ ٱلنَّفَّٰثَٰتِ فِى ٱلْعُقَدِ ﴿٤﴾

And from the evil of those who practise witchcraft when they blow in the knots.

Sūrah al-Falaq, verse 4

This refers to the magicians who tie knots in their magic and blow in them. Allāh would not have ordered the Muslims to seek refuge from magic were it not a reality.

Establishing the existence of magic:

The existence of magic has been established in the Qur'ān, *Sunnah* and by the consensus of the scholars.

Firstly – evidence from the Qur'ān:[212]

Allāh says:

وَٱتَّبَعُوا۟ مَا تَتْلُوا۟ ٱلشَّيَـٰطِينُ عَلَىٰ مُلْكِ سُلَيْمَـٰنَ ۖ وَمَا كَفَرَ
سُلَيْمَـٰنُ وَلَـٰكِنَّ ٱلشَّيَـٰطِينَ كَفَرُوا۟ يُعَلِّمُونَ ٱلنَّاسَ
ٱلسِّحْرَ وَمَآ أُنزِلَ عَلَى ٱلْمَلَكَيْنِ بِبَابِلَ هَـٰرُوتَ وَمَـٰرُوتَ ۚ
وَمَا يُعَلِّمَانِ مِنْ أَحَدٍ حَتَّىٰ يَقُولَآ إِنَّمَا نَحْنُ فِتْنَةٌ فَلَا تَكْفُرْ ۖ
فَيَتَعَلَّمُونَ مِنْهُمَا مَا يُفَرِّقُونَ بِهِۦ بَيْنَ ٱلْمَرْءِ وَزَوْجِهِۦ ۚ
وَمَا هُم بِضَآرِّينَ بِهِۦ مِنْ أَحَدٍ إِلَّا بِإِذْنِ ٱللَّهِ ۚ وَيَتَعَلَّمُونَ
مَا يَضُرُّهُمْ وَلَا يَنفَعُهُمْ ۚ وَلَقَدْ عَلِمُوا۟ لَمَنِ ٱشْتَرَىٰهُ
مَا لَهُۥ فِى ٱلْـَٔاخِرَةِ مِنْ خَلَـٰقٍ ۚ وَلَبِئْسَ مَا شَرَوْا۟ بِهِۦٓ
أَنفُسَهُمْ ۚ لَوْ كَانُوا۟ يَعْلَمُونَ ﴿١٠٢﴾

They followed what the shayāṭīn (devils) gave out (falsely of the magic) in the lifetime of Sulaymān. Sulaymān did not disbelieve, but the shayāṭīn disbelieved, teaching men magic and such things that came down at Babylon to the two angels, Hārūt and Mārūt, but neither of these two (angels) taught anyone (such things) till they had said, "We are only for trial, so disbelieve not (by learning this magic from us)". And from these (angels) people learn that by which they cause separation between man and his wife, but they could not thus harm anyone except by Allāh's Leave. And they learn that which harms them and profits them not. And indeed they knew that the buyers of it (magic) would have no share in the Hereafter. And how bad indeed was that for which they sold their own selves, if they but knew.

Sūrah al-Baqarah, verse 102

---

[212] Translator's note: The authors mention fifty verses from the Qur'ān which establish the existence of magic; I will suffice with mentioning ten verses.

وَقَالُوا۟ مَهْمَا تَأْتِنَا بِهِۦ مِنْ ءَايَةٍ لِّتَسْحَرَنَا بِهَا فَمَا نَحْنُ
لَكَ بِمُؤْمِنِينَ ﴿١٣٢﴾

They said [to Mūsā]: "Whatever Āyāt (proofs, evidences, verses, lessons etc) you may bring to us, to work therewith your sorcery on us, we shall never believe in you.

Sūrah al-A'rāf, verse 132

سَيَقُولُونَ لِلَّهِ ۚ قُلْ فَأَنَّىٰ تُسْحَرُونَ ﴿٨٩﴾

They will say: "(All that belongs) to Allāh." Say: "How then are you deceived and turn away from the truth?"

Sūrah al-Mu'minūn, verse 89

فَقَالَ ٱلَّذِينَ كَفَرُوا۟ مِنْهُمْ إِنْ هَـٰذَآ إِلَّا سِحْرٌ مُّبِينٌ ﴿١١٠﴾

And the disbelievers among them said: 'this is nothing but evident magic'.

Sūrah al-Mā'idah, verse 110

فَلَمَسُوهُ بِأَيْدِيهِمْ لَقَالَ ٱلَّذِينَ كَفَرُوٓا۟ إِنْ هَـٰذَآ إِلَّا سِحْرٌ مُّبِينٌ ﴿٧﴾

so they could touch it with their hands, the disbelievers would... have said: "This is nothing but obvious magic!"

Sūrah al-An'ām, verse 7

سَحَرُوٓا۟ أَعْيُنَ ٱلنَّاسِ وَٱسْتَرْهَبُوهُمْ وَجَآءُو
بِسِحْرٍ عَظِيمٍ ﴿١١٦﴾

They bewitched the eyes of the people, and struck terror into them, and they displayed a great magic.

Sūrah al-A'rāf, verse 116

وَقَالَ ٱلَّذِينَ كَفَرُوا۟ لِلْحَقِّ لَمَّا جَآءَهُمْ إِنْ هَٰذَآ إِلَّا سِحْرٌ مُّبِينٌ ﴿٤٣﴾

And those who disbelieve say of the truth when it has come to them: "This is nothing but evident magic!"
Sūrah Saba, verse 43

فَإِذَا حِبَالُهُمْ وَعِصِيُّهُمْ يُخَيَّلُ إِلَيْهِ مِن سِحْرِهِمْ أَنَّهَا تَسْعَىٰ

Then behold! Their ropes and their sticks, by their magic, appeared to him as though they moved fast.
Sūrah Ṭa-Ha, verse 66

وَأَلْقِ مَا فِى يَمِينِكَ تَلْقَفْ مَا صَنَعُوٓا۟ ۖ إِنَّمَا صَنَعُوا۟ كَيْدُ سَٰحِرٍ ۖ وَلَا يُفْلِحُ ٱلسَّاحِرُ حَيْثُ أَتَىٰ ﴿٦٩﴾

And throe that which is in your right hand! It will swallow up that which they have made. That which they have made is only a magician's trick, and the magician will never be successful, to whatever amount (of skill) he may attain.
Sūrah Ṭa-Ha, verse 69

أَسِحْرٌ هَٰذَا وَلَا يُفْلِحُ ٱلسَّٰحِرُونَ ﴿٧٧﴾

Is this magic? But the magicians will never be successful.
Sūrah Yūnus, verse 77

Secondly – evidence from the Sunnah:

On the authority of 'Ā'ishah: "*The Prophet (ﷺ) was bewitched to the extent that he would think he had done something when he had not. One day he supplicated and supplicated and then said: 'I feel Allāh has informed me as to the cure of my illness: Two men came to me, one sat by my head whilst the other at my feet. One of them asked the other: 'What is his illness?' He replied:*

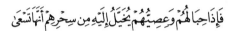

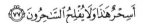

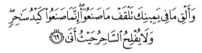

'Bewitchment'. He asked: 'Who bewitched him?' He replied: 'Labīd ibn Aʿṣam.' He asked: 'What with?' He replied: 'With a comb and his hair in the shape of a man.' He asked: 'So where is it?' He replied: 'In the well of Dharwān.' So the Prophet (ﷺ) went to it, and when he returned he said to 'Ā'ishah: 'Its trees are like the heads of shayāṭīn.' I asked: 'Did you remove it?' He replied: 'No, as for me then Allāh has cured me. However, I feared that the (well) would bring evil for people, so I buried the well.'"[213]

Thirdly – Consensus

Imām al-Qarāfī said: "Magic was known to the companions, and it was something agreed upon before the appearance of the Qadariyyah."[214]

Does magic have a reality?

Magic is real and has a reality, due to the saying of Allāh:

وَجَآءُو بِسِحۡرٍ عَظِيمٖ ﴿١١٦﴾

...and they displayed a great magic.
Sūrah al-Aʿrāf, verse 116

Likewise, the scholars of tafsīr have all agreed that the reason *Sūrah Falaq* was revealed, was because Labīd ibn Aʿṣam placed magic upon the Prophet (ﷺ), and the Prophet said after he was cured: *"Indeed Allāh has cured me."* A cure requires an illness to be removed. All this shows that magic has a reality; and we do not reject that magicians have the ability to do unnatural things, such as cause illnesses, madness, death etc.

Imām al-Qarāfī said: "Magic has a reality, and the bewitched may die or his habits change; this is the saying of Shāfiʿī and

---

[213] *Sahih al-Bukhari*, vol. 4, p. 49, no. 5766, and *Sahih Muslim*, vol. 4, p. 1719.

[214] *Al-Furūq*, vol. 4, p. 150.

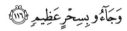

Aḥmad."[215] Al-Nawawī said: "The correct opinion is that magic has a reality; it is the saying of the scholars, and the majority have asserted this. It is also proven in the Qur'ān and authentic *Sunnah*."[216]

The ruling of learning magic

Learn magic is disbelief (*kufr*) because it cannot be achieved except with the assistance of the *shayāṭīn*, worshipping them, committing unlawful acts, and performing acts which more than likely a person may not understand. So, it is not allowed for one who believes in Allāh and the Last Day to learn magic. The evidence for this is much and includes:

1. The verse:

وَمَا يُعَلِّمَانِ مِنْ أَحَدٍ حَتَّىٰ يَقُولَا إِنَّمَا نَحْنُ فِتْنَةٌ فَلَا تَكْفُرْ

...but neither of these two (angels) taught anyone (such things) till they had said, "We are only for trial, so disbelieve not (by learning this magic from us)".

Sūrah al-Baqarah, verse 102

This verse clearly mentions that the one who learns magic has committed an act of disbelief.

2. The saying of the Prophet (ﷺ): "*Beware of the seven deadly sins....and from them he mentioned magic.*"[217]

3. There is no benefit in magic, rather it is pure evil; even if certain people believe it is beneficial. The *sharī'ah* has made unlawful anything which is purely harmful; indeed, it has made unlawful anything which has more harm than good in it.

---

[215] *Al-Furūq*, p. 89.

[216] *Rawḍah al-Ṭālibīn*, vol. 9, p. 346.

[217] Collected by al-Bukhārī and Muslim, see *Fatḥ al-Bārī*, vol. 5, p. 393.

Ibn Ḥajar said: "The verse ***'And Sulaymān did not disbelieve...'*** is evidence showing that magic is disbelief (*kufr*), and that the one who learns it has committed disbelief. Al-Nawawī said: 'Magic is unlawful, and from the major sins by agreement; the Prophet (ﷺ) mentioned it as one of the deadly sins.'"[218]

Ibn Qudāmah said: "To teach and learn magic is unlawful; we know of no difference of opinion in this between the scholars."[219] Al-Dhahabī said: "The third major sin is magic, for the magician must at some time disbelieve."[220]

The punishment for the magician

The punishment for the magician in Islām is beheading. This is due to the following *ḥadīth*: *"The punishment of the magician is that he be struck with the sword (i.e. he should be beheaded)."*[٢٢١]

Umar (رضي الله عنه) wrote two months before his death: "Kill each male and female magician."[222] It is reported that Ḥafṣah, the wife of the Prophet (ﷺ) ordered that a slave girl who placed magic upon her be killed.[223] Ibn Qudāmah said: "The magician who flies on a broom and his likes are to be killed."[224]

Repentance of the magician

The scholars have differed greatly in this matter; the *madhab* of Imām Aḥmad is that the magician is killed without being asked about his repentance. This is also the saying of Mālik,

---

[218] *Fatḥ al-Bārī*, vol. 10, p. 224.

[219] *Al-Mughnī*, vol. 8, p. 151.

[220] *Al-Kabā'ir*, p. 14.

[221] *Sunan al-Tirmidhī*, vol. 4, p. 60.

[222] Authentic, *Sunan Abū Dāwūd*, vol. 3, p. 228.

[223] Authentic, collected by Mālik and Bayhaqī, see *Muwaṭṭa'*, p. 543.

[224] *Al-Muqni'*, vol. 3, p. 523.

for the companions would not ask about the repentance of the magicians.

Another narration from Imām Aḥmad states that the magician is given the chance to repent; if he does so he is allowed to live. This is the saying of al-Shāfiʿī, because his sin is not more grave than associating partners with Allāh in worship (*shirk*), and one is allowed to repent from *shirk*, so likewise one is allowed to repent from magic.

This difference of opinion revolves around whether the repentance of the magician is sufficient in cancelling his punishment. As for the repentance between a person and his Lord, no-one can prevent this; this is between the slave and his Lord, and if it is sincere it will be accepted *Insha Allāh*.

Ways to protect oneself from magic

Indeed the *sharīʿah* mentions each and every way of attaining good and repelling evil. This includes ways in which to protect oneself from evil. This has already been mentioned. Here, we will mention that which protects one from magic.

1. *Adhkār* (Remembrances)

We mentioned this in the section entitled: Protective Shields. Ibn al-Qayyim said: "The best way to protect oneself against magic is to fill the heart with Allāh's remembrance, *duʿās*, *adhkār*, seeking refuge in Allāh and to ensure that the tongue conforms to that which is in the heart. This is from the best means of protecting oneself against magic before it befalls, and that which cures it after it befalls. Even the magicians accept that their magic only has an effect on those whose hearts are weak, and those who follow their desires. Magic most commonly affects those who have little of their religion, rarely trust in Allāh, and those who rarely make *duʿās* and remembrance."[225]

---

[225] *Al-Ṭibb al-Nabawī*, p. 270.

2. *ʿAjwah* (a type of date)

The Prophet (ﷺ) said in the *ḥadīth* of Saʿd: "*Whosoever awakes with (i.e. eats) seven ʿajwah dates will not be harmed that day by any poison or magic.*" In another narration of the same *ḥadīth*: "*When a person eats seven dates from between its (i.e. Madīnah) two mountain ranges and awakes, he will not be harmed by any poison until the night.*"[226]

ʿAjwah is a type of date from the dates of Madīnah, which is almost black in colour. It was planted by the Prophet (ﷺ), and it only has these benefits due to the blessing it received when the Prophet (ﷺ) planted it. This is like the two branches he placed in the graves of the two who were being punished. It was due to his blessing that their punishment was eased.[227]

Al-Nawawī said: "In this *ḥadīth*, there is something specific which is only applicable to the dates of Madīnah. The reason for the number seven is unknown, just as the reason for a certain number of *rakʿahs* in a prayer is unknown."[228] Ibn Ḥajr said: "It is more likely that it is something exclusive to the *ʿajwah* of Madīnah. Is it specific to that time only or is it for all time? This is possible, and is known by experience."[229]

What is correct is that it is for all time until the Day of Judgement, due to the general *ḥadīth* of Saʿd. It is also the case that it is appliacble to all the dates of Madīnah, and not just *ʿajwah*, due to the saying of the Prophet (ﷺ): "*...from that which is between its two mountain ranges...*"[230]

---

[226] *Sahih al-Bukhari*, vol. 4, p. 49, no. 5768, and *Sahih Muslim*, vol. 3, p. 1618, no. 2047.

[227] *Al-Manhal al-Rawiyy fī al-Ṭibb al-Nabawī*, p. 190.

[228] *Sharḥ al-Nawawī ʿalā Muslim*, vol. 14, p. 3.

[229] *Fatḥ al-Bārī*, vol. 10, p.2.

[230] This paragraph is an addition made by Shaykh Ibn Bāz.

The cure to magic

Magic is cured in two main ways:

1. By utilising means which are unlawful (*ḥarām*) like going to the magicians and asking them to remove the magic; this is impermissible.

2. Utilisng means which are lawful (*ḥalāl*), by using the following methods:

A) Extracting and nullifying it - this is the best method.

B) Ejecting the *jinnī* that is responsible for the magic from the body of the afflicted.

C) Removing it (cupping).

D) Permissible forms of incantation (*ruqyah*).

Firstly: Extracting and nullifying the magic

This is the best cure for magic. Here it may be asked: If it is not permissible to go to the magicians in order to nullify the magic, how is this achieved? The answer - in a number of ways:

1. Turning sincerely to Allāh, and asking Him to reveal the place of magic. When the Prophet (ﷺ) was bewitched, he asked Allāh to reveal to him the place of magic. Consequently, he found a comb with his hair in the appearance of a male in a well, so when he removed it, the magic left.[231]

Ibn al-Qayyim stated: "This is the best way to cure the bewitched; it is like removing the evil from the body."

[231] *Sahih al-Bukhari*, vol. 10, p. 199.

It may be asked however: The Prophet (ﷺ) was told about the magic due to revelation, but how are we to know? The answer to this is through the following:

a) A dream – this includes being shown by the grace of Allāh the place of magic. So after a person makes *duʿā* to his Lord, Allāh shows him the place of the magic in a dream. This is from the great blessing of Allāh upon His slave as it is a simple and easy way.

b) To be granted success in finding it, after searching for the magic.[232]

2. To learn about its place from the *jinn* by reciting upon the afflicted. When the *jinn* speak, they reveal its place. Once, when we recited upon a girl, the *jinn* spoke and informed us that she was bewitched, so we asked where the magic was. It informed us that it was buried near a tree in their house, so her uncle went and removed it. Likewise, in another incident, when we recited upon a woman who had been bewitched, the *jinn* informed us that the magic was in her pillow. Her husband went and found it there.

Secondly: Ejecting the *jinnī* that is responsible for the magic from the body of the ill

Sending a *jinnī* into the body of a person to harm it is from the types of magic that magicians use. If it is possible to eject the *jinnī* from the body, the the magic will be removed *inshā' Allāh*. This can be done by using permissible forms of incantations (*ruqyah*) which we will mention shortly, *inshā' Allāh*.

---

[232] *Al-Ṭibb al-Nabawī*, p. 267.

Thirdly: Removing the magic[233]

This is done by removing the magic from the part of the body which has been afflicted. Magic has effects upon a person's nature, and it agitates him, so if its effects are seen in a specific limb and it is possible to remove the evil substance from it, then this is beneficial. One of the most beneficial ways of doing this is by cupping.[234]

Cupping

'Cupping' is taken from the Arabic word '*ḥajm*' meaning size. This is due to the skin increasing in size when it is cupped; cupping is the sucking of blood.

The effects of cupping

It has been reported that the Prophet (ﷺ) was cupped on his head using a horn when he was treated.

Ibn al-Qayyim said: "Cupping is from the most beneficial of cures so he (ﷺ) used it. This was before it was revealed to him that it was magic. When he was informed of it being magic, he turned to the cure of extracting it. He asked Allāh to show him its place and he removed it."[235]

The best time for cupping

On the authority of Abū Hurayrah (ﷺ), the Prophet (ﷺ) said: "*Whosoever gets cupped on the seventeenth, nineteenth, and*

---

[233] Ibn al-Qayyim said: "The ways of removing magic are five: diarrhoea, vomiting, removal of blood, incense and sweating."

[234] We know of a girl who had been bewitched for eight years, and she used to feel a great deal of pain in her head, so we advised her to get it cupped; she did and was cured by the will of Allāh.

[235] *Al-Ṭibb al-Nabawī*, p. 118.

twenty first[236] *will be cured from any illness."*[237]

Cure by '*nashrah*'

'*Nashrah*' is a form of incantation (*ruqyah*) with which the ill and insane are cured. It is to sprinkle or pour over them, and it is similar to '*ruqyah*'.[238]

The author of *Taysīr* mentions: "Abū Sa'dāt said: '*Nashrah* is a form of cure which is used on the one who is thought to be possessed by the *jinn*; it is so named because it moves the illness away from him.' Ḥasan (al-Baṣrī) said: '*Nashrah* is from magic.' Ibn al-Jawzī said: '*Nashrah* is to remove magic from the bewitched. It is rarely done except by those who know magic.'"[239]

Types of 'nashrah' and their rulings

In *Sahih al-Bukhari*, it is stated that: "Qatādah said: 'I asked Sa'īd ibn al-Musayyib concerning a man who was bewitched, is it better to separate him from his wife or to cure him with *nashrah*?' He replied: 'There is no harm in it (i.e. *nashrah*). They only wish to benefit him, and that which is beneficial is not forbidden.'"[240]

Ibn al-Qayyim said: "*Nashrah* is to remove the magic from the bewitched. It is of two types; the first type is to remove it with its likes - this is from the work of *shayṭān*, and this is what is being referred to in the statement of Ḥasan. So the one performing nashrah and the possessed both perform acts (of worship) to *shayṭān* which please him, and he then removes the magic. The second type is to use incantations, *du'ās* and lawful medicines; this is permissible."

---

236 Translator's note: The dates referred to here are the Islamic dates of each month.

237 *Ṣaḥīḥ al-Jāmi'*, vol. 2, p. 1035, no. 5968.

238 *Lisān al-'Arab*, vol. 5, p. 209.

239 *Taysīr al-'Azīz al-Ḥamīd*, p. 416.

240 *Ṣaḥīḥ al-Bukhārī: Fatḥ al-Bārī*, vol. 10, p. 232.

In *Taysīr*, it is mentioned that: "This second type is what is being referred to in the statement of Ibn al-Musayyib, and likewise in the narration reported by Imām Aḥmad regarding the permissibility of performing *nashrah*. The one who thinks he is referring to the *nashrah* of magic is mistaken."[241] On the authority of Jābir, the Prophet (ﷺ) was asked about *nashrah*. He replied: "*It is from the works of shayṭān.*"[242]

The permissible form of nashrah

Shaykh Ibn Baz said: "An effective cure for a person who is bewitched, or is restrained from having marital relations is to take seven leaves of green sidr, grind them, place them in a vessel, and pour enough water on them to bathe in. Then, recite over them *Āyat al-Kursī*, *Sūrah Kāfirūn*, *Sūrah Ikhlāṣ*, *Sūrah Nās*, and the following verses:

۞ وَأَوْحَيْنَآ إِلَىٰ مُوسَىٰٓ أَنْ أَلْقِ عَصَاكَ ۖ فَإِذَا هِىَ تَلْقَفُ مَا
يَأْفِكُونَ ﴿١١٧﴾ فَوَقَعَ ٱلْحَقُّ وَبَطَلَ مَا كَانُوا۟ يَعْمَلُونَ ﴿١١٨﴾ فَغُلِبُوا۟
هُنَالِكَ وَٱنقَلَبُوا۟ صَٰغِرِينَ ﴿١١٩﴾

And we revealed to Mūsā (saying): "Throw your stick," and behold! It swallowed up straight away all the falsehood which they showed. Thus truth was confirmed, and all that they did was made of no effect. So they were defeated there and returned disgraced.

Sūrah al-Aʿrāf, verses 117-119

[241] *Taysīr al-ʿAzīz al-Ḥamīd*, p. 419.

[242] Collected by Aḥmad and Abū Dāwūd, see *Musnad Aḥmad*, vol. 3, p. 294.

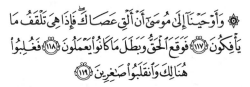

وَقَالَ فِرۡعَوۡنُ ٱئۡتُونِي بِكُلِّ سَٰحِرٍ عَلِيمٖ ﴿٧٩﴾ فَلَمَّا جَآءَ ٱلسَّحَرَةُ
قَالَ لَهُم مُّوسَىٰٓ أَلۡقُواْ مَآ أَنتُم مُّلۡقُونَ ﴿٨٠﴾ فَلَمَّآ أَلۡقَوۡاْ قَالَ
مُوسَىٰ مَا جِئۡتُم بِهِ ٱلسِّحۡرُۖ إِنَّ ٱللَّهَ سَيُبۡطِلُهُۥٓۖ إِنَّ ٱللَّهَ لَا يُصۡلِحُ
عَمَلَ ٱلۡمُفۡسِدِينَ ﴿٨١﴾ وَيُحِقُّ ٱللَّهُ ٱلۡحَقَّ بِكَلِمَٰتِهِۦ وَلَوۡ كَرِهَ
ٱلۡمُجۡرِمُونَ ﴿٨٢﴾

And Pharaoh said: "Bring me every well-versed sorcerer." And when the sorcerers came, Mūsā said to them: "Cast down what you want to cast!" Then when they had cast down, Mūsā said: "What you have brought is sorcery; Allāh will surely make it of no effect. Verily, Allāh does not set right the work of the evil-doers. And Allāh will establish and make apparent the truth by His Words, however much the Mujrimūn (polytheists, criminals, sinners etc.) may hate it."

Sūrah Yūnus, verses 79-82

قَالُواْ يَٰمُوسَىٰٓ إِمَّآ أَن تُلۡقِيَ وَإِمَّآ أَن نَّكُونَ أَوَّلَ مَنۡ أَلۡقَىٰ ﴿٦٥﴾ قَالَ
بَلۡ أَلۡقُواْۖ فَإِذَا حِبَالُهُمۡ وَعِصِيُّهُمۡ يُخَيَّلُ إِلَيۡهِ مِن سِحۡرِهِمۡ أَنَّهَا تَسۡعَىٰ
﴿٦٦﴾ فَأَوۡجَسَ فِي نَفۡسِهِۦ خِيفَةٗ مُّوسَىٰ ﴿٦٧﴾ قُلۡنَا لَا تَخَفۡ إِنَّكَ
أَنتَ ٱلۡأَعۡلَىٰ ﴿٦٨﴾ وَأَلۡقِ مَا فِي يَمِينِكَ تَلۡقَفۡ مَا صَنَعُوٓاْۖ إِنَّمَا صَنَعُواْ
كَيۡدُ سَٰحِرٖۖ وَلَا يُفۡلِحُ ٱلسَّاحِرُ حَيۡثُ أَتَىٰ ﴿٦٩﴾

They said: "O Mūsā! Either you throw first or we be the first to throw?" [Mūsā] said: "Nay, throw you (first)!" Then behold! Their ropes and their sticks, by their magic, appeared to him as though they moved fast. So Mūsā conceived fear in himself. We (Allāh) said: "Fear not! Surely, you will have the upper hand. And throw that which is in your right hand! It will swallow up that which they have made. That which they have made is only a magician's trick, and the magician will never be successful, to whatever amount (of skill) he may attain.

Sūrah Ṭa-Ha, verses 65-69

After he recites what has been mentioned, he drinks some of it, and bathes with the rest, and *inshā' Allāh* with that he will be cured. There is no harm in repeating this twice or more if there is a need to do so."[243]

Ibn al-Qayyim said: "From the most beneficial cures for magic are the divine cures. These are beneficial in and of themselves, for the effects of evil and low spirits are only repelled by that which opposes them from the *adhkār*, *du'ās* and verses which nullify and weaken their effects."[244]

---

[243] *Risālah fī Ḥukm al-Saḥarah wal-Kahānah*, p. 7-9.

[244] *Al-Ṭibb al-Nabawī*, p. 269.

CHAPTER 13

The Evil-Eye

The reality of it is to look at something with admiration, whilst feeling jealousy and envy; this causes harm to the one being looked at.[245]

Ibn al-Qayyim said: "It is like an arrow which leaves the heart of the envious towards the one being envied. Sometimes it will hit its target and sometimes it will miss. If it finds him without any armour or protection it will strike him, however, if it finds him with shields and armour which has no gaps, it will not affect him. It is similar to a real arrow, for one is from the soul and heart, whilst the other is from the body and limbs."[246]

---

[245] *Fatḥ al-Bārī*, vol. 10, p. 200.

[246] *Zād al-Maʿād*, vol. 4, p. 167.

Evidence establishing the reality of the evil-eye

Firstly – Proofs from the Qur'ān:

1. Allāh says in the story of Ya'qūb:

﴿٦٦﴾ وَقَالَ يَٰبَنِيَّ لَا تَدۡخُلُواْ مِنۢ بَابٖ وَٰحِدٖ وَٱدۡخُلُواْ مِنۡ أَبۡوَٰبٖ
مُّتَفَرِّقَةٖۖ وَمَآ أُغۡنِي عَنكُم مِّنَ ٱللَّهِ مِن شَيۡءٍۖ إِنِ ٱلۡحُكۡمُ إِلَّا
لِلَّهِۖ عَلَيۡهِ تَوَكَّلۡتُۖ وَعَلَيۡهِ فَلۡيَتَوَكَّلِ ٱلۡمُتَوَكِّلُونَ ﴿٦٧﴾

And he (Ya'qūb) said: "O my sons! Do not enter by one gate, but enter by different gates, and I cannot avail you against Allāh at all. Verily! The decision rests only with Allāh. In Him, I put my trust and let all those that trust, put their trust in Him."

Sūrah Yūsuf, verse 67

Ibn 'Abbās, Muḥammad ibn Ka'b, Mujāhid, Ḍaḥḥāk, Qatādah and al-Suddī all said: "He feared for them the evil-eye, for they were all handsome and possessed beauty. The evil-eye is real; it causes the horse rider to fall from his horse."[247]

2. Allāh says:

وَإِن يَكَادُ ٱلَّذِينَ كَفَرُواْ لَيُزۡلِقُونَكَ بِأَبۡصَٰرِهِمۡ
لَمَّا سَمِعُواْ ٱلذِّكۡرَ وَيَقُولُونَ إِنَّهُۥ لَمَجۡنُونٞ ﴿٥١﴾ وَمَا هُوَ إِلَّا ذِكۡرٞ لِّلۡعَٰلَمِينَ ﴿٥٢﴾

And verily, those who disbelieve would almost make you slip with their eyes (through hatred) when they hear the Reminder (the Qur'ān), and they say: Verily, he (Muḥammad) is a madman. But it is nothing else than a Reminder to all the 'Ālamin (mankind and jinn).

Sūrah al-Qalam, verses 51-52

---

[247] *Tafsīr al-Qur'ān al-'Aẓīm*, vol. 2, p. 419.

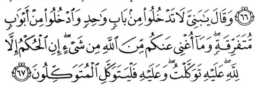

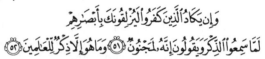

[Ibn Kathīr states:] "Ibn ʿAbbās said: 'This means that they will give you the evil-eye, i.e. become envious of you due to their hatred of you, were it not that Allāh had protected and shielded you.' In this is evidence showing that the evil-eye and its effects are real, if Allāh wills it."[248]

3. Allāh says:

بِسْمِ ٱللَّهِ ٱلرَّحْمَٰنِ ٱلرَّحِيمِ

قُلْ أَعُوذُ بِرَبِّ ٱلْفَلَقِ ﴿١﴾ مِن شَرِّ مَا خَلَقَ ﴿٢﴾ وَمِن
شَرِّ غَاسِقٍ إِذَا وَقَبَ ﴿٣﴾ وَمِن شَرِّ ٱلنَّفَّٰثَٰتِ فِى
ٱلْعُقَدِ ﴿٤﴾ وَمِن شَرِّ حَاسِدٍ إِذَا حَسَدَ ﴿٥﴾

Say: "I seek refuge with (Allāh), the Lord of the daybreak. From the evil of what He has created. And from the evil of the darkening (night) as it comes with its darkness. And from the evil of those who practise witchcraft when they blow in the knots. And from the evil of the envier when he envies."

Sūrah al-Falaq

Here Allāh says: ***"And form the evil of the envier when he envies."***

Secondly – Proofs from the Sunnah:

1. The *ḥadīth* of Abū Hurayrah (رضي الله عنه) in which the Prophet (ﷺ) said: *"The evil-eye is true"* and he forbade tattoos.[249]

2. The *ḥadīth* of ʿĀ'ishah in which the Prophet (ﷺ) said: *"Seek refuge in Allāh from the evil-eye, for verily it is true."*[250]

---

[248] Ibid, vol. 4, p. 357.

[249] *Sahih al-Bukhari*, vol. 4, p. 44, no. 5740.

[250] Collected by Ḥākim, see *Ṣaḥīḥ al-Jāmiʿ al-Ṣaghīr*, vol. 3, p. 337.

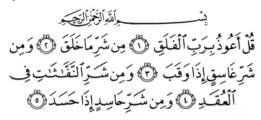

3. The *ḥadīth* of Ibn 'Abbās (☺) that the Prophet (☻) said: *"The evil-eye is true, and was anything to precede the decree of Allāh it would be the evil-eye, and if you are asked to bathe then do so."*[251]

4. The saying of the Prophet (☻): *"Indeed the evil-eye can have an effect with the will of Allāh upon a man, until he ascends (i.e. a mountain) and then falls from it."*[252]

5. The saying of the Prophet (☻): *"The majority of people from my Ummah (nation) will die after the decree of Allāh as a result of the evil-eye."*[253]

6. The *ḥadīth* of 'Ā'ishah that when the Prophet (☻) would feel unwell, Jibrīl would read over him and say: *"In the name of Allāh may you recover, and from all illnesses be cured, and from the evil of the envier when he envies, and from the evil of the one who gives the evil-eye."*[254]

7. The *ḥadīth* of Jābir (☺) in which the Prophet (☻) said to Asmā' bint 'Umays: *"'Why is it that I see the bodies of my brother's children weak and lean, thus causing them illness? She replied: 'They are afflicted with the evil-eye.' He said: 'Recite over them,' so they were brought to him and he said: 'Recite over them.'"*[255]

So, the Qur'ān and *Sunnah* mention that a single breath from the envious one is harmful for the envied. The envied are harmed through his eyes and his thoughts, even if they are not harmed by his tongue and hands. This is why Allāh says: *"and from the evil of the envier when he envies"* showing that the evil comes simply from the feeling of jealousy and envy. It may be that a

---

[251] *Sahih Muslim*, vol. 4, p. 1719, no. 2188.

[252] Collected by Aḥmad and Abū Ya'lā, see *Ṣaḥīḥ al-Jāmi'*, vol. 3, p. 338.

[253] Collected by Bazzār, see *Ṣaḥīḥ al-Jāmi'*, vol. 1, p. 386.

[254] *Sahih Muslim*, vol. 4, p. 1718, no. 2185.

[255] Collected by Muslim.

person who is envious by nature may not always be mindful of this, but when he is, the fire of envy strikes and harms the envied. Hence, one needs to protect himself and seek refuge in Allāh, say the relevant *du'ās* and remembrances, and turn to Allāh so that this evil is repelled based upon his turning to Allāh, otherwise, the evil of envy will affect him.

Types of evil-eye (*'ayn*):

1. The evil-eye which comes from humans.

2. The evil-eye which comes from the *jinn*.

Both types have been proven. As for the first type: The saying of the Prophet (ﷺ) to 'Āmir ibn Rabī'ah when he gave the evil-eye to Sahl ibn Ḥanīf: *"Over what does one of you kill his brother?"*[256]

As for the second type it is supported from the *ḥadīth* of Umm Salamah when the Prophet (ﷺ) saw a salve girl in her house who had a scar on her face, and said: *"Make incantation upon her for she has the evil-eye."*[257]

Al-Farā' said, "*ṣaf'ah* is the evil-eye from the *jinn*."[258] Ibn Qutaybah said, "*ṣaf'ah* is a colour which differs from the colour of the face." Ibn al-Qayyim said: "The evil-eye is of two types: one from the humans and the other from the *jinn*."[259]

Shaykh Muḥammad ibn 'Abdul Wahhāb said: "From the evil of the envier when he envies, includes those from the *jinn* and mankind, for *shayṭān* and his party are jealous of the believers and that which they have received from the blessings of Allāh."[260]

---

[256] Collected by Mālik, see *al-Muwaṭṭa'*, vol. 2, p. 938.

[257] Collected by al-Bukhārī, no. 4739, and Muslim, no. 2197.

[258] *Zād al-Ma'ād*, vol. 4, p. 164.

[259] Ibid, vol. 4, p. 164.

[260] *Tafsīr Sūrah al-Falaq*, p. 30.

How does the evil-eye affect?

First and foremost, it is important to know and realise that the evil-eye does not affect a person except by the will of Allāh. It is also important to realise that a person may inflict the evil-eye upon himself or others; it may be unintentional, and sometimes the evil-eye comes about without actually seeing. Examples include a blind person or when something absent is being described to a person.

Also, it can be as a result of seeing something amazing without actually envying. It may even come from a righteous person or a loved one. Therefore, it is recommended for the one who sees something he likes, whether from himself, his family or others to say that which has been narrated.

Ibn al-Qayyim said: "The evil-eye is not necessarily the result of seeing something, for something may be described to the one who is blind, and he may affect it, and many times those who give the evil-eye do so from description and not seeing."[261]

Ibn Ḥajr said: "This confuses certain people: How is it possible to give the evil-eye from a distance, and harm others? The answer to this is that people's natures differ; it could be as a result of poison which leaves the eye of the envious, and reaches the body of the envied. Certain people who are known to give the evil-eye mention that when they see something they feel heat emerging from their eyes.....so that which leaves the eye of the envious is like an arrow. If this arrow strikes something unprotected, it will affect it, otherwise, it will miss and may even return to the shooter, it is just like a real arrow."[262]

Shaykh Muḥammad ibn 'Abdul-Wahhāb said: "The evil-eye only affects due to the evil soul. It is similar to a snake which can only

---

[261] *Zād al-Ma'ād*, vol. 3, pp. 117-118.

[262] *Fatḥ al-Bārī*, vol. 10, pp. 210-211.

release its poison if it bites. The evil-eye takes the form of hatred, and this hatred brings about a poison which affects others; it can become strong enough to affect others from a single glance..."[263]

The role of the *imām* (leader) towards those who inflict the evil-eye

Ibn al-Qayyim mentioned that our scholars and others have said: "Whosoever is known to inflict the evil-eye on others must be imprisoned, and the leader should provide for him until he dies; this is undoubtedly the correct opinion."[264]

Qaḍī ʿIyāḍ said: "Some of the scholars stated: If one is known to inflict the evil-eye, it is necessary to avoid that person; the leader should prevent him from mingling with people, and he orders him to remain in his house. If he is poor he is given what is sufficient for him. His harm is greater than the harm caused by the one who eats onions and garlic, and hence has been ordered by the Prophet (ﷺ) to refrain from coming to the mosque so as not to harm others, or the harm posed by the leper who was prevented by ʿUmar."[265] Imām al-Nawawī also mentions this.[266]

Ways to protect oneself from the evil-eye, and how to repel the evil of the envious

The *sharīʿah* has mentioned many ways in which one can protect oneself from the evil-eye. From them are the following:

1. To seek refuge in Allāh from the evil of the envious one and to recite the *muʿawwidhatayn* (*Sūrahs Falaq* and *Nās*). Allāh says:

---

263 *Tafsīr Sūrah al-Falaq*, pp. 27-29.

264 *Zād al-Maʿād*, vol. 4, p. 168.

265 *ʿUmdah al-Qārī': Sharḥ Ṣaḥīḥ al-Bukhārī*, vol. 17, p. 405.

266 *Ṣaḥīḥ Muslim: Sharḥ al-Nawawī*, vol. 14, p. 173.

وَمِن شَرِّ حَاسِدٍ إِذَا حَسَدَ ﴿٥﴾

And from the evil of the envier when he envies.
Sūrah al-Falaq, verse 5

The *ḥadīth* of Abū Saʿīd mentions that the Prophet (ﷺ) used to seek refuge in Allāh from the *jinn* and the evil-eye of humans, until the *muʿawwidhatān* were revealed. Then, these became sufficient and all else was left.[267]

2. To make the *duʿā* of blessing if one sees something he likes. Imām al-Nawawī said: "It is recommended for the one who sees something he likes, to make *duʿā* for that person, and say: "O Allāh bless him and do not harm him."
One should also say:

مَا شَاءَ اللهُ لَا قُوَّةَ إِلَّا بِاللهِ

Ibn Kathīr said in the commentary of the verse:

وَلَوْلَآ إِذْ دَخَلْتَ جَنَّتَكَ قُلْتَ مَا شَآءَ ٱللَّهُ لَا قُوَّةَ إِلَّا بِٱللَّهِ

"It was better for you to say, when you entered your garden: 'That which Allāh wills (will come to pass)! There is no power but with Allāh!'
Sūrah al-Kahf, verse 39

"When you entered your garden, and saw that which amazed you, you should have praised Allāh for that which He had blessed you with, and given to you from wealth and children, which He has not given to others, and said *māshā' Allāh*."[268]

The Prophet (ﷺ) said: "*Whosoever sees something which amazes him, and says: 'That which Allāh wills, there is no power except*

[267] *Sunan al-Tirmidhī*, no. 2059, see also *Rawḍah al-Ṭālibīn*, vol. 9, p. 348.

[268] *Tafsīr al-Qur'ān al-ʿAẓīm*, vol. 3, p. 75.

with Allāh,' it will not harm him."[269] He (ﷺ) also said: *"If one of you sees from himself or his wealth that which amazes him, let him ask Allāh to bless it."*[270]

'*Tabrīk*' (asking for blessing) is to say:

تَبارَكَ اللهُ أَحْسَنَ الخالِقِيْنَ، اللّٰهُمَّ بارِكْ فِيْه

Tabārak Allāh aḥsan al-khāliqīn, Allāhumma bārik fīh
May Allāh be blessed, the best of creators, O Allāh! Bless it.

اللّٰهُمَّ بارِكْ فِيْهِ وَلا تَضُرُّه

Allāhumma bārik fīh, wa lā taḍurruh
O Allāh! Bless it and do not make it harmful.

3. To be patient with the one who inflicts the evil-eye, and not to harm him, due to the saying of Allāh:

وَمَنْ عَاقَبَ بِمِثْلِ مَا عُوقِبَ بِهِۦ ثُمَّ بُغِىَ عَلَيْهِ
لَيَنصُرَنَّهُ ٱللَّهُ

And whoever has retaliated with the like of that which he was made to suffer, and then has again been wronged, Allāh will surely help him.
Sūrah al-Ḥajj, verse 60

4. To be good to the one who has been inflicted with the evil-eye. This is like the wealthy being good to the poor who are in need of his assistance.

5. To conceal that which a person feels may be in danger of being inflicted with the evil-eye, for the evil-eye is the yearning of the soul towards that which amazes it. So, if a person possesses that which he fears will be envied, he should conceal it and not show

---

[269] *Al-Wābil al-Ṣayyib*, p. 307.

[270] Ibid.

it off, especially in front of those who are known to be envious. At the same time, he should know that all that happens is by the will of Allāh, as He says:

$$وَمَاهُم بِضَآرِّينَ بِهِۦ مِنۡ أَحَدٍ إِلَّا بِإِذۡنِ ٱللَّهِ$$

...but they could not thus harm anyone except by Allāh's Leave.
Sūrah al-Baqarah, verse 102

It is reported that 'Uthmān (☸) saw a handsome boy, and said: "Blacken or darken his cheeks."[271]

6. To be cautious of the envious.

7. To assist one's own self in fulfilling ones needs by concealment and secrecy.

8. To fear Allāh, and to preserve His commandments, for whosoever fears Allāh, He will protect him and not leave him to others. Allāh says:

$$وَإِن تَصۡبِرُواْ وَتَتَّقُواْ لَا يَضُرُّكُمۡ كَيۡدُهُمۡ شَيۡئًا$$

But if you remain patient and become pious, not the least harm will their cunning do to you.
Sūrah Āl-'Imrān, verse 120

9. To be patient against one's enemy, and not fight him, complain about him or harm him in any way.

10. To trust in Allāh, for whosoever trusts in Allāh, He is sufficient for him.

11. To turn to Allāh sincerely, and to love Him, be pleased with Him and repent to Him. If he does this, he will realise it is not befitting of him to waste his time thinking of the one who is envious of him.

---

[271] *Sharḥ al-Sunnah*, al-Baghawī, vol. 12, p. 166.

12. To make his repentance to Allāh pure of any sins. These are the reasons why his enemies have overpowered him, for Allāh says:

وَمَآ أَصَٰبَكُم مِّن مُّصِيبَةٍ فَبِمَا كَسَبَتْ أَيْدِيكُمْ

And whatever of misfortune befalls you, it is because of what your hands have earned.

Sūrah al-Shūrā, verse 30

13. This point is from the most difficult to adhere to, and the most severe upon a person. The only one who is successful in it, is the one who is close to Allāh. It is to extinguish the fire inside the envious by doing good to him, so the more he increases in his harm, evil and envy the more you increase in your goodness and kindness to him.

14. Making one's *tawḥīd* purely for Allāh and turning to the One who has power over all causes is the most comprehensive of these points, and the one that unifies them all. If a person has sincere *tawḥīd*, fear of everything else will leave him, for whosoever fears Allāh, all else will fear him, and whosoever does not fear Allāh, fears all else, and whosoever fears other than Allāh, will be overpowered by it.[272]

Psychological illnesses

We are not specialists in the field of psychological illnesses; these illnesses have their specialists whom we respect, but this does not mean we cannot identify certain psychological conditions, which can be apparently seen when a person does not have peace of mind and contentment.

---

[272] *Badā'i al-Fawā'id*, vol. 2, p. 238.

There are a number of reasons for this:

Turning away from Allāh, avoiding his remembrance and committing sins, all cause a lack of relief and contentment. Allāh says:

وَمَنْ أَعْرَضَ عَن ذِكْرِى فَإِنَّ لَهُۥ مَعِيشَةً ضَنكًا

But whosoever turns away from My Reminder verily, for him is a life of hardship.

Sūrah Ṭa-Ha, verse 124

Also, constant pressures and difficulties in life may also cause certain psychological problems, for a person witnesses many things throughout his life which cause his affairs to be reversed. For example, if a person is informed of the death of a relative or a loved one, and he does not have the faith (*īmān*) that causes him to submit to the decree of Allāh, this will cause him distress, and he may becomes saddened for a long period of time.

Rather, even physical illnesses cause a person to become distressed, and this distress causes him to change the way he deals with his family and other people. If for example, a person stayed awake all night due to some pain he was feeling, what would his situation be in the morning? Even too much free time can lead to uneasiness.

This book also relates to these psychological conditions, for magic can cause a psychological illness which will not allow the afflicted to be content in any matter. In certain cases, this is also applicable to the one who has convulsions, so psychological conditions cover a vast territory.

The cure to any illness is through *īmān*, the Qur'ān, returning to Allāh and submitting to His decree. One can also seek modern cures for psychological illnesses as long as they are not unlawful (*ḥarām*).

However, it should be known that so long as psychological cures are not connected with *īmān* in Allāh then their success will be limited. A specialist in psychology once informed us that certain people come to him with illnesses, and he tries to cure them, but some people do not benefit from this. Then, after some time he sees them and they are better, and when he asks about this, they reply that they used the Qur'ān.

Sins and their evil effects

Indeed, sins have an immense impact upon the one who commits them, both in this life and the Hereafter. Ibn al-Qayyim said: "Is there a single evil in this world whose cause is not sins and misdeeds?"

Today, many people have become prisoners of their own sins which have restricted and held them back. The *shayāṭīn* from the humans and *jinn* have overpowered them until their lives have become unbearable, and the majority of those afflicted by magic and its likes are usually far and distanced from Allāh. Let us travel with Ibn al-Qayyim as he mentions the ill effects of sins:

"From it, is a wilderness the sinner feels in his heart between him and his Lord. This is not matched by the joy of leaving those sins; were one to know this he would leave those sins to escape from this wilderness. A man once complained to someone about a feeling of wilderness that he would find himself in, so it was said to him: 'If sins have caused this feeling of wilderness, leave them and become content. There is nothing more bitter for the heart than the wilderness of sin upon sin.'

From it, is a wilderness he feels between himself and others, especially the pious from amongst them. The stronger this feeling becomes, the further he parts from them and their benefit. The further one becomes from the party of the Most Merciful, the closer he becomes to the party of *shayṭān*. This continues in strength until it comes between him and his wife, children, relatives and even his own self, until you see him discontent with himself.

From it, is darkness in his heart, which is as real as the darkness of the night. The darkness of sins envelops his heart just as the darkness of night covers his eyes, for obedience is light, and sins are darkness; the stronger the darkness becomes the more his bewilderment increases."[273]

The cure for the evil-eye

Firstly: To ask the one who inflicted the evil-eye, if he is known, to bathe.

This is the best way to cure the evil-eye. If the inflictor bathes, the same water is taken and poured over the head of the afflicted. Also, a pot can be brought to the one who inflicted the evil-eye. He should enter his hand in it, then gargle and spit the water back into the pot. He should then wash his face in the pot, and then put his left hand in it and use the right hand to wash it with. The right hand should be used to wash the left hand. This should all be done once. Next, the right forearm should be washed and then the left. The right foot should be washed next followed by the left. Lastly, the right shin should be washed and then the left. All of this should be done in the pot of water, which should then be poured once over the head of the afflicted from behind.[274]

The evidence for this bathing is established by the Prophet (ﷺ) in the *ḥadīth* of Abū Umāmah ibn Sahl ibn Ḥanīf: "*My father was bathing, so he removed his cloak and ʿĀmir ibn Rabīʿah saw him. Sahl was very fair and handsome, and ʿĀmir said: 'I have never seen the flesh of a virgin to be similar to what I am seeing today.' Sahl became severely ill on the spot. The Prophet (ﷺ) was*

[273] *Al-Jawāb al-Kāfī.*

[274] *Al-ʿAyn Ḥaqq*, p. 44.

informed of his illness; he was told that Sahl was even unable to lift his head. The Prophet (ﷺ) asked: 'Do you blame anyone?' They replied: "Āmir ibn Rabīʿah.' So the Prophet (ﷺ) called him and became angry with him saying: 'Over what does one of you kill his brother? You should have asked that he be blessed. Bathe for him.' So ʿĀmir washed his face, hands, forearms, shins, feet and under his lower robe all in a pot, then it was poured over Sahl from behind him, and he was cured instantly."[275] The Prophet (ﷺ) said: "*If you are asked to bathe then do so.*" This *ḥadīth* has already been mentioned.

ʿĀ'ishah said: "The one who used to inflict the evil-eye would be ordered to make *wuḍu*, and the afflicted would wash from it."[276]

How to identify the person who has inflicted the evil-eye

He can be known by a number of ways:

1. He is well known amongst people to inflict the evil-eye with the permission of Allāh. Someone he was sitting with may have been afflicted.

2. When someone speaks about someone else, either in their presence or absence. If it is in their presence, he is ordered to bathe, and if it was in their absence, he is told to fear Allāh. If it is known that the person has become afflicted, he is also told to bathe.

How to approach the one who has inflicted the evil-eye

One of the major problems that people face is how they should approach the one who has inflicted them with the evil-eye. They fear this may cause him to become angry, or it may result in the severance of ties. We say to them:

---

[275] Collected by Mālik and Nasā'ī, see *Ṣaḥīḥ al-Jāmiʿ*, vol. 4, p. 37.

[276] Collected by Abū Dāwūd.

Firstly: One should be certain that it is that person who inflicted the evil-eye, for the Prophet (ﷺ) asked the companions in the story of Sahl: "*Do you blame anyone?*" They mentioned ʿĀmir ibn Rabīʿah. A person becomes certain due to that person having said something, or someone informs them of what he said.

Secondly: If one is not certain, they should at least be very confident.

Thirdly: To look at that person and see whether he is someone who fears Allāh and accepts advice? If so, he is told what has taken place.

Fourthly: If he is a person who becomes angry when approached, then he should be reminded of Allāh, and advised to fear Him. Those who are close to him and those whom he respects are asked to help in this matter.

Fifthly: If he refuses, should he be forced? The scholars have differed in this. Al-Māzirī said: "What is correct is that he is forced, especially if the afflicted will die as a consequence because then, it is a case of saving someone's life."[277]

Secondly: Incantation (*ruqyah*) from the evil-eye:

It has been established by the authentic *Sunnah* that one can make incantation from the evil-eye. Evdience for this includes:

1. The *ḥadīth* of ʿĀ'ishah who said: "*The Prophet (ﷺ) would order me, or order that we make incantation from the evil-eye.*"[278]

2. The *ḥadīth* of Anas (رضي الله عنه): "*The Prophet (ﷺ) allowed incantation from fever, the evil-eye and ants.*"[279]

---

[277] *Ṣaḥīḥ Muslim: Sharḥ al-Nawawī*, vol. 5, p. 37.

[278] *Sahih al-Bukhari*, vol. 7, p. 23, and *Sahih Muslim*, vol. 4, p. 1725.

[279] *Sahih Muslim*, vol. 4, p. 1725.

3. The *ḥadīth* of Ibn ʿAbbās (رضي الله عنهما): *"The Prophet (ﷺ) would recite upon Ḥasan and Ḥussayn and say: 'I seek refuge for you in the perfect and complete words of Allāh from both every shayṭān and every vermin, and from every evil-eye which harms.' He would say: 'This is how Ibrāhīm would seek refuge for Isḥāq and Ismāʿīl.'"*[280]

Incantation (*ruqyah*) from the evil-eye

بِسْمِ اللهِ أُرْقِيكَ، مِنْ كُلِّ داءٍ يُؤْذِيكَ، وَمِنْ شَرِّ كُلِّ نَفْسٍ أَوْ عَيْنٍ حاسِدٍ، اللهُ يَشْفِيكَ بِسْمِ اللهِ أُرْقِيكَ

Bismillāh urqīk, min kulli dāʾin yu'dhīk, wa min sharri kulli nafsin aw ʿaynin ḥāsid, Allāhu yashfīk, bismillāh urqīk.
In the name of Allāh I make '*ruqyah*' over you, from every illness which harms you, and from the evil of every envious soul or eye, may Allāh cure you, in the name of Allāh I make '*ruqyah*' over you.[281]

بِسْمِ اللهِ يُبْرِيكَ، وَمِنْ كُلِّ داءٍ يَشْفِيكَ، وَمِنْ شَرِّ حاسِدٍ إِذا حَسَدَ، وَمِنْ شَرِّ كُلِّ ذِي عَيْنٍ

Bismillāh yubrīk, wa min kulli dāʾin yushfīk, wa min sharri hāsidin idhā ḥasad, wa min sharri kulli dhī ʿayn.
In the name of Allāh may He cause you to recover, and from every illness cure you, and from the evil of the envier when he envies, and from the evil of the one who inflicts the evil-eye.[282]

أَعُوذُ بِكَلِماتِ اللهِ التَّامَّاتِ مِنْ شَرِّ ما خَلَقَ

Aʿūdhu bi-kallimāt illāhi at-tāmmāt min sharri mā khalaq.
I seek refuge in the complete and perfect Words of Allāh from the evil of what He has created.

أَعُوذُ بِكَلِماتِ اللهِ التَّامَّةِ مِنْ كُلِّ شَيْطانٍ وَهامَّةٍ وَمِنْ كُلِّ عَيْنٍ لامَّةٍ

---

[280] *Sahih al-Bukhari*, vol. 4, p. 119.

[281] *Sahih Muslim*, vol. 4, p. 1718, no. 2186.

[282] Ibid, no. 2185.

Aʿūdhu bi-kallimāt illāhi at-tāmmah min kulli shayṭānin wa hāmmah wa min kulli ʿaynin lāmmah.
I seek refuge in the complete and perfect Words of Allāh from every devil and every vermin, and from the evil-eye which harms.

أَعُوْذُ بِكَلِماتِ اللهِ التَّامَّاتِ الَّتِي لا يُجاوِزُهُنَّ بَرٌّ وَلا فاجِرٌ وَمِنْ شَرِّ ما خَلَقَ وَذَرَأَ وَبَرَأَ وَمِنْ شَرِّ ما ذَرَأَ فِي الأَرْضِ وَمِنْ شَرِّ ما يَخْرُجُ مِنْها وَمِنْ شَرِّ فِتَنِ اللَّيْلِ وَالنَّهارِ وَمِنْ شَرِّ طَوارِقِ اللَّيْلِ وَالنَّهارِ إِلا طارِقٌ يَطْرُقُ بِخَيْرٍ يا رَحْمَن

Aʿūdhu bi-kallimāt illāhi at-tāmmāt allatī lā yujāwizuhunna barrun wa lā fājir, wa min sharri mā khalaqa wa dhara'a wa bara'a, wa min sharri mā dhara'a fil arḍ, wa min sharri mā yakhruju minhā wa min sharri fitan al-layli wan-nahār, wa min sharri ṭawāriq al-layli wan-nahār illā ṭāriqun yaṭruqu bikhayr yā Raḥmān.
I seek refuge in the complete and perfect Words of Allāh which cannot be passed by any pious or impious, from the evil of what He has created, made and originated, and from the evil of what He has sowed in the earth and the evil of what sprouts from it, and from the evil trials of the night and day, and from the evil of those who visit by night and day except the one who visits with good, O the Most Gracious.

أَعُوْذُ بِكَلِماتِ اللهِ التَّامَّاتِ مِنْ غَضَبِهِ وَعِقابِهِ وَمِنْ شَرِّ عِبادِهِ وَمِنْ هَمَزاتِ الشَّياطِيْنِ وَأَنْ يَحْضُرُوْن

Aʿūdhu bi-kallimāt illāhi at-tāmmāt min ghaḍabihi wa ʿiqābihi wa min sharri ʿibādihi wa min hamazāt ash-shayāṭīn wa an yahḍarūn.
I seek refuge in the complete and perfect Words of Allāh from His anger, His punishment, and from the evil of His slaves, and from the whisperings of the devils and that they should come near me.

اللَّهُمَّ إِنِّي أَعُوْذُ بِوَجْهِكَ الكَرِيْمِ وَكَلِماتِكَ التَّامَّاتِ مِنْ شَرِّ مَا أَنْتَ آخِذٌ بِناصِيَتِه ، اللَّهُمَّ أَنْتَ تَكْشِف

المَأْثَمِ وَالمَغْرَمِ، اللَّهُمَّ لَا يَهْزِمُ جُنْدُكَ وَلَا يُخْلَفُ وَعْدُكَ سُبْحَانَكَ وَبِحَمْدِكَ

Allāhumma innī a'ūdhu bi-wajhika al-karīm wa kalimātika at-tāmmāt min sharri mā anta ākhidhun bi-nāṣiyatih, Allāhumma anta takshifu al-ma'tham wal-maghram, Allāhumma lā yuhzamu junduka wa lā yukhlafu wa'duka, subhānaka wa bi-ḥamdik.

O Allāh! I seek refuge in Your Noble Face and Your complete and perfect Words from the evil of that which requires Your provision, O Allāh You uncover sin and debt, O Allāh Your army is not defeated, and Your promise is not broken, Glory be to You and be You Praised.

أَعُوذُ بِوَجْهِ اللهِ العَظِيْمِ الَّذِي لَا شَيْءَ أَعْظَمُ مِنْهُ وَبِكَلِمَاتِهِ التَّامَّاتِ الَّتِي لَا يُجَاوِزُهُنَّ بَرٌّ وَلَا فَاجِرٍ، وَ

بِأَسْمَاءِ اللهِ الحُسْنَى مَا عَلِمْتُ مِنْهَا وَمَا لَا أَعْلَم، وَمِنْ شَرِّ مَا أَنْتَ آخِذٌ بِنَاصِيَتِهِ إِنَّ رَبِّي عَلَى صِرَاطٍ

مُسْتَقِيْم

A'ūdhu bi-wajh illāhi al-'aẓīm alladhī lā shay'a a'ẓamu minh, wa bi-kallimātihi at-tāmmāt allatī lā yujāwizuhunna barrun wa lā fājir, wa bi-asmā illāhi al-ḥusnā mā 'alimtu minhā wa mā lā a'lam, wa min sharri mā anta ākhidun bi-nāṣiyatih, inna rabbī 'alā sirāṭ mustaqīm.

I seek refuge in the Great Face of Allāh which there is nothing greater than, and in His complete and perfect Words which cannot be passed by the pious or impious, and in the beautiful Names of Allāh, those which I know and those which I do not know, and from the evil of that which requires Your provision. Verily, my Lord is on the Straight Path.

اللَّهُمَّ أَنْتَ رَبِّي لَا إِلَهَ إِلَّا أَنْتَ عَلَيْكَ تَوَكَّلْتُ وَأَنْتَ رَبُّ العَرْشِ العَظِيْمِ، مَا شَاءَ اللهُ كَانَ وَمَا لَمْ يَشَأْ لَمْ

يَكُنْ، وَلَا حَوْلَ وَلَا قُوَّةَ إِلَّا بِاللهِ، أَعْلَمُ أَنَّ اللهَ عَلَى كُلِّ شَيْءٍ قَدِيْرٌ، وَأَنَّ اللهَ قَدْ أَحَاطَ بِكُلِّ شَيْءٍ

عِلْمًا وَأَحْصَى كُلَّ شَيْءٍ عَدَدًا اللَّهُمَّ إِنِّي أَعُوذُ بِكَ مِنْ شَرِّ نَفْسِي وَشَرِّ الشَّيْطَانِ وَشِرْكِهِ، وَمِنْ شَرِّ

كُلِّ دَابَّةٍ أَنْتَ آخِذٌ بِنَاصِيَتِهَا إِنَّ رَبِّي عَلَى صِرَاطٍ مُسْتَقِيْم

Allāhumma anta rabbī lā ilāha illā anta, ʿalayka tawakkaltu wa anta rabbul ʿarsh al-ʿaẓīm. Mā shā' Allāh kān, wa mā lam yasha' lam yakun, wa lā ḥawla wa lā quwwata illā billāh, aʿlamu anna Allāh ʿalā kulli shay'in qadīr, wa anna Allāha qad aḥāṭa bi-kulli shay'in ʿilmā, wa aḥṣā kulla shay'in ʿadadā, Allāhumma innī aʿūdhu bika min sharri nafsī wa sharri ash-shayṭān wa shirkih, wa min sharri dābbatin anta ākhidhun bi-nāṣiyatihā, inna rabbī ʿalā sirāṭ mustaqīm.

O Allāh, You are my Lord, none has the right to be worshipped but You, in You I trust, and You are the Lord of the exalted Throne, that which Allāh wills happens, and that which He does not will does not happen, and there is no power nor might except by Allāh, I know that Allāh is able to do all things, and that Allāh surrounds all things in (His) knowledge, and that He has enumerated everything. O Allāh! I seek refuge in You from the evil of myself, and from the evil of *shayṭān* and his partners, and from the evil of that which requires Your provision. Verily, my Lord is on the Straight Path.

تَحَصَّنْتُ بِالإِلَهِ الَّذِي لَا إِلَهَ إِلَّا هُوَ وَإِلَيْهِ كُلُّ شَيْءٍ وَاعْتَصَمْتُ بِرَبِّي وَرَبُّ كُلِّ شَيْءٍ ، وَتَوَكَّلْتُ عَلَى الْحَيِّ الَّذِي لَا يَمُوْت ، وَاسْتَدْفَعْتُ الشَّرَّ بِلَا حَوْلَ وَلَا قُوَّةَ إِلَّا بِاللهِ ، حَسْبِيَ اللهُ وَنِعْمَ الْوَكِيل ، حَسْبِيَ الرَّبُّ مِنَ الْعِبَاد ، حَسْبِي الْخَالِقُ مِنَ الْمَخْلُوْق ، حَسْبِي الرَّازِقُ مِنَ الْمَرْزُوق ، حَسْبِي اللهُ هُوَ حَسْبِي ، الَّذِي بِيَدِهِ مَلَكُوتُ كُلِّ شَيْءٍ ، وَهُوَ يُجِيْرُ وَلَا يُجَارُ عَلَيْه ، حَسْبِي اللهُ وَكَفَى ، سَمِعَ اللهُ لِمَنْ دَعَا ، وَلَيْسَ وَرَاءَ اللهِ مَرْمَى حَسْبِيَ اللهُ لَا إِلَهَ إِلَّا هُوَ عَلَيْهِ تَوَكَّلْتُ وَهُوَ رَبُّ الْعَرْشِ الْعَظِيْم

Taḥaṣṣantu bil-ilāh alladhī lā ilāha illā huwa, wa ilayhi kullu shay', waʿtaṣamtu bi-rabbī wa rabbi kulli shay', wa tawakkultu ʿalā al-Ḥayy alladhī lā yamuwt, wastadfʿatu ash-sharr bi-lā ḥawla wa lā quwwata illā billāh, ḥasbiy Allāh wa niʿm al-wakīl, ḥasbiy ar-rabb min al-ʿibād, ḥasbiy al-khāliq min al-makhlūq, ḥasbiy ar-rāziq min al-marzūq, ḥasbiy Allāh huwa ḥasbiy, alladhī biyadihi malakūtu kulli shay', wa huwa yujīru wa lā yujāru ʿalayh, ḥasbiy Allāh wa kafā, samiʿ Allāh liman daʿā, wa laysa warā' Allāhi marmā, ḥasbiy Allāh lā ilāha illā huwa, ʿalayhi tawakkaltu wa

huwa rabbul ʿarsh al-ʿaẓīm.
I seek strength from the true God, none has the right to be worshipped but Him, to Him belongs everything, I rely upon my Lord and the Lord of everything, and I trust in the Ever-Living who will never die, and I seek to repel evil by the power and might which is not except for Allāh, Allāh is sufficient for me, and He is the Best Disposer of affairs, the Lord suffices me from the slaves, the Creator suffices me from the creation, the Provider suffices me from the provided, Allāh is sufficient for me, in whose Hand is the sovereignty of everything, and He protects (all) and there is none to protect from Him, Sufficient is Allāh for me, Allāh hears the one who invokes Him, there is nothing beyond Allāh, Allāh is sufficient for me, none has the right to be worshipped except Him, in Him I place my trust, and He is the Lord of the Magnificent Throne.

Whosoever utilises these *duʿās* will realise the great benefit they possess, and the great need people have of them. They prevent the evil-eye, and remove it after it has befallen. All of this is dependent upon the strength of *īmān* one possesses and the strength of his heart and soul, for it is a weapon, and the weapon is only as strong as the one yielding it.

CHAPTER 14
Jealousy

Definition

Linguistically, it means to wish to have what someone else has been blessed with, or to take it from him, or to see someone else with a blessing and wish for its removal, or to wish that he has less than it. '*Ghabṭ*' is to hope to have a similar blessing whilst not wishing for its removal from that person.[283]

In the *sharīʿah* jealousy means 'to wish for the removal of the blessing the envied possesses, even if the envier does not receive it. It can also be to wish that others do not receive blessings.

Its reality

The reality of jealousy is that it comes as a result of hatred, which stems from anger.

[283] *Lisān al-ʿArab*, vol. 3, p. 148-149.

Establishing the existence of jealousy

The Qur'ān and *Sunnah* have both mentioned the existence of jealousy amongst people.

Evidence from the Qur'ān:

Allāh says:

وَدَّكَثِيرٌۭ مِّنۡ أَهۡلِ ٱلۡكِتَٰبِ لَوۡ يَرُدُّونَكُم مِّنۢ
بَعۡدِ إِيمَٰنِكُمۡ كُفَّارًا حَسَدًا مِّنۡ عِندِ أَنفُسِهِم

Many of the people of the Scripture (Jews and Christians) wish that if they could turn you away as disbelievers after you have believed, out of envy for their own selves.

Sūrah al-Baqarah, verse 109

He also says:

أَمۡ يَحۡسُدُونَ ٱلنَّاسَ عَلَىٰ مَآ ءَاتَىٰهُمُ ٱللَّهُ مِن فَضۡلِهِۦ فَقَدۡ ءَاتَيۡنَآ
ءَالَ إِبۡرَٰهِيمَ ٱلۡكِتَٰبَ وَٱلۡحِكۡمَةَ وَءَاتَيۡنَٰهُم مُّلۡكًا عَظِيمًا ٥٤

Or do they envy men (Muḥammad and his followers) for what Allāh has given them of His Bounty? Then We had already given the family of Ibrāhīm the Book and Al-Ḥikmah (Divine Revelation to those Prophets not written in the form of a book), and conferred upon them a great kingdom.

Sūrah al-Nisā', verse 54

Evidence from the Sunnah:

"Jealousy eats good deeds just as fire eats wood."[284]

"Do not be jealous of one another, nor cut off from one another, nor hate one another, nor desert one another, rather be the slaves of Allāh as brothers."[285]

---

[284] Collected by Abū Dāwūd and Ibn Mājah.

[285] Collected by al-Bukhārī and Muslim.

"'Verily my nation will be afflicted with the illness of all nations.' They asked: 'What is the illness of all nations?' He replied: 'Evil, arrogance and greed, and competing for this world and becoming distanced, and jealousy until there is oppression and then turmoil.'"[286]

The difference between jealousy and the evil-eye

The jealous and those who give the evil-eye are similar in one respect, and differ in another. They are similar in that they both turn and adjust themselves to the one they wish to harm. They both inflict their harm upon others, whether they are present or not.

They differ in that the one who gives the evil-eye may do so without being jealous of him, even though he has some form of jealousy in him, for he may give the evil-eye to an animal or even himself. This is because he has seen something which amazes him. Therefore, jealousy is more general than the evil-eye, for everyone who has the evil-eye possesses some jealousy, but the jealous do not always inflict the evil-eye. Seeking refuge from the jealous also includes those who inflict the evil-eye.

The levels of jealousy

There are three levels of jealousy:

1. To wish that a blessing is removed from another – this level is the most dangerous and the most impermissible.

2. To wish that another does not receive blessings – a person dislikes that Allāh should bestow His blessings upon others. Instead, he wishes they resume their weak state of poverty, ignorance etc. This is also impermissible.

---

[286] Authentic, collected by al-Ṭabarānī.

3. The jealousy of '*ghabṭ*': This is to wish for a similar blessing, without its removal from others. This is allowed and is similar to competing, as Allāh says:

وَفِي ذَٰلِكَ فَلْيَتَنَافَسِ ٱلْمُتَنَٰفِسُونَ ﴿٢٦﴾

...and for this let (all) those strive who want to strive (i.e. hasten earnestly to the obedience of Allāh).

Sūrah al-Muṭaffifīn, verse 26

The Prophet (ﷺ) said: "*There is no jealousy except in two: the one to whom Allāh has given wealth and he spends it upon his dependants with truth and fairness, and the one to whom Allāh has given knowledge and wisdom, so he judges according to it and teaches it to the people.*"[287]

The causes of jealousy

Jealousy has causes which make a person's heart fill with hatred and it makes a person despise other people. This hatred may even cause him to kill.

Some of these causes are:

1. Lack of contentment with what Allāh has given to him from the affairs of this world. You will find such a person is always angry: Why does so and so have wealth and I do not? Why is it that so and so has a better job than me? etc.

2. Hatred and enmity - the one who has enmity does not the want the person he hates to be blessed by Allāh, rather he wants the opposite for him. Allāh says:

وَإِن تُصِبْكُمْ سَيِّئَةٌ يَفْرَحُوا۟ بِهَا

...but if some evil overtakes you, they rejoice at it.

Sūrah Āl-'Imrān, verse 120

---

[287] *Sahih al-Bukhari*, vol. 1, p. 6 and *Sahih Muslim*, vol. 1, p. 559.

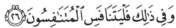

This enmity may cause a person to steal or even kill.

3. Amazement - this is a dangerous ailment which causes a person to become jealous, indeed, it causes him to reject the truth, as Allāh says:

أَوَعَجِبْتُمْ أَن جَآءَكُمْ ذِكْرٌ مِّن رَّبِّكُمْ عَلَىٰ رَجُلٍ مِّنكُمْ

Do you wonder that there has come to you a Reminder from your Lord through a man from amongst you.

Sūrah al-A'rāf, verse 63

Therefore, the one who is amazed by his own self dislikes that another should be better than him.

4. The presence of rivalry between certain groups in society, such as a businessman being jealous of other businessmen; this is impermissible.

The cure to jealousy

Now that we know that jealousy is a grave illness, what is its cure? The answer is in the following:

1. The jealous should know that they have participated with the enemies of Allāh in their hatred of the believers, for the enemies dislike that the blessings of Allāh should be bestowed upon the believers. The one who has jealousy is similar to them in this regard.

2. To know that their jealousy does not harm anyone except themselves, for they are the ones who feel anxiety, despair and sadness. Were Allāh to answer the wishes of the jealous, no-one would receive any blessings.

3. To be fully content with what Allāh has given, for one does not grieve over what has passed from this world, for it will all be destroyed one day. He should know that this jealousy and lack

of contentment is in opposition to what Allāh has ordered. Allāh says:

أَهُمْ يَقْسِمُونَ رَحْمَتَ رَبِّكَ ۚ نَحْنُ قَسَمْنَا بَيْنَهُم مَّعِيشَتَهُمْ فِي الْحَيَوٰةِ
الدُّنْيَا ۚ وَرَفَعْنَا بَعْضَهُمْ فَوْقَ بَعْضٍ دَرَجَٰتٍ لِّيَتَّخِذَ بَعْضُهُم
بَعْضًا سُخْرِيًّا ۗ وَرَحْمَتُ رَبِّكَ خَيْرٌ مِّمَّا يَجْمَعُونَ ﴿٣٢﴾

Is it they who would portion out the Mercy of your Lord? It is We Who portion out between them their livelihood in this world, and We raised some of them above others in ranks, so that they may employ others in their work. But the Mercy (Paradise) of your Lord is better than the (wealth of this world) which they amass.

Sūrah al-Zukhruf, verse 32

The effects of jealousy upon society

Jealousy is the disease of all nations, as the Prophet (ﷺ) said: "*The illness of those nations before you has spread to you: jealousy and enmity.*"[288]

When jealousy becomes apparent in a society it splits, becomes weakened, lacks in motivation, its members plot against one another, and the members of such a society continuously compete with and hate one another; thus life in such a society becomes unbearable. So, it is the duty of the Muslim to fear Allāh, wash his heart from the evils of hate and jealousy so that he may become upright, and be good in his dealings with others. The Prophet (ﷺ) said: "*The believer to the believer is like a building, each part of it supports the other.*"[289] He (ﷺ) also said: "*None of you truly believes until he loves for his brother what he loves for himself.*"[290]

---

[288] Collected by al-Tirmidhī.

[289] *Sahih al-Bukhari*, vol. 3, p. 98, and *Sahih Muslim*, vol. 8, p. 9.

[290] Al-Bukhārī, see *Ṣaḥīḥ al-Jāmiʿ*, vol. 6, p. 208.

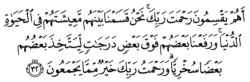

Allāh says:

وَلَا تَتَمَنَّوْا۟ مَا فَضَّلَ ٱللَّهُ بِهِۦ بَعْضَكُمْ عَلَىٰ بَعْضٍ ۚ لِّلرِّجَالِ
نَصِيبٌ مِّمَّا ٱكْتَسَبُوا۟ ۖ وَلِلنِّسَآءِ نَصِيبٌ مِّمَّا ٱكْتَسَبْنَ ۚ
وَسْـَٔلُوا۟ ٱللَّهَ مِن فَضْلِهِۦٓ ۗ إِنَّ ٱللَّهَ كَانَ بِكُلِّ شَىْءٍ
عَلِيمًا ﴿٣٢﴾

And wish not for the things in which Allāh has made some of you to excel others. For men there is reward for what they have earned, (and likewise) for women there is reward for what they have earned, and ask Allāh of His Bounty. Surely, Allāh is Ever All-Knower of everything.

Sūrah al-Nisā', verse 32

So it is necessary for the jealous, those who inflict the evil-eye, and others similar to them to know that these are dangerous diseases which not only harm them, but harm society as a whole. The jealous and those who give the evil-eye are more in need of a cure than others.

CHAPTER 15

True Incidents Relating to Convulsions, Magic, the Evil-Eye and Fortune Tellers

These are a number of incidents relating to convulsions, magic and the evil-eye, the majority of which we have witnessed personally, and the rest are stories we were told by people we trust. We have tried our best to only mention what we know to be true, for such incidents are more often than not exaggerated. We are certain of what we mention here because we know the people involved by their names. We ask Allāh to protect us from all evil.

1. During the month of Dhul-Ḥijjah (the 12th Islamic month) in the year 1411 AH, one of us recited upon an old woman. After a short while, the *jinnī* began to mutter in an unintelligible, incoherent manner. Then he began to make sense, and the following conversation took place:

Reciter: Why have you entered into this woman?
Jinnī: O shaykh, may Allāh reward you with good.
Reciter: Do you know me?
Jinnī: Yes, you are our shaykh, and I know you from last year

when the family of this woman brought some Zamzam water for you to recite upon, and then she drank from it.
Reciter: Then you are a Muslim?
Jinnī: Yes, I am a Muslim and I pray.
Reciter: Then why did you enter into this poor woman?
Jinnī: Six years ago, this woman went with a group to perform *Ḥajj*. When they were returning they stopped close to Riyadh to pray the *Fajr* prayer. This woman got off the bus and whilst she was walking she tripped and fell on me hurting me. So I entered her, and since then I have harmed her.
Reciter: Do you gain any benefit in harming her?
Jinnī: No.
Reciter: Did she intentionally fall on you and harm you?
Jinnī: No.
Reciter: So Allāh says:

وَالْكَاظِمِينَ الْغَيْظَ وَالْعَافِينَ عَنِ النَّاسِ ۗ وَاللَّهُ يُحِبُّ الْمُحْسِنِينَ ﴿١٣٤﴾

"...who repress anger and who pardon men."

You are also not being just in your oppression, for you harmed her intentionally, and have continued to do so; this is unlawful.
Jinnī: That is true. Do you know what I used to do to her? I used to cause her pain in her neck, and she would complain of this regularly. Her sons would take her to the hospital, but I would leave her at the door of the hospital, and when they checked her they would find her well. When she would leave I would enter her again and continue to harm her.
Reciter: Are you married?
Jinnī: Yes, and I have children. I visit them and then return to this woman.
Reciter: And now?
Jinnī: As you wish.
Reciter: I want you to leave this woman and never return to her.
Jinnī: I will leave for you.
Reciter: Rather, you will leave out of obedience to Allāh.
Jinnī: Do you know that we actually wanted to kill her?
Reciter: Do you own the souls?

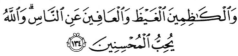

Jinnī: No.
Reciter: Then leave this talk; leave her and repent to Allāh.

After this, the *jinnī* left and the woman became well, but after a few months, it returned again, and the following conversation took place:

Reciter: Why have you returned when you promised not to do so?
Jinnī: I am the son of that *jinnī* who left this woman. When she fell, she fell on us both.
Reciter: What's your name?
Jinnī: Muḥammad, and my father is ʿAbdul-Qādir.
Reciter: O Muḥammad, we don't want a long conversation. Fear Allāh, leave her and return to your father. So he left, and the woman became well, by the grace and blessings of Allāh.

2. In another instance, one of us recited upon a young man who had been possessed, and the following conversation took place:

Shaykh: Who are you?
Jinnī: I am Shaykh Faraj, the leader of a tribe.
Shaykh: Why have you possessed this man?
Jinnī: Why do you make the man angry? Do you want me to harm those who make him angry?
Shaykh: Are you a Muslim?
Jinnī: Yes, I am a Muslim and I fear Allāh.
Shaykh: Do you not know that happiness, sadness and anger are all temporary states, for they can come upon a person at any time and for any reason, and that they happen to humans and *jinn*?
Jinnī: Yes, that is so, but I want to stretch my legs, as I am an old man.
Shaykh: How old?
Jinnī: 360 years, most of my friends have died.
Shaykh: O Shaykh Faraj, why do many of you harm people?
Jinnī: Due to their distancing themselves from the religion and

Allāh.
Shaykh: But many of you harm people who are practising, so why don't you advise them?
Jinnī: We have no power over the *jinn*.
Shaykh: Will you now leave this man?
Jinnī: I will now leave without you having to recite, but do you want to go with me to Yemen?
Shaykh: How?
Jinnī: I will fly with you.
Shaykh: We ask Allāh for His protection, leave this man and don't fly with us and we won't fly with you. After this, the *jinnī* left the man, and the man did not realise what had happened.

3. A *jinnī* once possessed a woman, so I went to recite upon her. After I began, the *jinnī* spoke, and the following conversation took place:

Shaykh: What is your name?
Jinnī: Mukhlid.
Shaykh: Are you a Muslim?
Jinnī: No, but I wish to accept Islām, 'I testify that none has the right to be worshipped except Allāh, and that Muḥammad is His Messenger.'
Shaykh: How many years have you possessed this woman? And for what reason?
Jinnī: For twenty years, and the reason is because whilst she was young she used to urinate in the open, but she never used to seek refuge in Allāh so I possessed her.
Shaykh: Now that Allāh has blessed you with Islām, and Islam forbids oppression, will you leave her?
Jinnī: Yes, I will leave and I promise not to return.

So he left, and after two hours he returned asking for the Shaykh, so the Shaykh returned:

Shaykh: Why have you returned?

Jinnī: O Shaykh, you know that a child learns how to make *wuḍu* and pray. I've accepted Islām but you haven't taught me anything about the religion; teach me how to make *wuḍu* and pray.

One of the brothers present brought some water and showed him how to make *wuḍu*, and how to pray, and certain other things about the religion. We advised him to find other pious *jinn* who would help him learn about the religion. He said he knew no-one, and if his family found out that he had accepted Islām, they would kill him. We advised him to be patient and seek Allāh's assistance; he then left.

4. Once a *jinnī* possessed a married woman during the first Gulf war, and after reciting upon her in the presence of her husband, the *jinnī* spoke and said:

Jinnī: I love her, and want her to leave this area as it will be demolished.
Shaykh: And who told you that?
Jinnī: A magician.
Shaykh: Are you a Muslim or a disbeliever?
Jinnī: I am a disbeliever, and so is the magician.
Shaykh: You and the magician have lied.
Jinnī: We do not lie, we only steal news by listening.
Shaykh: You have lied, for Allāh says:
Then, the Shaykh began to recite from *Sūrah al-Ṣāffāt*, and he repeatedly recited the verse:

لَّا يَسَّمَّعُونَ إِلَى ٱلْمَلَإِ ٱلْأَعْلَىٰ وَيُقْذَفُونَ مِن كُلِّ جَانِبٍ ﴿٨﴾

They cannot listen to the higher group (angels) for they are pelted from every side.

Jinnī: I testify that none has the right to be worshipped except Allāh, and that Muḥammad is His Messenger, I ask for Allāh's forgiveness, and I repent to Him. Then, he learned about Islām, and changed his name from Joshua to ʿAbdur-Raḥmān.
Shaykh: Is it true this area will be demolished?
Jinnī: Allāh know best...(three times)

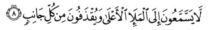

He then left the woman with great difficulty, due to his love for her, but he was reminded of Allāh and that this type of love is unlawful, so he left.

Incidents relating to magic

One of the shaykhs whom we trust informed us that he saw magic[291] at the top of a tree. It was made of two small stones, each the size of a hazelnut, and also a bandage and a rolled up charm. All of this was placed inside a cement ball on the top of the tree. So when the cement ball was broken, it was discovered that everything inside it had been burned. When they tried to open the bandage, it began to crumble. The bewitched happened to be someone well known to us, who had memorised the Qur'ān, and would constantly recite upon himself, and would turn to Allāh frequently, so Allāh cured him from his illnesses.

I once recited upon a young man who had studied in America. I continued to recite upon him for nearly a whole year due to the problems he was having, which caused his wife to leave him and return to her family. She gave birth to a daughter who he had not seen. Every time he would be recited upon he would shake, and do strange things. We were confused as to whether he was afflicted by magic, possession, or the evil-eye. All this caused much pain for his family, especially his mother. After nearly a year, I recited upon him with severity, and struck him. The *jinnī* began to scream and speak; the more I struck him the more he screamed, until it said it wanted to leave.

I said: Before you leave, who are you? And why did you come?
Jinnī: I have possessed him due to magic.
I said: Who bewitched him?
It said: I don't know.
So I struck it and said: You know.

[291] Perhaps the one who told him about the location of the magic, was the magician after he repented to Allah.

It replied: It was Judy, she bewitched him in America.[292]
So I said: Leave him.
It replied: I can't. So I struck him severely, and it said: Ok, ok, I will leave, so it left, and promised not to return.

I advised this man to repent to Allah, and observe the five daily prayers, and recite the Qur'an. Consequently, he became better. However, he did not continue this, so the magic returned, and the reason for this and Allah knows best, is that when he became negligent of the advice given to him, he was bewitched again.

Incidents relating to the evil-eye

The first incident:

One of the brothers whom we trust informed us, that a man who was well known to give the evil-eye went to his friend's farm, and saw the chickens he had. They were ninety five in number. He said: 'What's with all the traffic?' The next day all the chickens died.

The second incident:

A.L. told us whilst crying: I have been destroyed, I have been inflicted with the evil-eye, and he told the following story:

I used to sit with my family in the garden every day enjoying the serenity and peacefulness of last summer. One day just before sunset, so and so knocked on the door. I met him in the guest room, and one of my sons brought us coffee, dates, tea and fruit. The guest spent his time looking around the room, admiring the furniture and decorations, and I could feel arrows leaving his eyes aimed for my heart. Before he left, he said: 'You are a fortunate man, you have gathered much in a small period of time, and you have a big family and much wealth.' After this visit, everything

---

[292] It seems Judy was someone he met in America, who bewitched him before he left so that he would return.

changed; my business became stagnant, and the son who served us was injured, and nearly died were it not for the mercy of Allāh. My health deteriorated, so I closed my business and had to see many doctors.

Stories of fortune tellers

1. I once met a young man from the Gulf in India, and I sat with him at 'Arrivals.' He was determined to go to a famous fortune teller in that country, so I advised him and told him that the Prophet (ﷺ) said: "*Whosoever goes to a fortune teller and asks him something, and believes him, his prayer will not be accepted for forty days.*" However, he insisted on going, so I asked if I could go with him to prove to him their lies, and he agreed. When we entered upon the fortune teller, I began to speak to him and made up a false story regarding the man with me. After I finished he said: 'What you have said is true, for this man has been bewitched.' The man was astonished knowing it was all false, so he left and repented to Allāh and realised that they are just impostors.

2. A man facing marital problems went to one of these fortune tellers thinking his problems were due to work etc, so the fortune teller asked them to return the following day. They returned the next day, and the fortune teller informed him he had been bewitched, so the fortune teller was asked: "How long have these problems existed?" He replied: "For seven years, since he got married." In reality he had only been married for two years.

An amazing story

Shaykh Yāsīn Aḥmad 'Ayn said: "Some time ago, a man passed away and left a beautiful house, which had many rooms, was very spacious, and was decorated with embroidery, ornaments, and a marble courtyard, all surrounded by different coloured decorations and water features.

This man had no children to inherit from him, so the house was abandoned. His relatives agreed to sell the house believing it would be worth a small fortune, but as soon as they put the house on the market, news spread that the house had been overtaken by *jinn*. This news spread so much that it was the main topic amongst people for days and nights. Whoever disbelieved the story would go to the house, only to return the next day agreeing that the house had *shayāṭīn* in it.

So, people refused to buy the house, and the relatives of the deceased feared many problems as a result of this, especially since one prospective buyer had already paid a quarter of the price. So, a strong man who had heard of the news, but was not daunted by the prospect of the *jinn* went to the relatives and told them he would eject the *jinn* from the house if they paid him for it. They agreed and gave him half of the price.

That evening, the man went to the house armed with a gun. When he arrived, he rested for a while, and after the candle extinguished, he fell asleep. After a while, he felt something pulling his quilt, so he grabbed the quilt and asked: 'Who is it that is pulling the quilt?' A reply came: 'I am the *ʿifrīt* (*jinn*), and I must take the quilt or else I will possess you.' The man let the quilt go, and the *jinn* fell on its back. The man moved to pin him down, and put the gun to its head, and said: 'Tell me, who are you?' At this it became frightened and replied: 'Let me go, and I will tell you.'

The man said: 'Speak O *ʿifrīt*.' It replied: 'I am neither an *ʿifrīt* nor a *jinnī*, but a man like you; the only difference between us is my dark complexion and ugly features.' So, he let him go and lit the candle, whereupon he saw a naked, black man. He said: 'Tell me, what you are doing here.'

He replied: 'I am here out of necessity; I am a poor and unemployed man, who has a large family dependant upon him. I was looking for someone to employ me, and I found a man who told me to come to this house every night, and whenever someone approaches to clap and strike a tinplate which I brought for this purpose. If that does not deter the visitor I turn on the water features, and shout and scream from around the house in different voices. He then made me promise to keep this a secret.'

When the young man heard this, he took him to the relatives of the deceased and told them the full story. They discovered that the man who had employed him was the prospective buyer, who had wanted the house for a cheap price." (Summarised)

Chapter 16

Fatāwā (Rulings)

Firstly: *Fatāwā* from the Permanent Committee of Scholars in Saudi Arabia

These are a collection of *fatāwā* we have chosen from the book: *Fatāwā of the Permanent Committee of Scholars* gathered by Shaykh Aḥmad al-Duwaysh, from the first volume, relating to matters of *ʿaqīdah* (belief).

Question 5, from *fatwā* no. 1515

Q: What is the ruling of writing Qur'ānic verses and hanging them on the upper arm, for example. What about placing them in water and then sprinkling the water on a persons body, or bathing in it. Is this from *shirk*? Is this permissible?

A: To write Qur'ānic verses or all of the Qur'ān and hang it on the upper arm or somewhere else, in order to repel some harm, or in the hopes of curing harm, is something the scholars of the past differed over. Some of them forbade it, and included it amongst the amulets which are forbidden, because of the saying of the Prophet (ﷺ): "*Verily incantations, amulets and tiwalah (love charms) are shirk.*" Collected by Aḥmad and Abū Dāwūd. They state that there is nothing which exempts the Qur'ān from this ruling, so it is also forbidden to use the Qur'ān in this way, so as not to open the doors of hanging that which is from other than the Qur'ān.

Thirdly, they say, that it is very likely that the one who wears such things will forget to remove them whilst relieving himself etc. This is the saying of ʿAbdullāh ibn Masʿūd (⬥), his students, and it is the opinion supported by Imām Aḥmad in a narration chosen by some of his followers, especially the latter ones.

From the scholars who have allowed the hanging of amulets taken from the Qur'ān, or from the names of Allāh, or His attributes, are ʿAbdullāh ibn ʿAmr ibn al-ʿĀs (⬥), Abū Jaʿfar al-Bāqir, and Imām Aḥmad in one narration; they see the previous *hadīth* as only referring to those things which include *shirk*.

The first opinion is the strongest and safest for a person's *ʿaqīdah*, because it is more cautious in preserving one's *tawḥīd*. That which has been reported by Ibn ʿAmr refers to the memorisation of the Qur'ān, by writing the verses on tablets and then hanging them around the neck. It is not meant as a means of preventing evil or attaining benefit.

As for placing these verses in water, and then sprinkling it on the body or bathing from it, there is nothing authentically reported from the Prophet (⬥) about this. It is reported that Ibn ʿAbbās (⬥) would write words from the Qur'ān and *duʿās* and tell the ill to drink from it, but this is not authentically reported from him. Imām Mālik narrates that ʿĀmir ibn Rabīʿah saw Sahl ibn Ḥanīf bathing. ʿĀmir said: *"I have never seen the flesh of a virgin similar to what I am seeing today."* Sahl immediately became severely ill. The Prophet (⬥) was informed of his illness, and the fact that he was unable to lift his head. The Prophet (⬥) asked: *"Do you blame anyone?"* They replied: *"ʿĀmir ibn Rabīʿah."* So the Prophet (⬥) called him and became angry with him saying: *"Over what does one of you kill his brother? You should have asked that he be blessed. Bathe for him."* So, ʿĀmir washed his face, hands, forearms, shins, feet and under his lower robe in a pot, then it was poured over Sahl from behind, and he was cured instantly.

This incident is also collected by Aḥmad and al-Ṭabarānī. Some of the scholars, based upon this, have allowed the writing of verses and bathing from it etc. They base it either on an analogy with this incident or on what has been reported from Ibn ʿAbbās (☙), even though it is a weak narration.

Shaykh al-Islām Ibn Taymiyyah mentions that it is permissible in the second volume of *Majmūʿ Fatāwā*. He says: "Aḥmad and others have mentioned it is permissible." Ibn al-Qayyim says in *Zād al-Maʿād*: "A number of the scholars of the past allowed it, such as Ibn ʿAbbās, Mujāhid and Abū Qilābah." Whatever the case, this action is not from *shirk*.

May the peace and blessings of Allāh be upon our Prophet Muḥammad, his family and companions.

Deputy Head of the Committee: ʿAbdur-Razzāq ʿAfīfī
Member: ʿAbdullāh ibn Ghudayyān
Member: ʿAbdullāh ibn Munīʿ

Question 2 from *fatwā* no. 4015

Q: Was the Prophet (ﷺ) bewitched?

A: The Prophet (ﷺ) was human, so it is possible for him to be afflicted with that which humans are afflicted with. This includes pain, illnesses, oppression from others and similar things from the affairs of this world for which he was not sent, nor was the message he received due to it. So it is not far fetched to believe he fell ill, or that someone bewitched him etc. In the affairs of the world, this would cause him to think for example, he had had relations with one of his wives when he had not. However, these illnesses and bewitchment did not affect the revelation he received, or his conveying of the message from Allāh. This has been stated many times in the Qur'ān and *Sunnah*, and it was also the consensus of the scholars that he was perfect and safeguarded in these affairs and the affairs of the religion.

Witchcraft is a type of illness which the Prophet (ﷺ) was afflicted with, for it is established that ʿĀ'ishah (ؓ) said: "*The Prophet (ﷺ) was bewitched by a man from Banū Zurayq, known as Labīd ibn Aʿṣam, to the extent that the Prophet (ﷺ) would think he had done something when he had not. One day, he supplicated and supplicated and then said: 'I feel Allāh has informed me of the cure of my illness: Two men came to me, one sat by my head whilst the other at my feet. One of them asked the other: 'What is his illness?' He replied: 'Bewitchment.' He asked: 'Who bewitched him?' He replied: 'Labīd ibn Aʿṣam.' He asked: 'With what?' He replied: 'With a comb and his hair all in the shape of a man.' He asked: 'So where is it?' He replied: 'In the well of Dharwān.*" *The Prophet (ﷺ) went to it, and when he returned he said to ʿĀ'ishah: 'Its trees are like the heads of devils (shayāṭīn).' I asked: 'Did you remove it?' He replied: 'No, as for me, Allāh has cured me. I feared that the well would bring evil for people, so I buried it.'*" Collected by al-Bukhārī and Muslim.

The person who rejects this has opposed the evidence, as well as the consensus of the companions and scholars of the past. Instead, he has chosen to hold onto whims and doubts which have no authenticity, and cannot therefore be relied upon. This matter has been mentioned in great detail by Ibn al-Qayyim in *Zād al-Maʿād*, and by Ibn Ḥajr in *Fatḥ al-Bārī*.

May the peace and blessings of Allāh be upon our Prophet Muḥammad, his family and his companions.

Head of the Committee: ʿAbdul-ʿAzīz ibn Bāz
Deputy Head: ʿAbdur-Razzāq ʿAfīfī
Member: ʿAbdullāh ibn Ghudayyān
Member: ʿAbdullāh ibn Quʿūd

Q: Is it allowed to recite the Qur'ān for the ill, for the sake of Allāh or for a fee?

A: If the purpose is to make incantations upon the ill, then this is allowed, indeed, it is recommended, because of the saying of the Prophet (ﷺ): *"Whosoever from amongst you can benefit his brother, let him do so."* Collected by Muslim. Due to this being the action of the companions, it is better to do it without taking a fee, and if one takes a fee then it is allowed because it has been mentioned in the *Sunnah*.

If the purpose here is to recite, with the intention that the reward is going to the ill, it is best to avoid this as it is not mentioned in the *sharīʿah*. The Prophet (ﷺ) said: *"Whosoever brings into this affair of ours that which is not from it, will have it rejected."* Al-Bukhārī and Muslim.

May the peace and blessings of Allāh be upon our Prophet Muḥammad, his family and his companions.

Head of the Committee: ʿAbdul-ʿAziz ibn Bāz
Deputy Head: ʿAbdur-Razzāq ʿAfīfī
Member: ʿAbdullāh ibn Ghudayyān
Member: ʿAbdullāh ibn Quʿūd

Question 1 from *fatwā* no. 4804

Q: A woman was bewitched by a magician because of her marriage; she became insane, and the magician was caught by the authorities and confessed, so what is his punishment?

A: If a magician does something in his magic which comprises of disbelief, then he is killed as an apostate. If as a result of his magic, he killed someone, then he is killed as a murderer. However, if he did not commit an act of disbelief in his magic, or kill anyone, then there is a difference of opinion as to whether he should be executed or not. The correct opinion is that he is killed as an apostate; this is the saying of Abū Ḥanīfah, Mālik and Aḥmad, because he is a disbeliever due to his magic. This is mentioned in the following verse:

They followed what the shayāṭīn (devils) gave out (falsely of the magic) in the lifetime of Sulaymān. Sulaymān did not disbelieve, but the shayāṭīn disbelieved, teaching men magic.

The *ḥadīth* in Bukhārī of Bajālah ibn ʿAbdah also mentions this: *"ʿUmar wrote to us ordering that every male and female magician be killed, so we killed three."* Likewise, Ḥafṣah, the mother of the believers, ordered that a slave girl who had bewitched her be killed, so she was (collected by Mālik). Also, Jundub said: *"The punishment of the magician is beheading."* Collected by al-Tirmidhī.

Therefore, the ruling for the magician you are inquiring about is that he is killed because this is the correct opinion of the scholars. The one who verifies this claim of magic, and then carries out its punishment is the Muslim ruler. This is in order to preserve harmony and prevent chaos.

May the peace and blessings of Allāh be upon our Prophet Muḥammad, his family and his companions.

Deputy Head of the Committee: ʿAbdul-ʿAzīz ibn Bāz
Member: ʿAbdur-Razzāq ʿAfīfī
Member: ʿAbdullāh ibn Quʿūd

Q: What is the ruling of writing Qur'ānic verses and drinking from them, for I have seen people do this?

A: This has not been established by the Prophet (ﷺ), nor by his Khalīfahs nor his companions, so it is best to refrain from it. Allāh knows best.

May the peace and blessings of Allāh be upon our Prophet Muḥammad, his family and his companions.

Head of the Committee: ʿAbdul-ʿAzīz ibn Bāz
Deputy Head: ʿAbdur-Razzāq ʿAfīfī
Member: ʿAbdullāh ibn Ghudayyān
Member: ʿAbdullāh ibn Quʿūd

Secondly: *Fatāwā* from Shaykh Ibn ʿUthaymīn

Q: What is the ruling of incantations (*ruqyah*) and writing verses and hanging them on the neck of the patient?

A: Performing incantations on the one who has been bewitched or afflicted with other illnesses is allowed if it is from the Qur'ān and those *duʿās* which have been mentioned in the *Sunnah*, which the Prophet (ﷺ) would say on his companions, such as:

رَبُّنا اللهُ الَّذِيْ فِي السَّماءِ تَقَدَّسَ اسْمُكَ، أَمْرُكَ فِي السَّماءِ وَالأَرْضِ، كَما رَحْمَتُكَ فِي السَّماءِ فَاجْعَلْ رَحْمَتَكَ فِي الأَرْضِ، أَنْزِلْ رَحْمَةً مِنْ رَحْمَتِكَ وَشِفاءً مِنْ شِفائِكَ عَلَى هَذا الوَجَعِ

Rabbun Allāh alladhī fis-samā'i taqaddasa ismuk, amruka fis-samā'i wal-arḍ, kamā raḥmatuka fis-samā'i fajʿal raḥmatuka fil-arḍ, anzil raḥmatan min raḥmatik, wa shifā'an min shifā'ik ʿalā hādha al-wajaʿ.
Our Lord is Allāh whose name in heaven is glorified, Your decree is in the heavens and the earth, and just as Your Mercy is in the heavens then place Your Mercy on the earth, send down a mercy from Your Mercy, and a cure from Your cure upon this afflicted.

بِسْمِ اللهِ أُرْقِيْكَ، مِنْ كُلِّ داءٍ يُؤْذِيْكَ، وَمِنْ شَرِّ كُلِّ نَفْسٍ أَوْ عَيْنٍ حاسِدٍ، اللهُ يَشْفِيْكَ بِسْمِ اللهِ أُرْقِيْكَ

Bismillāh urqīk min kulli dā'in yu'dhīk, wa min sharri kulli nafsin aw ʿaynin ḥāsid, Allāhu yashfīk, bismillāh urqīk.
In the name of Allāh, I make '*ruqyah*' over you, from every illness which harms you, and from the evil of every envious soul or eye, may Allāh cure you, in the name of Allāh I make '*ruqyah*' over you.

Likewise, it is allowed to place one's hand on the part of the body which is in pain, and say:

أَعُوذُ بِاللهِ وَعِزَّتِهِ مِنْ شَرِّ مَا أَجِدُ وَأُحَاذِر

A'ūdhu billāhi wa 'izzatihi min sharri mā ajidu wa uḥādhir.
I seek refuge in Allāh and in His Might from the evil that I feel and am wary of.

Other such similar *du'ās* which the scholars have mentioned as coming from the *ḥadīths* can also be recited.

As for writing verses and *du'ās* and hanging them, the scholars have differed over this. Some of them allowed it and others forbade it. The stronger opinion is to forbid it, because it has not been reported by the Prophet (ﷺ). Rather what has been reported is to recite over the ill. As for hanging verses and *du'ās* on the neck or hand, or placing them under ones pillow etc., the correct opinion is that this is also not allowed due to it not having been reported. By using something which is not from the *sharī'ah*, a person commits a form of *shirk*, as he is placing as a means that which Allāh has not placed.[293]

Q: What is the ruling of hanging amulets and charms?

A: Hanging amulets and charms is of two types:

Firstly - that which is from the Qur'ān.

Secondly - that which is from other than the Qur'ān, from that which has no meaning.

The first type is something the scholars have differed over both in the past and present: Some have allowed it, considering it to be included in the verse:

---

[293] *Fatāwā Shaykh Ibn 'Uthaymīn*, vol. 1, p. 65, no. 30.

وَنُنَزِّلُ مِنَ ٱلْقُرْءَانِ مَا هُوَ شِفَآءٌ وَرَحْمَةٌ لِّلْمُؤْمِنِينَ

And We send down of the Qur'ān that which is a healing and a mercy to those who believe.

Sūrah al-Isrā', verse 82

And in His saying:

كِتَٰبٌ أَنزَلْنَٰهُ إِلَيْكَ مُبَٰرَكٌ

This is) a Book (the Qur'ān) which We have sent down to you,) full of blessings.

Sūrah Ṣād, verse 29

From the blessing of the Qur'ān is that it should be hung to protect from evil.

Others from the scholars have forbidden it because it has not been established by the Prophet (ﷺ) as being a permissible means of preventing evil. The correct opinion in these matters is to refrain from this, as it is not allowed to hang such amulets even if they are from the Qur'ān, or to place them under one's pillow, or hang them on the wall etc. Rather, one should make *du'ā* for the ill and recite upon them as the Prophet (ﷺ) used to.

The second category, (that which has no meaning from other than the Qur'ān) is not permissible in any situation, due to one not knowing what has been written. Certain people write incantations and joined words which cannot be read or distinguished; this is an innovation and unlawful in any situation. Allāh knows best.[294]

Q: What is the ruling of the bride placing her foot in the blood of a slaughtered sheep?

A: This custom has no permissible (*shar'ī*) foundation, rather, it is an evil custom, for it is:

---

[294] Ibid, vol. 1, pp. 66-67, no. 32.

1. A false belief not based on divine law (*sharīʿah*).

2. It makes her foot impure because of the blood. One is ordered to remove impurities, and stay away from them.

Here, I would like to mention to my Muslim brothers that it is appropriate that when one has some impurity on them, they hasten in its removal. This is the guidance of the Prophet (ﷺ). When the Bedouin entered the mosque and urinated in it, the Prophet (ﷺ) ordered that water be poured on it. Likewise, when the child urinated in the lap of the Prophet (ﷺ), he asked for water and cleaned it. Delaying the removal of impurities may cause a person to forget about it. This may cause him to pray whilst in a state of impurity, even though the correct opinion states that he is excused and his prayer is correct. However, if he remembers whilst in the prayer and is unable to clean the impurity whilst praying, then, he must break his prayer and start anew after the removal of this impurity.

Either way, the evil custom which is being referred to in the question is from foolishness, for the *sharīʿah* has ordered one to remove impurities and clean them. I also fear that the sacrifice may have been performed for some other reason, like sacrificing it to the *jinn* or devils (*shayāṭīn*) etc; this is from *shirk*, and it is well known that *shirk* is a sin which is not forgiven by Allāh.[295]

Q: Someone moved into a new house and began to be afflicted with illnesses. This has caused him and his family to become pessimistic regarding the house, so is it allowed for him to leave due to this reason?

A: Certain houses, vehicles and spouses may possess misfortune due to the wisdom of Allāh. This may cause some harm, or the removal of some benefit etc, so if this is the case then there is nothing wrong with moving to another house. Allāh may place

[295] Ibid, vol. 1, pp. 69-70, no. 34.

good for him in his new abode. It has been reported that the Prophet (ﷺ) said: *"Misfortune is in three: a house, a woman and a horse."* So, certain vehicles possess misfortune, likewise certain wives and houses. So if a person sees this, he should know it is from the decree of Allāh, and that Allāh has decreed this in His wisdom so that the person may move to another place. Allāh knows best.[296]

Q: What is the ruling of '*nafath*' (lightly spitting) in water?

A: Spitting in water is of two types:

Firstly - To want some blessing from the saliva of that person. Without doubt, this is impermissible and a form of *shirk* for a person's saliva does not possess any blessing or cure, so one should not seek blessing from anyone else's traces except the Prophet (ﷺ). People used to seek blessings from his traces during his lifetime. Likewise, after his death, if those traces were still present, (Umm Salamah would have hairs of the Prophet (ﷺ) in a silver container) they would be used to cure the ill by placing water on them, then giving the water to the ill.

However, this is not allowed for anyone other than the Prophet (ﷺ). Using a person's saliva, sweat or clothes is unlawful and a form of *shirk*, as the one who brings a cure which is not from the *sharī'ah* or a natural cure, has brought a form of *shirk*. If a person does this, he has made himself similar to Allāh in placing a cure, for these cures are only taken from the *sharī'ah*, so the one who relies upon a means and cure other than that which is natural or from the *sharī'ah*, he has brought a form of *shirk*.

Secondly - To spit after having recited the Qur'ān, such as reciting *Sūrah Fātiḥah*, (which is from the best '*ruqyahs*' to recite over the ill). He recites it and then spits into the water; this is allowed, and some of the pious predecessors would do it. It has been tried and

[296] Ibid, vol. 1, pp. 70-71, no. 36.

is beneficial by the will of Allāh. The Prophet (ﷺ) before sleeping, would recite *Sūrahs Ikhlāṣ*, *Falaq* and *Nās* and then spit into his hands, and wipe his face and whatever he could of his body. Success is with Allāh.

Q: Does magic have a reality? And was the Prophet (ﷺ) bewitched?

A: Magic exists without a doubt, and it has a reality, as is mentioned in the Qur'ān and *Sunnah*. In the Qur'ān, Allāh mentions the sorcerers of Pharaoh who threw their sticks and ropes, and bewitched the eyes of those watching, to the extent that even Musa (عليه السلام) thought the serpents would bite due to the magic. He became frightened, so Allāh ordered him to throw his staff, which turned into a serpent and ate their magic. There is no confusion in this, and there are also many *ḥadīths* which establish magic and its effects.

The Prophet (ﷺ) was bewitched as has been established in the *ḥadīth* of 'Ā'ishah and others that the Prophet (ﷺ) was bewitched, to the extent he would think he had done something which he had not, but Allāh revealed to him *Sūrahs Falaq* and *Nās*, and he was cured by them.[297]

Q: Is it allowed to remove magic from the bewitched (i.e. '*nashrah*')?

A: The correct opinion is that this '*nashrah*' is of two types:

The first: By using the Qur'ān and authentic *du'ās* - there is nothing wrong with this due to its benefits, and it possesses no harm, rather sometimes it may even be necessary.

The second type: If it is by doing something impermissible, like nullifying the magic by using other magic, the scholars have

---

[297] Ibid, vol. 1, pp. 71-72, no. 37.

differed over this - some have allowed it due to necessity whilst others forbid it due to the saying of the Prophet (ﷺ) when he was asked about *'nashrah'*: *"It is from the work of shayṭān."* Collected by Abū Dāwūd with a sound chain of narration. Therefore, using magic against magic is unlawful, instead, one should turn to Allāh making *du'ā* with humility and ask Him to remove this harm. He says:

وَإِذَا سَأَلَكَ
عِبَادِي عَنِّي فَإِنِّي قَرِيبٌ أُجِيبُ دَعْوَةَ الدَّاعِ إِذَا دَعَانِ

And when My slaves ask you (O Muḥammad) concerning Me, then (answer them), I am indeed near (to them by My Knowledge). I respond to the invocations of the supplicant when he calls on Me.

Sūrah al-Baqarah, verse 186

He also says:

أَمَّن يُجِيبُ الْمُضْطَرَّ إِذَا دَعَاهُ وَيَكْشِفُ السُّوءَ وَيَجْعَلُكُمْ
خُلَفَاءَ الْأَرْضِ أَإِلَٰهٌ مَّعَ اللَّهِ قَلِيلًا مَّا تَذَكَّرُونَ ٦٢

Is not He (better than your gods) Who responds to the distressed one, when he calls on Him, and Who removes the evil, and makes you inheritors of the earth, generations after generations? Is there any god with Allāh? Little is that you remember!

Sūrah al-Naml, verse 62

Q: What is the ruling of reconciliation between a husband and wife using magic?

A: This is impermissible and not allowed. It is known as *'aṭf'*, and that which causes a husband and wife to separate is known as *'ṣarf'*; this is also impermissible, and can be disbelief or *shirk* at times. Allāh says:

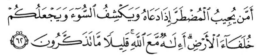

وَمَا يُعَلِّمَانِ مِنْ أَحَدٍ حَتَّىٰ يَقُولَا إِنَّمَا نَحْنُ فِتْنَةٌ فَلَا تَكْفُرْ ۖ
فَيَتَعَلَّمُونَ مِنْهُمَا مَا يُفَرِّقُونَ بِهِ بَيْنَ الْمَرْءِ وَزَوْجِهِ ۚ
وَمَا هُم بِضَارِّينَ بِهِ مِنْ أَحَدٍ إِلَّا بِإِذْنِ اللَّهِ ۚ وَيَتَعَلَّمُونَ
مَا يَضُرُّهُمْ وَلَا يَنفَعُهُمْ ۚ وَلَقَدْ عَلِمُوا لَمَنِ اشْتَرَاهُ
مَا لَهُ فِي الْآخِرَةِ مِنْ خَلَاقٍ ۚ

But neither of these two (angels) taught anyone (such things) till they had said: "We are only for trial, so disbelieve not (by learning this magic from us)." And from these (angels) people learn that by which they cause separation between man and his wife, but they could not thus harm anyone except by Allāh's Leave. And they learn that which harms them and profits them not. And indeed they knew that the buyers of it (magic) would have no share in the Hereafter.

Sūrah al-Baqarah, verse 102

Q: Certain people call on the *jinn* using incantations and make them discover buried treasures, which have been buried for a long time. What is the ruling of this?

A: This is not allowed, because in the majority of cases, these incantations they use to call the *jinn* with involve *shirk*, and *shirk* is a dangerous matter. Allāh says:

إِنَّهُ مَن يُشْرِكْ بِاللَّهِ فَقَدْ حَرَّمَ اللَّهُ عَلَيْهِ
الْجَنَّةَ وَمَأْوَاهُ النَّارُ ۖ وَمَا لِلظَّالِمِينَ مِنْ أَنصَارٍ ﴿٧٢﴾

Verily, whosoever sets up partners (in worship) with Allāh, then Allāh has forbidden Paradise to him, and the Fire will be his abode. And for the Ẓālimūn (polytheists and wrong-doers) there are no helpers.

Sūrah al-Mā'idah, verse 72

Those who go to these people deceive them and their own selves. They deceive them by making them think they are on the truth, and they deceive themselves by giving them money. What is obligatory is that one severs all ties with them, refrains from going to them and tells his Muslim brothers to do the same, for in the majority of cases, these types of people cheat others and extort their money. They tells lies, and in some cases when these lies are actually manifested, they spread the news and tell people how what they said has taken place. If it fails to happen, they falsely claim that they are the ones who prevented it from happening.

I advise these people and say: Beware of spreading lies amongst people, and committing *shirk* with Allāh, and taking peoples money without just cause, for the duration of this world is short, and the accounting of the Day of Judgement is severe, so it is necessary for you to repent to Allāh, rectify your actions and purify your wealth, and Allāh is the One who grants success.[298]

Q: Does the evil-eye inflict people? And how is it cured? And if one is cautious about it, does this disavow his trust (*tawakkul*) in Allāh?

A: We know that the evil-eye is true; it is established by the *sharīʿah* and by experience. Allāh says:

وَإِن يَكَادُ ٱلَّذِينَ كَفَرُوا۟ لَيُزْلِقُونَكَ بِأَبْصَـٰرِهِمْ

And verily, those who disbelieve would almost make you slip with their eyes (through hatred)
Sūrah al-Qalam, verse 51

Ibn ʿAbbās and others said in its explanation: "give you the evil-eye by their sight." The Prophet (ﷺ) said: *"The evil-eye is true and was anything to precede the decree of Allāh it would be the evil-eye, and if you are asked to bathe then do so."* Collected by Muslim.

---

[298] Ibid, vol. 1, pp. 154-155, no. 111.

Likewise, al-Nasāʾī and others report that ʿĀmir ibn Rabīʿah passed by Sahl ibn Ḥanīf whilst he was bathing. *"ʿĀmir said: 'I have never seen the flesh of a virgin to be similar to what I am seeing today.' Sahl became severely ill on the spot. The Prophet (ﷺ) was informed of his illness, and he was told that Sahl was unable to lift his head. The Prophet (ﷺ) asked: 'Do you blame anyone?' They replied: "ʿĀmir ibn Rabīʿah.' So the Prophet (ﷺ) called him and became angry with him saying: 'Over what does one of you kill his brother? You should have asked that he be blessed. Bathe for him.' So ʿĀmir washed his face, hands, forearms, shins, feet and under his lower robe in a pot. It was poured over Sahl from behind, and he was cured instantly."* Reality also supports this, and one cannot reject it.

Once it befalls, one uses the permissible cures for it. They are:

1. Recitation - the Prophet (ﷺ) said: *"There is no 'ruqyah' except from the evil-eye or fever."* Jibrīl would make '*ruqyah*' over the Prophet (ﷺ) and say: *"In the name of Allāh I make 'ruqyah' over you, from every illness which harms you, and from the evil of every envious soul or eye, may Allāh cure you, in the name of Allāh I make 'ruqyah' over you."*

2. To ask the one who inflicted it to bathe, just as the Prophet (ﷺ) ordered ʿĀmir in the previous *ḥadīth*, then to pour this water on the afflicted.

As for using his urine or faeces or other traces, there is no foundation for this. What has been reported is that one should wash his limbs, and under his garments; Allāh knows best.

Being cautious of the evil-eye does not disavow one's trust in Allāh, for *tawakkul* is to rely upon Allāh whilst taking the necessary means which one is allowed to take, or has been ordered to take. The Prophet (ﷺ) would seek refuge for Ḥasan and Ḥusayn and say: *"I seek refuge for you both in the perfect and complete words of Allāh from every shayṭān and every vermin, and from every eye which harms,"* and he would say:

"This is how Ibrāhīm would seek refuge for Isḥāq and Ismāʿīl." Collected by al-Bukhārī.[299]

Q: Certain people differ with regards to the evil-eye. Some say, 'It has no effects due to it opposing the Qur'ān.' What is the correct opinion in this matter?.

A: The true opinion is what the Prophet (ﷺ) said, *"Verily the evil-eye is true."* This is also something reality attests to. I know of no verse which contradicts this *ḥadīth*, in order for people to claim it contradicts the Qur'ān. Rather Allāh has placed for everything its cure. Some scholars of *tafsīr* state in the explanation of the verse:

وَإِن يَكَادُ الَّذِينَ كَفَرُوا لَيُزْلِقُونَكَ بِأَبْصَارِهِمْ

And verily, those who disbelieve would almost make you slip with their eyes (through hatred)

Sūrah al-Qalam, verse 51

"It is referring to the evil-eye." Whether it is what is being referred to in the verse or not, the evil-eye is without doubt real. Reality attested to it in the time of the Prophet (ﷺ) and continues to do so today. What should the one who has been afflicted by the evil-eye do? The answer:

He should recite upon himself. The one who inflicted it (if he is known), should be asked to make *wuḍu*, and this water is then poured over the head and body of the afflicted; with this he will be cured *inshā' Allāh*. It has become the custom here, to take certain possessions of the person who inflicted the evil-eye, such as his hat etc, and place it in water, then give the water to the afflicted. We have heard that this is also beneficial, so if this is the case, then there is nothing wrong with doing this. If a means is established as being a cure in the *sharīʿah* or naturally, then it is correct. As for that which is neither *sharʿī* nor natural, then it

---

[299] Ibid, vol. 1, pp. 155-156, no. 112.

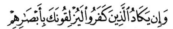

is impermissible, such as those who rely upon amulets and its likes, hanging them on themselves to repel the evil-eye; this has no foundation to it, whether it is from the Qur'ān or other than it. Certain scholars allow amulets from the Qur'ān if there is a need for it.[300]

Q: Can the *jinn* affect people? And how does one protect themselves from them?

A: There is no doubt that the *jinn* can affect people by harming them which can at times lead to death, or by throwing stones at them, or maybe frightening them etc. from that which has been mentioned in the *Sunnah* or has been witnessed. It has been established that the Prophet (ﷺ) allowed some of his companions to return to their families during one of the expeditions, and I believe it was the Battle of the Trench. Among them was a young man who was a newly wed. When he returned home he found his wife on the roof of the house, so he rebuked her. She said: "Enter", so he did and found a snake which had coiled itself up on the ground. He struck it with his spear until it died, and he also died. It was unknown which of them died first. When the Prophet (ﷺ) heard this, he forbade the killing of the *jinn* in the house except the '*abṭar*' (short-tailed or mutilated-tailed snake) and '*dhū ṭaftayn*' (the snake with two white lines on its back).

This is evidence to show that the *jinn* may attack people and that they cause harm; reality also attests to this, for it has been reported on many occasions that a person has come to a ruin, and been hit by a stone, even though he sees no-one there, and he may hear a rustling like that of leaves etc., all which frightens and harms him. Likewise, the *jinn* may possess a human due to love, or out of harm, or due to another reason, and Allāh points to this in His saying:

---

[300] Ibid, vol. 1, pp. 155-156, no. 113.

ٱلَّذِينَ يَأْكُلُونَ ٱلرِّبَوٰاْ لَا يَقُومُونَ إِلَّا كَمَا يَقُومُ ٱلَّذِى يَتَخَبَّطُهُ ٱلشَّيْطَٰنُ مِنَ ٱلْمَسِّ

Those who eat ribā (usury) will not stand (on the Day of Resurrection) except like the standing of a person beaten by Shayṭān leading him to insanity.
Sūrah al-Baqarah, verse 275

At times the *jinnī* may speak from within the person, to the one who recites over that person, and at times it may take an oath not to return, and other such things which are well known and have spread amongst people. Therefore, the way to protect oneself from the *jinn* is to recite what has been mentioned in the *Sunnah*, such as *Āyat al-Kursī*, for if one recites it at night, a guardian from Allāh will remain with him until the morning, so no *shayṭān* will be able to approach. Allāh is the Protector.[301]

Q: Is there any reality to the *jinn*? Do they have any effects? What is the cure to that?

A: Allāh knows best with regards to the reality of the *jinn*, but we know that they have real bodies made from fire, and that they eat, drink, marry and have children. Allāh says regarding *shayṭān*:

أَفَتَتَّخِذُونَهُۥ وَذُرِّيَّتَهُۥٓ أَوْلِيَآءَ مِن دُونِى وَهُمْ لَكُمْ عَدُوٌّۢ

Will you then take him (Iblīs) and his offspring as protectors and helpers rather than Me while they are enemies to you?
Sūrah al-Kahf, verse 50

Likewise, they are also ordered to perform acts of worship, for Allāh sent to them the Prophet (ﷺ), and they attended and heard the Qur'ān, as Allāh says:

---

[301] Ibid, vol. 1, pp. 156-157, no. 114.

قُلْ أُوحِىَ إِلَىَّ أَنَّهُ ٱسْتَمَعَ نَفَرٌ مِّنَ ٱلْجِنِّ فَقَالُوٓا۟ إِنَّا سَمِعْنَا قُرْءَانًا
عَجَبًا ﴿١﴾ يَهْدِىٓ إِلَى ٱلرُّشْدِ فَـَٔامَنَّا بِهِۦ ۖ وَلَن نُّشْرِكَ بِرَبِّنَآ أَحَدًا ﴿٢﴾

Say (O Muḥammad): "It has been revealed to me that a group (from three to ten in number) of jinn listened (to this Qur'ān). They said: verily we have heard a wonderful Recitation (this Qur'ān)! It guides to the Right Path, and we have believed therein, and we shall never join (in worship) anything with our Lord (Allāh).

Sūrah al-Jinn, verse 1-2

He also says:

وَإِذْ صَرَفْنَآ إِلَيْكَ نَفَرًا مِّنَ ٱلْجِنِّ يَسْتَمِعُونَ ٱلْقُرْءَانَ فَلَمَّا
حَضَرُوهُ قَالُوٓا۟ أَنصِتُوا۟ ۖ فَلَمَّا قُضِىَ وَلَّوْا۟ إِلَىٰ قَوْمِهِم مُّنذِرِينَ
﴿٢٩﴾ قَالُوا۟ يَٰقَوْمَنَآ إِنَّا سَمِعْنَا كِتَٰبًا أُنزِلَ مِنۢ بَعْدِ مُوسَىٰ
مُصَدِّقًا لِّمَا بَيْنَ يَدَيْهِ يَهْدِىٓ إِلَى ٱلْحَقِّ وَإِلَىٰ طَرِيقٍ مُّسْتَقِيمٍ

And (remember) when We sent towards you (Muḥammad) a group (three to ten persons) of the jinn, (quietly) listening to the Qur'ān. When they stood in the presence thereof, they said: "Listen in silence!" and when it was finished, they returned to their people, as warners. They said: "O our people! Verily, we have heard a Book (this Qur'ān) sent down after Mūsā, confirming what came before it: it guides to the truth and to the straight Path (i.e. Islām)."

Sūrah al-Aḥqāf, verse 29-30

It has been established that the Prophet (ﷺ) said to the *jinn* who came to him and asked him for provisions: *"In every bone that the name of Allāh has been recited upon, you will find it with the fattest of meat."*

The *jinn* participate with a person whilst he is eating, if he does so without taking the name of Allāh. This is why saying *'bismillāh'* is obligatory before eating and drinking as the Prophet (ﷺ) ordered. Therefore, the *jinn* are real and exist, and to deny them is to deny the Qur'ān and disbelieve in Allāh. The *jinn* have been ordered to do good and forbidden from evil, and their disbelievers will enter the Fire, as Allāh says:

قَالَ ٱدْخُلُوا۟ فِىٓ أُمَمٍ قَدْ خَلَتْ مِن قَبْلِكُم مِّنَ ٱلْجِنِّ وَٱلْإِنسِ
فِى ٱلنَّارِ ۖ كُلَّمَا دَخَلَتْ أُمَّةٌ لَّعَنَتْ أُخْتَهَا ۖ

Allāh) will say: "Enter you in the company of nations who) passed away before you, of men and jinn, into the Fire." Every time a new nation enters, it curses its sister nation (that went before)

Sūrah al-A'rāf, verse 38

The believing *jinn* will enter Paradise, due to the saying of Allāh:

وَلِمَنْ خَافَ مَقَامَ رَبِّهِۦ جَنَّتَانِ ﴿٤٦﴾ فَبِأَىِّ ءَالَآءِ رَبِّكُمَا تُكَذِّبَانِ
﴿٤٧﴾ ذَوَاتَآ أَفْنَانٍ ﴿٤٨﴾ فَبِأَىِّ ءَالَآءِ رَبِّكُمَا تُكَذِّبَانِ ﴿٤٩﴾

But for him who fears the standing before his Lord, there will be two gardens (i.e. in Paradise). Then which of the Blessings of your Lord will you both (jinn and men) deny? With spreading branches. Then which of the Blessings of your Lord will you both (jinn and men) deny?

Sūrah al-Raḥmān, verse 46-49

This includes both mankind and *jinn*. Allāh also says:

يَـٰمَعْشَرَ ٱلْجِنِّ وَٱلْإِنسِ أَلَمْ يَأْتِكُمْ رُسُلٌ مِّنكُمْ يَقُصُّونَ
عَلَيْكُمْ ءَايَـٰتِى وَيُنذِرُونَكُمْ لِقَآءَ يَوْمِكُمْ هَـٰذَا ۚ قَالُوا۟
شَهِدْنَا عَلَىٰٓ أَنفُسِنَا ۖ وَغَرَّتْهُمُ ٱلْحَيَوٰةُ ٱلدُّنْيَا وَشَهِدُوا۟ عَلَىٰٓ
أَنفُسِهِمْ أَنَّهُمْ كَانُوا۟ كَـٰفِرِينَ ﴿١٣٠﴾

O you assembly of jinn and mankind! Did not there come to you Messengers from amongst you, reciting unto you My verses and warning you of the meeting of this Day of yours? They will say: We bear witness against ourselves. It was the life of this world that deceived them. And they will bear witness against themselves that they were disbelievers.

Sūrah al-Anʿām, verse 130

There are other such verses and *ḥadīths* which show that they will enter paradise if they believe and the Fire if they disbelieve.

As for their effects on humans, this is also real and it exists. Sometimes, they enter a person and cause convulsions and pain, or they affect him by frightening him.

The cure to protect oneself from their effects is to recite the *sharʿī duʿās*, such as *Āyat al-Kursī*, for if one recites it at night, a guardian from Allāh will remain with him until morning, so no *shayṭān* will be able to approach him.[302]

Q: What is magic? And what is the ruling of learning it?

A: The scholars mention that magic linguistically means: 'All that which has a hidden cause, like all that which people do not see or realise.' This term includes astrology and fortune telling and the effects of speech and eloquence, as the Prophet (ﷺ) said: "*Verily in speech there is magic.*" So, everything which has a hidden effect is magic.

In the *sharīʿah*, it has been defined by some as: "Amulets, incantations, and knots which affect the hearts, minds and bodies; it takes away ones intellect, causes love and hatred, separates a husband and wife, causes illness to the body, and takes away ones thoughts."

---

302 Ibid, vol. 1, pp. 157-159, no. 115.

Learning magic is impermissible; indeed, it is disbelief if one uses it to associate partners using the *shayāṭīn*. Allāh says:

وَٱتَّبَعُوا۟ مَا تَتْلُوا۟ ٱلشَّيَـٰطِينُ عَلَىٰ مُلْكِ سُلَيْمَـٰنَ ۖ وَمَا كَفَرَ
سُلَيْمَـٰنُ وَلَـٰكِنَّ ٱلشَّيَـٰطِينَ كَفَرُوا۟ يُعَلِّمُونَ ٱلنَّاسَ
ٱلسِّحْرَ وَمَآ أُنزِلَ عَلَى ٱلْمَلَكَيْنِ بِبَابِلَ هَـٰرُوتَ وَمَـٰرُوتَ ۚ
وَمَا يُعَلِّمَانِ مِنْ أَحَدٍ حَتَّىٰ يَقُولَآ إِنَّمَا نَحْنُ فِتْنَةٌ فَلَا تَكْفُرْ ۖ
فَيَتَعَلَّمُونَ مِنْهُمَا مَا يُفَرِّقُونَ بِهِۦ بَيْنَ ٱلْمَرْءِ وَزَوْجِهِۦ ۚ
وَمَا هُم بِضَآرِّينَ بِهِۦ مِنْ أَحَدٍ إِلَّا بِإِذْنِ ٱللَّهِ ۚ وَيَتَعَلَّمُونَ
مَا يَضُرُّهُمْ وَلَا يَنفَعُهُمْ ۚ وَلَقَدْ عَلِمُوا۟ لَمَنِ ٱشْتَرَىٰهُ
مَا لَهُۥ فِى ٱلْـَٔاخِرَةِ مِنْ خَلَـٰقٍ ۚ

They followed what the shayāṭīn (devils) gave out (falsely of the magic) in the lifetime of Sulaymān. Sulaymān did not disbelieve, but the shayāṭīn disbelieved, teaching men magic and such things that came down at Babylon to the two angels, Hārūt and Mārūt, but neither of these two (angels) taught anyone (such things) till they had said, "We are only for trial, so disbelieve not (by learning this magic from us)". And from these (angels) people learn that by which they cause separation between man and his wife, but they could not thus harm anyone except by Allāh's Leave. And they learn that which harms them and profits them not. And indeed they knew that the buyers of it (magic) would have no share in the Hereafter.

Sūrah al-Baqarah, verse 102

This type of magic i.e. by using the *shayāṭīn*, is disbelief, and using it is a form of disbelief, oppression and tyranny against the creation. This is why the magician is killed either due to his apostasy or as a punishment. If his magic is disbelief, then he is killed as an apostate, and if it is not disbelief then he is killed as punishment, and to protect people from his harm.[303]

---

[303] Ibid, vol. 1, pp. 159-160, no. 116.

Q: Does magic have a reality?

A: There is no doubt that magic has a reality, and that its effects are real. However, the idea that it turns things, or causes what is still to move, or that which moves to be still, is untrue. Look at the saying of Allāh in the story of the sorcerers of Pharaoh:

سَحَرُوٓا۟ أَعْيُنَ ٱلنَّاسِ وَٱسْتَرْهَبُوهُمْ وَجَآءُو بِسِحْرٍ عَظِيمٍ ﴿١١٦﴾

...they bewitched the eyes of the people, and struck terror into them, and they displayed a great magic.

Sūrah al-A'rāf, verse 116

How did they place magic on people's eyes? They placed magic on them when people watched the ropes of the sorcerers move as though they were serpents, as Allāh says:

يُخَيَّلُ إِلَيْهِ مِن سِحْرِهِمْ أَنَّهَا تَسْعَىٰ

...by their magic, appeared to him as though they moved fast

Sūrah Ṭa-Ha, verse 66

So, magic in turning things, or moving others, or causing others to be still has no effect, but magic affects the bewitched by causing him to see that which is still as moving, and that which is moving as still. These effects are very apparent, and have an impact on the body and senses of the bewitched; it may even kill him.[304]

Q: What are the categories of magic? Is the magician a disbeliever?

A: Magic is of two types:

The first type is knots and incantations, meaning phrases and mutterings the magician uses as a means to associate partners

---

[304] Ibid, vol. 1, pp. 164-165, no. 121.

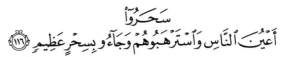

with Allāh using the *shayāṭīn* so as to harm the bewitched. Allāh says:

وَٱتَّبَعُواْ مَا تَتْلُواْ ٱلشَّيَٰطِينُ عَلَىٰ مُلْكِ سُلَيْمَٰنَّ وَمَا كَفَرَ
سُلَيْمَٰنُ وَلَٰكِنَّ ٱلشَّيَٰطِينَ كَفَرُواْ يُعَلِّمُونَ ٱلنَّاسَ
ٱلسِّحْرَ

They followed what the shayāṭīn (devils) gave out (falsely of the
magic) in the lifetime of Sulaymān. Sulaymān did not disbelieve,
but the shayāṭīn disbelieved, teaching men magic
Sūrah al-Baqarah, verse 102

The second type is remedies and drugs which affect the body, mind, inclinations and willpower of the bewitched; this is known as *'aṭf* and *'ṣarf*. They make a person succumb to his wife or another woman, to the extent that he becomes like an animal, and she can lead him as she pleases. *'Ṣarf* is the opposite; it affects the body of the bewitched weakening it little by little until he is destroyed. It also causes him to believe things which are untrue.

The scholars have differed over the disbelief of the magician. Some have said he is a disbeliever whilst others have said he is not. In using the categorisation we have mentioned we can say that the ruling is: the one who uses *shayāṭīn* in his magic is a disbeliever, and as for the one who uses remedies and drugs, then he is not a disbeliever but is still sinful.[305]

Q: Is the magician killed due to his apostasy or as a punishment?

A: A magician may be killed due to his apostasy, or as a punishment, depending upon what we have mentioned concerning whether or not he is a disbeliever. When it is ruled that he is a disbeliever, he is killed as an apostate, otherwise he is killed as a punishment for his magic. Magicians should be killed whether they are considered

---

[305] Ibid, vol. 1, pp. 165-166, no. 122.

disbelievers or not, due to the immense harm they bring about, for they cause a husband and wife to separate. They can cause friendship between enemies for their own personal gratification, such as wanting to fornicate with a woman. It is the duty of the ruler to kill them without asking whether they repent or not, if it is a punishment, because once a punishment comes before the ruler he carries it out without asking about repentance. From this, we can see the mistake of those who put 'apostasy' in the chapter of punishments, for the killing of an apostate is not considered from the punishments. This is because if he repents he is allowed to live. Likewise, punishments are expiation for those who commit sins, but not for the disbeliever, so the killing of an apostate is not expiation. He is a disbeliever and hence is not washed, prayed over or buried with the Muslims.

Thus, saying that the magician should be killed is in accordance with the principles of the *sharīʿah*, for they cause evil on the earth and their evil is of the worst kind. If they are killed people will be saved from their harm, and likewise people will refrain from approaching them.[306]

Q: Has it been established that the Prophet (ﷺ) was bewitched?

A: Yes, it has been established in al-Bukhārī, Muslim and other than them that the Prophet (ﷺ) was bewitched. However, this did not affect him with regard to matters of revelation and religion, rather the extent of it was that he would think he had done something when he had not. He was bewitched by a Jew known as Labīd ibn Aʿṣam, but Allāh saved him and revealed to him *Sūrahs Falaq* and *Nās*. The bewitchment did not affect his station as a Prophet, as it did not affect him (ﷺ) with regard to matters of revelation and worship.

Certain people have denied that the Prophet (ﷺ) was bewitched, saying that this would imply that the disbelievers were truthful in their statement:

---

[306] Ibid, vol. 2, pp. 130-131, no. 230.

إِن تَتَّبِعُونَ إِلَّا رَجُلًا مَّسْحُورًا ﴿٤٧﴾

You follow none but a bewitched man.
Sūrah al-Isrā', verse 47

However, there is no doubt that this does not mean that they were truthful in their description of the Prophet (ﷺ). They claimed that the Prophet (ﷺ) was bewitched in matters of revelation, and that he raved as the magicians do. The bewitchment of the Prophet (ﷺ) did not affect anything to do with matters of revelation and the religion. It is not allowed for us to deny authentic narrations just because certain people misunderstand them.[307]

Q: What is the ruling of asking a soothsayer?

A: Asking soothsayers can be divided into three categories:

The first category: To ask them and then to believe them; this is impermissible (*ḥarām*), and is disbelief. This is because believing what they mention from the unseen is a denial of what has been mentioned in the Qur'ān.

The second category: To ask them in order to see whether they are truthful or liars, and not in order to believe them. This is allowed, for the Prophet (ﷺ) asked Ibn Siyād: "*What have I hidden from you?" He replied: "Al-dukh." The Prophet (ﷺ) said: "Shame be on you! You cannot cross your limits.*" So, the Prophet (ﷺ) asked him about that which he had hidden in order to test him, not to believe him.

The third category: To ask them so that their lies and weakness becomes apparent, and this is something which should be done, and may even be obligatory.[308]

---

[307] Ibid, vol. 2, pp. 134-135, no. 234.

[308] Ibid, vol. 2, pp. 135-136, no. 235.

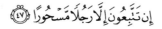

Q: What is fortune telling? And what is the ruling of going to fortune tellers?

A: Fortune telling is taken from '*takahhun*', meaning to guess and search for the truth using methods which have no foundation. In the days of ignorance (*jāhiliyyah*) it was the work of people who would be contacted by the *shayāṭīn* who would steal news from the heavens. These people would take this news and add to it what they pleased, then tell it to people. If something they said conformed to reality, people would be deceived by them and take them as a source of authority. They used them to learn about matters of the future. Therefore, we say, a fortune teller is the one who informs others regarding matters of the unseen in the future.

Those who come to fortune tellers are of three types:

The first type: To ask a fortune teller without believing him - this is unlawful, and the punishment of the questioner is that his prayer will not be accepted for forty days. This is mentioned in the *ḥadīth* of *Ṣaḥīḥ Muslim* that the Prophet (ﷺ) said: "*Whosoever comes to a fortune teller and asks him, his prayer will not be accepted for forty days or forty nights.*"

The second type: To ask the fortune tellers and believe in what they claim - this is disbelief, for he has believed them regarding what they have claimed from the matters of the unseen. To believe men in these claims of the unseen is to deny the saying of Allāh:

قُل لَّا يَعۡلَمُ مَن فِي ٱلسَّمَٰوَٰتِ وَٱلۡأَرۡضِ ٱلۡغَيۡبَ إِلَّا ٱللَّهُۚ

Say: "None in the heavens and the earth knows the Unseen except Allāh"

Sūrah al-Naml, verse 65

This is why the Prophet (ﷺ) said: "*Whosoever comes to a fortune teller and believes what he says, has disbelieved in that which has been revealed to Muḥammad (ﷺ).*"

The third type: To ask the fortune teller in order to expose his lies, guesses and fabrications; this is allowed; the evidence for this is that Ibn Siyād came to the Prophet (ﷺ), and the Prophet thought of something and then asked him about what he had hidden from him. Ibn Siyād replied: "*Al-dukh*" meaning *Sūrah al-Dukhān* [he guessed incorrectly], so the Prophet (ﷺ) said *"Shame be on you! You cannot cross your limits."* These are the three types of people who approach the fortune teller:

1. To ask them without believing them and without wanting to test them; this is *ḥarām*, and the punishment of the questioner is that his prayer is not accepted for forty days.

2. To ask them and believe them; this is disbelief, and one must repent to Allāh from this, or else he dies upon disbelief.

3. To ask them in order to test them and make their condition apparent to people; this is allowed.[309]

Q: What is '*tanjīm*' (astrology)? And what is its ruling?

A: The word '*tanjīm*' comes from '*najm*' (star); it is to use the condition and state of the universe as a sign for predicting what will take place on the earth. The astrologer connects that which takes place, or will take place on the earth with the movement of the stars; it's rising, descent and patterns etc. This form of astrology is a type of magic and fortune telling, and it is unlawful, for it is based upon illusions which have no basis, as there is no connection between that which takes place on the earth with that which takes place in the heavens.

It was from the beliefs of pre-Islām (*jāhiliyyah*) that the sun and moon only eclipse when someone important dies. When the sun eclipsed during the time of the Prophet (ﷺ) on the same day his son, Ibrāhīm, passed away, people said: "The sun has eclipsed

[309] Ibid, vol. 2, pp. 136-137, no. 236.

due to the death of Ibrāhīm." So, the Prophet (ﷺ) gave a sermon after praying the eclipse prayer, and said: "*Verily the sun and moon are two signs from the signs of Allāh; they do not eclipse due to the death or birth of anyone.*" Hence, the Prophet (ﷺ) rejected the connection between incidents which take place on earth and the state of the universe. Just as this type of astrology is a form of magic, it is also a reason for certain psychological illusions which have no basis, so a person falls into a maze of illusions and pessimism which have no end.

There is also another type of astrology, and it is to use the stars as signs for times, periods and seasons. There is no harm in this type, for example, to say that if such and such star is seen, then it means the rain season will enter, or that it is the season of ripened fruits etc. There is nothing wrong with this.[310]

Q: What is the connection between '*tanjīm*' (astrology) and fortune telling? And which of the two is more dangerous?

A: The connection between the two is that both are based on illusions and deception, unlawfully eating people's wealth, and filling their lives with sorrow and grief, and such similar things.

As for which of the two is more dangerous than the other, this depends on how widespread they are, for it may be that in a certain society *tanjīm* has no effect, nor do they bother with it or believe in it, but fortune telling is widespread amongst them and therefore more dangerous, and vice versa. However, if both are present, then fortune telling is the more dangerous of the two.[311]

---

[310] Ibid, vol. 2, pp. 138-139, no. 237.

[311] Ibid, vol. 2, p. 139, no. 238.

Q: What is the ruling of the *jinn* serving humans?

A: Shaykh al-Islām mentions in the eleventh volume of *Majmūʿ Fatāwā* that the *jinn* serving humans is of three types:

The first type: To use them in the obedience of Allāh or in the assistance of those affairs which are needed. For example, using them to convey Islām, just as if he had a believing *jinnī* which he teaches. The *jinn* then call other *jinn* and teach them; this is from *daʿwah* (calling) to Allāh. The *jinn* attended a gathering with the Prophet (ﷺ), and he recited for them the Qur'ān and they then returned to their people as warners. Amongst the *jinn* there are those who are pious, worshippers, and scholars; a warner must be knowledgeable with regards to that which he is warning about.

The second type: To use them in matters which are lawful; this is allowed on the condition that the means in achieving this is also lawful. If it is unlawful then to use them is also unlawful, for example, being unable to use the *jinnī* unless a person makes *shirk* with Allāh by sacrificing to the *jinnī*, or bowing or prostrating to it, etc.

The third type: To use them in that which is impermissible, such as to steal people's money and frighten them etc., - this is impermissible due to it being oppression and tyranny, and if the means to it is via *shirk* then it is more severe.[312]

Q: What is the ruling of asking questions to the *jinn* and believing in what they say?

A: Shaykh al-Islām said in *Majmūʿ Fatāwā*: "To ask the *jinn*, or to ask those who speak to the *jinn*, in order to believe them is unlawful. However, if it is to test them, and if one is able to differentiate between truth and falsehood, it is allowed." He then mentions evidence for this, and states what has been reported by

[312] Ibid, vol. 2, pp. 239-240, no. 318.

Abū Mūsā, that the news of 'Umar was delayed in reaching him, and there was a woman who had a friend from the *jinn*, so he asked it, and it informed him that he left 'Umar poisoning the camels.[313]

Q: Do the *jinn* know the unseen?

A: The *jinn* do not know the unseen; no one knows the unseen of the heavens and earth except Allāh, as is mentioned in the following verse:

فَلَمَّا قَضَيْنَا عَلَيْهِ الْمَوْتَ مَا دَلَّهُمْ عَلَىٰ مَوْتِهِ
إِلَّا دَابَّةُ الْأَرْضِ تَأْكُلُ مِنسَأَتَهُ ۖ فَلَمَّا خَرَّ تَبَيَّنَتِ الْجِنُّ
أَن لَّوْ كَانُوا يَعْلَمُونَ الْغَيْبَ مَا لَبِثُوا فِي الْعَذَابِ الْمُهِينِ ﴿١٤﴾

Then when We decreed death for him (Sulaymān), nothing informed them (jinn) of his death except a liitle worm of the earth which kept (slowly) gnawing away at his stick. So when he fell down, the jinn saw clearly that if they had known the Unseen, they would not have stayed in the humiliating torment.

Sūrah Saba', verse 14

Whosoever claims to know the unseen is a disbeliever, and likewise so are those who believe the claims of such people. This is because of the following saying of Allāh:

قُل لَّا يَعْلَمُ مَن فِي السَّمَاوَاتِ وَالْأَرْضِ الْغَيْبَ إِلَّا اللَّهُ ۚ

Say: "None in the heavens and the earth knows the Unseen except Allāh"

Sūrah al-Naml, verse 65

Only Allāh knows the unseen of the heavens and the earth. As for those who claim such knowledge, they are from the fortune tellers. The Prophet (ﷺ) said: "*Whosoever comes to a fortune teller and*

[313] Ibid, vol. 2, p. 240, no. 319.

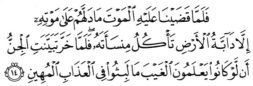

asks him, his prayer will not be accepted for forty days." If he believes in what he says, this is disbelief, for he has believed what he has said of the unseen, and thus denied the verse:

قُل لَّا يَعۡلَمُ مَن فِي ٱلسَّمَٰوَٰتِ وَٱلۡأَرۡضِ ٱلۡغَيۡبَ إِلَّا ٱللَّهُۚ

Say: "None in the heavens and the earth knows the Unseen except Allāh"

Sūrah al-Naml, verse 65

Q: Certain people who cure others by reciting do things which we are unsure of. Some of them sell particular vessels for a higher price due to someone having recited in it seven times, whilst other vessels are cheaper because it has only been recited in once. Likewise, some of them tell the patients that they must capture pigeons and hold them for the night, and that the patients cannot recite upon themselves, rather they must be taken to these people in order for them to be recited upon. Please inform us of the ruling of all of this.

A: All that has been mentioned in this question has no basis in it. Likewise, reciting in vessels, regardless of how many times it is done has no foundation. Rather, what is known from some of the scholars of the past is that they would write verses from the Qur'ān in saffron, such as *Sūrah al-Fātiḥah* and *Āyat al-Kursī*, then pour water over this and give it to the ill to drink from. As for reciting seven times, this has no basis to the best of my knowledge. Due to the increase of psychological illnesses in these times, these people bring things which have no foundation.

Our advice to such people is that they should not overstep what the pious predecessors would do, for they were closer to the truth and their opinions were more correct.[314]

---

[314] *Daʿwah* magazine, issue no. 1455, 18th Rabīʿ al-Awwal, 1415 AH.

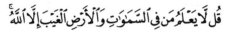

Q: A person has been diagnosed with chronic neurosis. This illness has caused him many problems, such as raising his voice to his parents, severing the ties of kinship, anxiety, embarrassment and fear, so is such a person exempt from the rulings of the *sharīʿah*? And will he be held to account for these actions? What is your advice to him?

A: He is not exempt from the rulings of the *sharīʿah* so long as he is sane. When he loses his sanity, and is unable to control his mind, he is excused. My advice to him is to increase his *duʿā* to Allāh, increase his remembrance of Allāh, ask for His forgiveness, and seek refuge in Allāh from *shayṭān* when he becomes angry. May Allāh cure him.

Conclusion

All praise is due to Allāh, with whose blessing does one complete righteous actions.

The completion of this book has been made easy for us, by the grace and bounty of Allāh. Through it we have endured much, and as Allāh knows, it has taken much effort and time from us.

It pleases us, dear reader, to place a summary of what we have mentioned at the end for you:

1. This topic is very important due to the need people have for a book comprising of both the theological and practical aspects, in a subject which is both old and new, and which affects people in every time and place.

2. There are a certain number of important principles the Muslim should be aware of, and which he should apply throughout life. These include belief in Allāh, the unseen, the pre-decree, patience upon calamities etc.

3. The *jinn* were created before mankind from fire. They are ordered with the worship of Allāh, and are included in the *sharīʿah* of the Prophet (ﷺ). Whosoever from amongst them believes, performs righteous actions, and dies upon that will

enter Paradise, and whosoever from them disbelieves, rejects, and chooses other than the Straight Path will enter the Fire, and what an evil abode that is.

4. The *jinn* are part of a hidden world which one must believe in; their existence has been established by the Qur'ān, *Sunnah* and by the agreement of the scholars. Whosoever denies this, has denied something in the Qur'ān and *Sunnah*, and whosoever twists this has taken a dangerous path.

5. The *jinn* reside in many places, such as open spaces, caves, deserts and ruins etc, so one should protect himself with the *duʿās* mentioned in order to be safe from harm.

6. There are many ways in which one can protect themselves from the evil and harm of the *jinn*. Whosoever takes and preserves these means will be protected by the will of Allāh, and will be safe from them, and whosoever is negligent and lazy in this has only himself to blame when calamity befalls.

7. The touching and possession of humans by the *jinn* is established in the *sharīʿah*, intellectually and by reality. It has many symptoms which are apparent on the afflicted, such as convulsions, fainting, screaming and bodily pains which have no apparent reason.

8. The reasons for convulsions are many. Sometimes they come as a test and trial from Allāh, sometimes because the afflicted is distant from Allāh, and sometimes becuase the *jinn* possesses love for the afflicted, such as a male *jinnī* loving a woman or vice versa. In some cases, it is due to the foolishness and oppression of the *jinn*; this is common (and sometimes as a result of humans harming them; this is also common).[315]

9. Seeking medication is permissible as is mentioned in the Qur'ān and *Sunnah*. Allāh has pointed to many types of cures, and there

---

[315] What is in between the brackets was added by Shaykh Ibn Bāz.

is no illness except that it has a cure. Know it those who know it, and be ignorant of it those who are ignorant of it.

10. Not every person is suitable to make incantation (*ruqyah*). There are certain matters which must be present in the one reciting the incantation, and the one being recited upon. When these conditions have been met, the cure will be beneficial, by the will of Allāh.

11. There are many medicines which are beneficial in the curing of convulsions, and these cures have been tested and their benefit has been established, *inshā' Allāh*.

12. The daily prayers, patience and other such things have many beneficial effects in curing the ill, no matter what the illness is. We have witnessed these benefits ourselves on many occasions.

13. Magic consists of invented incantations and murmurings which the magician submits to *shayṭān*, and thus the *shayṭān* does the magicians bidding regardless of whether it is lawful or unlawful.

14. Magic has been established in the Qur'ān, *Sunnah*, and by the consensus of the scholars; it is real and exists.

15. It is impermissible to learn magic in any situation, and the punishment of the magician is beheading.

16. There are many ways to prevent magic, before or after it occurs, and whosoever takes these means whilst relying upon Allāh, and trusting in Him, will be cured by Allāh.

17. The evil-eye is true, and was anything to precede the decree of Allāh, it would be the evil-eye; its effects are mentioned in the Qur'ān and *Sunnah*.

18. Jealousy is the illness of all nations, and it is most commonly between people. It has split nations and communities, destroyed families and relations, and it only stems from evil souls which dislike good and crave evil.

19. There are many ways to protect oneself from the evil-eye. These comprise of permissible (*shar'ī*) incantations and natural medicines, which will cure the one afflicted by it, *inshā' Allāh*. We have tried many of them ourselves and have seen their benefit, by Allāh's grace.

20. The evil-eye can occur from one who does not normally inflict it, when he hears of something, or wishes for it. This results in the evil-eye which is not from his nature, and this is something well known and witnessed.

21. We have dedicated a chapter to incidents which we have witnessed without adding or subtracting from them, and have tried our utmost in only mentioning that which we are certain of. This is the most truthful thing we can use as evidence from reality, and many of our friends know these incidents to be true, as we mentioned it to them, or they witnessed them, or it happened to one of their relatives.

Finally:

Dear brother, here is the cure in your hands, from the Book of Allāh and the *Sunnah* of the Prophet (ﷺ), and from the actions of the pious predecessors and those who have followed in their way. It has been tested and is without doubt beneficial. Whosoever does not benefit from it, let him examine himself. Does he rely upon Allāh, trust in Him, and make a covenant with Allāh not to go to those impostors and deceivers who will only fill his heart with grief and remorse, extort his money, and distance him from Allāh and cause him to commit that which is unlawful?

We hope and pray that is the case and we ask Allāh that He gives us all good health and protection in this life and the Hereafter, and may Allāh's peace, blessings and mercy be upon you.

May the peace and blessings of Allāh be upon our Prophet Muḥammad, his family and all his companions.

Appendices

Two Short Treatises
by
Shaykh ʿAbdul-Azīz ibn ʿAbdullāh ibn Bāz
(may Allāh have mercy upon him)

Treatise 1:
A clarification regarding the *jinn* entering humans, and a refutation of those who deny it

Treatise 2:
Seeking cures from the magicians and fortune tellers poses a great danger for Islām and the Muslims

Appendix 1

A Clarification Regarding the *Jinn* Entering Humans, and a Refutation of Those who Deny it

All praise is due to Allāh, and may the peace and blessings of Allāh be upon His Messenger, his family, companions and all those who follow his guidance. To proceed:

Certain domestic newspapers reported in Shaʿbān 1407AH, various incidents wherein the *jinn* who had possessed a certain Muslim sister announced its Islām in my presence, after already having done so in the presence of ʿAbdullāh ibn Mushrif al-ʿAmrī, of Riyadh. He had recited upon this afflicted sister and spoken to the *jinnī*, reminding it of Allāh, and that oppression is unlawful and a major sin. Upon learning that the *jinnī* was a Buddhist, he called it to Islām and told it to leave the afflicted woman. The jinnī accepted this call to Islām and announced his Islām.

Br. ʿAbdullāh and the family of the woman then desired to bring the woman to me so that I may hear the *jinnī* announce his Islām. They came, and I asked the *jinnī* why he had possessed this woman, so he informed me. He was speaking through the woman, but with a male and not a female voice. She was sitting in a chair next to me in the presence of her brother, sister, Br.

ʿAbdullāh and other shaykhs who were present and heard the *jinnī* speak.

He then clearly announced his Islām, and mentioned that he was originally an Indian Buddhist. I advised him to fear Allāh, and that he should leave this woman and refrain from harming her, so he agreed. I also advised him to call his people to Islām now that Allāh had guided him. He promised to do so, and then left. His final words were, *'Assalām ʿAlaykum'*.

The woman then spoke with her own voice and said she felt much better. A month later, she returned with her two brothers, sister and uncle to inform me that she was still doing well and that the *jinn* had not returned *alḥamdulillāh*. I then asked her how she used to feel when she was possessed. She responded saying she would have evil thoughts contradictory to the teachings of Islām, and a clear inclination towards Buddhism. She said she would want to read books on that religion, but after she was cured by Allāh these thoughts and desires left her, and she returned to her normal state.

It then reached me that Shaykh Ṭanṭāwī had denied the occurrence of any such events; he argued that it was all deception and trickery, and maybe the voice was recorded and not from the woman. I asked to hear the cassette in which he had made these claims, and I was very surprised that he thought it all came from a recording, especially when I had asked the *jinnī* a number of questions and it answered. How is it possible for a cassette to ask and answer? This is from allowing the impossible.

He also claimed that the acceptance of Islām by the *jinnī* at the hands of a human contradicts the verse in the story of Sulaymān:

وَهَبْ لِي مُلْكًا لَّا يَنبَغِي لِأَحَدٍ مِّنۢ بَعْدِيٓ

...and bestow upon me a kingdom such as shall not belong to any other after me

Sūrah Ṣād, verse 35

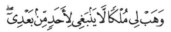

There is no doubt that he is mistaken in this, may Allāh guide him, and that he has misunderstood. There is no contradiction between a *jinnī* accepting Islām at the hands of a Muslim and the *duʿā* of Sulaymān, for many of the *jinn* accepted Islām at the hands of the Prophet (ﷺ).

This has been made clear by Allāh in *Sūrahs Aḥqāf* and *Jinn*; it has also been established in al-Bukhārī and Muslim, in the *ḥadīth* of Abū Hurayrah (ﷺ), in which the Prophet (ﷺ) said: *"Verily shayṭān came to me and tried to break my prayer, but Allāh enabled me to overpower him. I wished to tie him to a pillar so that you may see him in the morning, but I remembered the statement of my brother Sulaymān: "and bestow upon me a kingdom such as shall not belong to any other after me." So Allāh returned him (shayṭān) defeated."*

In the wording of Muslim: *"An ʿifrīt from the jinn tried to kill me last night in order to break my prayer, but Allāh enabled me to overpower him, and I wished to tie him to a pillar from the pillars of the mosque so that you may see him in the morning, but I remembered the statement of my brother Sulaymān: "and bestow upon me a kingdom such as shall not belong to any other after me." So Allāh returned him (shayṭān) defeated."*

Al-Nasā'ī reports from ʿĀ'ishah that whilst the Prophet (ﷺ) was praying, *shayṭān* came to him, so he took hold of him, knocked him down and choked him. The Prophet (ﷺ) said: "*...until I felt the wetness of his tongue on my hand, and were it not for the duʿā of Sulaymān he would have been tied up, so that the people could have seen him in the morning.*"

It is also reported by Aḥmad and Abū Dāwūd from the *ḥadīth* of Abū Saʿīd: "*...so I pinned him with my hand, and I continued to choke him until I felt the wetness of his saliva between my two fingers, the index finger and the one next to it.*"

Also, al-Bukhārī reports in his *Ṣaḥīḥ* that Abū Hurayrah (ﷺ) said: *"The Prophet (ﷺ) deputised me in the safeguarding of the charity of Ramaḍān. Someone came to me and continued to urge me for some food, so I took him and said: 'By Allāh, I will hand you over to the Prophet (ﷺ).' The man said: 'I am needy, and have many dependants and am in great poverty,' so I left him. In the morning, the Prophet (ﷺ) said: 'What did your prisoner do last night?' I replied: 'O Messenger of Allāh, he complained of poverty and many dependants, so I had mercy on him and released him.' He said: 'Indeed he lied to you, and he will return.' So I knew he would return because the Prophet (ﷺ) said so. I watched out for him, and he came looking for food, so I took him and said: 'By Allāh, I will hand you over to the Prophet (ﷺ).' But he said: 'Leave me for I am needy, and have many dependants and I will not return,' so again I felt mercy for him and released him. In the morning, the Prophet (ﷺ) again asked: 'O Abū Hurayrah, what did your prisoner do last night?' I replied: 'O Messenger of Allāh, he complained of poverty and many dependants, so I had mercy on him and released him.' He said: 'Indeed he lied to you, and he will return.' So I waited for him a third time, and he came looking for food, so I took him and said: 'By Allāh, I will hand you over to the Prophet (ﷺ). This is the last time; you say you will not return and then do so.' He said: 'Let me go and I will teach you something which will benefit you.' I said: 'What is it?' He said: 'Before you sleep recite Āyah al-Kursī, for if you do so a guardian from Allāh will remain with you until the morning, and no shayṭān will approach you.' So I released him, and in the morning the Prophet (ﷺ) asked: 'What did your prisoner do last night?' I replied: 'O Messenger of Allāh, he claimed he would teach me something beneficial, so I released him.' He said: 'What was it?' I replied: 'He said before you sleep recite Āyah al-Kursī, for if you do so a guardian from Allāh will remain with you until the morning, and no shayṭān will approach you' - and they used to be eager to do good - so the Prophet (ﷺ) said: 'He has told the truth even though he is a liar. Do you know who you were speaking to for three nights, O Abū Hurayrah?' I replied: 'No'. He said: 'That was shayṭān.'"*

The Prophet (ﷺ) has informed us in the authentic *ḥadīth* of Ṣafiyyah: "*Verily shayṭān runs in the son of Adam just as blood runs.*"

Imām Aḥmad reports in his *Musnad*, with an authentic chain of narration from 'Uthmān ibn Abil 'Āṣ (ﷺ) that he said: "O *Messenger of Allāh, shayṭān comes between me and my prayer and recitation." He replied: "That is a shayṭān known as khinzab, so if you feel his presence seek refuge in Allāh, and lightly spit on your left three times."*

Likewise, it has been authentically established from the Prophet (ﷺ) that every human has a companion from the *jinn*, even the Prophet (ﷺ) except that Allāh assisted him, so it became a Muslim and only ordered that which was good.

The Book of Allāh, the *Sunnah* of the Prophet (ﷺ) and the agreement of the scholars all show the possibility of the *jinn* possessing humans. How is it possible for those who consider themselves to have knowledge to deny this? They are not basing it upon knowledge or guidance, but rather they are blindly following the people of innovation? All assistance is from Allāh, and there is no power or might except with Allāh. I will mention to you what I am able to from the sayings of the scholars *inshā' Allāh*.

The sayings of the scholars of *tafsīr* regarding the verse:

ٱلَّذِينَ يَأْكُلُونَ ٱلرِّبَوٰاْ لَا يَقُومُونَ إِلَّا كَمَا يَقُومُ ٱلَّذِى
يَتَخَبَّطُهُ ٱلشَّيْطَٰنُ مِنَ ٱلْمَسِّ

Those who eat ribā (usury) will not stand (on the Day of Resurrection) except like the standing of a person beaten by Shayṭān leading him to insanity.

Sūrah al-Baqarah, verse 275

Imām al-Ṭabarī said: "This is how *shayṭān* besots him in this world; he causes his downfall and chokes him with possession." Imām al-Baghawī said: "It refers to possession; it is said one is possessed meaning he is insane."

Ibn al-Kathīr said: "It means that they will stand from their graves on the Day of Judgement, like the one who has convulsions (convulsions) stands from his condition after *shayṭān* has struck him; that is, he stands improperly."

Ibn ʿAbbās (ﷺ) said: "The one who eats *ribā* will be resurrected on the Day of Judgement insane and being choked." Collected by Ibn Abī Ḥātim, and he said: "The same has been reported from ʿAwf ibn Mālik, Saʿīd ibn Jubayr, al-Suddī, Rabīʿ ibn Anas, Qatādah and Muqātil ibn Ḥayyan."

Imām al-Qurṭubī said: "In this verse, there is evidence showing the futility of all those who deny convulsions from the *jinn*. Instead, they claim it is something natural, and they argue that *shayṭān* does not possess people and does not inflict insanity."

The sayings of the scholars of *tafsīr* regarding this issue are numerous. Those who wish to know it will find it. Shaykh al-Islām Ibn Taymiyyah says in *Majmūʿ al-Fatāwā*: "A group from the Muʿtazilah denied this, including al-Jubbā'ī, Abū Bakr al-Rāzī and others. They deny that the *jinn* enters the body of the afflicted, but they do not deny the existence of the jinn, as the former has not been as widely reported from the Messenger as the latter, even though they are mistaken in this. This is why al-Ashʿarī mentions from the sayings of Ahlus Sunnah: They state that the *jinnī* enters into the body of the afflicted, as Allāh says:

ٱلَّذِينَ يَأْكُلُونَ ٱلرِّبَوٰاْ لَا يَقُومُونَ إِلَّا كَمَا يَقُومُ ٱلَّذِى
يَتَخَبَّطُهُ ٱلشَّيْطَٰنُ مِنَ ٱلْمَسِّ

Those who eat ribā (usury) will not stand (on the Day of Resurrection) except like the standing of a person beaten by Shayṭān leading him to insanity.

Sūrah al-Baqarah, verse 275"

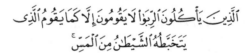

He also says in *Majmūʿ al-Fatāwā*: "The existence of the *jinn* is established in the Qur'ān, *Sunnah* and by the agreement of the scholars, likewise, the entering of the *jinn* into humans is agreed upon by the scholars of Ahlus Sunnah. Allāh says:

ٱلَّذِينَ يَأْكُلُونَ ٱلرِّبَوٰا۟ لَا يَقُومُونَ إِلَّا كَمَا يَقُومُ ٱلَّذِى
يَتَخَبَّطُهُ ٱلشَّيْطَٰنُ مِنَ ٱلْمَسِّ ۚ

Those who eat ribā (usury) will not stand (on the Day of Resurrection) except like the standing of a person beaten by Shayṭān leading him to insanity.

Sūrah al-Baqarah, verse 275

A *ḥadīth* also states: "*Verily shayṭān runs in the son of Adam just as blood runs.*"

'Abdullāh ibn Aḥmad ibn Ḥanbal said: "I said to my father, 'Certain people claim that the *jinn* do not enter the body of the afflicted.' He replied: 'O my son, they lie, he is the one who is speaking on their tongues.'" This is something that is well known, for the *jinnī* possesses a person and speaks in an unknown tongue. Also, he is beaten severely so much so that it would even greatly harm a camel, but the patient feels nothing. The *jinnī* may at times pull things, like the carpet, or change the furniture or go from place to place. Whoever witnesses this knows for certain that the one speaking and moving is a different being, and not from mankind.

There are no scholars from the Muslims who deny the entering of *jinn* into humans. Whoever denies this and claims that the *sharīʿah* also denies this, has himself contradicted the *sharīʿah*. There is no evidence proving his point."

Ibn al-Qayyim said in *Zād al-Maʿād*, "Convulsions are of two types: a type that is a result of the mixing of evil spirits, and the other type is that which the doctors discuss and cure.

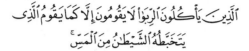

As for the convulsions caused by spirits, their leaders and intellectuals accept this and do not reject it, and they agree that the cure for it is to repel them using good and pious spirits, which nullify the effects of the evil spirits. This is something mentioned by Apocrates in some of his books in which he discusses certain cures for convulsions. He says: This is beneficial for the convulsions which are a result of physical ailments. It does not benefit that which is a result of spirits."

Those ignorant doctors who are involved in heresy deny the possession that can be caused by spirits, and that they affect the body of the afflicted, and they have nothing except ignorance for there is nothing in medicine which denies this, rather reality attests to it, and their claim that it is due to natural causes is true in certain instances, not in all.

"The cure for this is with two things, the first involves the patient and the second involves the one who is curing. As for the patient, a strong resolve is needed. Alongside this, the patient must sincerely turn to the One who has created these spirits, and seek protection from Him with both the heart and tongue in agreement. For indeed, it is a type of battle; and one can only win a battle if he has a weapon which fulfils the following criteria:

1. That the weapon itself is good and solid
2. That the arm which yields this weapon is strong

If one of these two characteristics is missing then the weapon is of no benefit even if it is big. This is even more so if both of these characteristics are absent, like the person who is devoid of tawḥīd, trust in Allāh and fear of Him, and he does not possess a weapon either.

These two characteristics should also be possessed by the one who is curing. From those who cure others are some who only need to say: 'leave', or '*bismillāh*' or 'there is no power or might except with Allāh.' The Prophet (ﷺ) would say: *'Leave O enemy of Allāh for I am the Messenger of Allāh.'*

I witnessed our shaykh send someone to speak to the spirit inside a person who had convulsions. He said: 'The shaykh tells you to leave for this is not something *ḥalāl* (permissible) for you.' So, it would leave, and sometimes he would speak to them himself. In some cases, the spirit would be a '*mārid*' so he would force it to leave by beating it. When it left the afflicted would awake without feeling any pain, and we have seen him do this many times."

Ibn al-Qayyim concludes by saying that this type of convulsion and its cure is only denied by those who have little knowledge, intellect and insight. "In the majority of cases, the possession occurs because the possessed has very little religion and their hearts and tongues have become negligent of the remembrance of Allāh, and seeking His protection. These evil spirits meet the one who has isolated himself and has no weapon and thus are able to affect him." This is what we intended to mention from him, may Allāh have mercy upon him.

From the evidence that has been mentioned from the *sharīʿah* and the sayings of the scholars, it is conceivable that the *jinn* can enter and possess a human being. This evidence is a sufficient refutation against those who deny this. It is also a refutation against the mistake made by Shaykh Ṭanṭāwī when he denied this. The shaykh promised in his statement to return to the truth when it is shown to him, so hopefully he will return to the truth after he reads what we have mentioned. We ask Allāh to guide us and him, and give us success.

Dr. Muḥammad ʿArfān mentioned in the '*Nadwah*' newspaper, dated 14/10/1407 AH, page 8, that the word 'madness' has been concealed from the medical dictionary, and that the possession of humans by *jinn* is a total and complete misunderstanding. All this is wrong; it stems from a lack of knowledge concerning the affairs of the *sharīʿah*, and that which the scholars have agreed upon from Ahlus Sunnah. If such a thing is not known by a large number of doctors, it is not proof of its non-existence. Rather, it shows their great ignorance with regard to what is known by scholars who are recognised as truthful, trustworthy and are known to have insight in the affairs of the religion. The possession of humans by *jinn* is a phenomenon whose existence is agreed upon by Ahlus Sunnah. Ibn Taymiyyah mentions this, and states that it was related by Abul Ḥasan al-Ashʿarī. Likewise, it was related by al-Ashʿarī through Abū ʿAbdullāh Muḥammad ibn ʿAbdullāh al-Shiblī al-Ḥanafī, who died in 799AH.

It has already been mentioned that Ibn al-Qayyim stated that this is something attested to by the intellectual and leading doctors. It is only denied by the ignorant ones who have chosen the path of heresy. So know all this, dear reader, and hold onto that which we have mentioned from the truth, and do not be deceived by the ignorant doctors and their likes, nor by those who speak in these matters without knowledge or insight. Do not blindly follow these ignorant doctors and those from the people of innovation; Allāh is the One who helps and from Him alone is assistance sought.

Important Note

What we have mentioned from the authentic *ḥadīths* and the statements of the scholars, regarding speaking to the *jinnī*, reminding him, calling him to Islām and his acceptance of this invitation, all shows that it is not in contradiction to the verse in *Sūrah Ṣād*, (in the story of Sulaymān) which states:

رَبِّ ٱغْفِرْ
لِى وَهَبْ لِى مُلْكًا لَّا يَنۢبَغِى لِأَحَدٍ مِّنۢ بَعْدِىٓ ۖ إِنَّكَ أَنتَ ٱلْوَهَّابُ ﴿٣٥﴾

My Lord! Forgive me, and bestow upon me a kingdom such as shall not belong to any other after me: Verily, You are the Bestower.

Sūrah Ṣād, verse 35

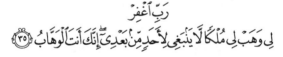

Likewise, for one to order the *jinn* with good, forbid it from evil, and strike it if it refuses, does not contradict the aforementioned verse; rather, it is obligatory to do so. If one does this, he prevents evil, helps the oppressed, orders good and forbids evil. It is done with the *jinn* just as it is done with humans.

We have already mentioned the authentic *ḥadīth* of the Prophet (ﷺ) in which he choked *shayṭān* until he felt his saliva on his hands, and said: "*Were it not for the du'ā of Sulaymān I would have tied him, so the people could see him in the morning.*"

In a narration in Muslim from the *ḥadīth* of Abū Dardā', the Prophet (ﷺ) said: "*Verily the enemy of Allāh, Iblīs came to me with a star from fire in order to place it in my face, so I said: 'I seek refuge in Allāh' from you three times, and then said: 'I curse you with the complete curse of Allāh', but he did not leave. I did this three times. I wanted to capture him, and were it not for the du'ā of our brother Sulaymān, he would have awoken restrained, and the children of Madīnah would have been playing about with him.*"

These are the sayings of the scholars; I hope that what we have mentioned is sufficient and in it is contentment for the one who seeks the truth. I ask Allāh by His most beautiful Names and lofty Attributes, that He grants us and all the Muslims the ability to understand the religion, be firm upon it, and that He graces us by guiding us to the truth in sayings and actions, and to protect us from speaking about that which we have no knowledge of. He is the one who is able to do all things.

May the peace and blessings of Allāh be upon His slave and Messenger, our Prophet Muḥammad, his family, companions and all those who follow in their way.

Appendix 2

Seeking Cures from the Magicians and Fortune Tellers Poses a Great Danger for Islām and the Muslims

There has been an increase in the number of impostors and deceivers in these latter times. These people claim to have medical knowledge, and cure using magic and fortune telling. Their practices are spreading in certain countries; and these people take advantage of those who are naïve and mostly ignorant. Therefore, I saw that it is from sincere advice to Allāh and His slaves to clarify the great danger this poses for Islām and the Muslims, due to it comprising of relying upon other than Allāh, and opposing the order of Allāh and His Messenger (ﷺ). I say this while asking Allāh for His assistance:

By consensus, it is allowed to seek cures for illnesses. It is also permissible for the Muslim to go to a doctor who specialises in psychological, physical or neural illnesses, in order to diagnose his condition and cure it with the appropriate and lawful medication. This is from taking the necessary means; it does not disavow one's trust in Allāh, because Allāh has sent down illnesses and their cures. These cures are known to those who know it, and unknown to those who do not know it. However, Allāh has not placed as a cure for His slaves that which He has made unlawful for them.

So, it is not allowed for the one who is ill to go to fortune tellers who claim to know the unseen, in order to diagnose his illness, just as it is not allowed for him to believe in their claims as they only guess, or seek the presence of the *jinn* so that they can assist them in their needs. These people are upon disbelief and misguidance due to the fact that they claim to know the unseen. Muslim has reported in his *Ṣaḥīḥ* that the Prophet (ﷺ) said: "*Whosoever goes to a fortune teller and asks him something, his prayer will not be accepted for forty days.*"

Abū Hurayrah (ﷺ) narrated that the Prophet (ﷺ) said: "*Whosoever approaches a fortune teller and believes in what he says, has disbelieved in what has been revealed to Muḥammad (ﷺ).*" This has been reported by Abū Dāwūd and others and authenticated by Ḥākim. Also, on the authority of ʿImrān ibn Huṣayn (ﷺ) that the Prophet (ﷺ) said: "*He is not from among us who flies or is flown for, the one who fortune tells or it is done for him, and the one who practises magic or it is practised for him. Whosoever approaches a fortune teller and believes in what he says has disbelieved in what has been revealed to Muḥammad.*" Collected by Bazzār with a good chain of narration.

So, these *ḥadīths* forbid people from approaching fortune tellers and their likes, asking them, and believing them; they also mention the relevant punishment for those who do so. It is the duty of the Muslim rulers and people in a position of authority to reject these visits to the fortune tellers and their likes. Some of them are present in the markets; this should be forbidden severely.

One should not be deceived when they are correct in some of their claims, nor by the amount of people who go to them from those who claim to have knowledge. Such people have no knowledge; they are ignorant because they are doing something impermissible. The Prophet (ﷺ) has forbidden approaching them, asking and believing them due to the great sin and immense dangers it involves for they are liars.

Likewise, these *ḥadīths* show the disbelief of magicians and fortune tellers. These people claim to have knowledge of the unseen; this is disbelief. They cannot achieve their goals unless they serve and worship the *jinn*; and this is *kufr* and *shirk*. The one who believes their claims of knowing the unseen and attests to this is like them. The Prophet (ﷺ) freed himself from all those who perform such actions those who take from them.

It is not allowed for the Muslim to succumb to their claims of being able to cure. Their muttering of incantations, pouring lead and other superstitious acts is all from trickery and the deception of people. Whosoever accepts and is pleased with this has assisted them in their evil and disbelief.

Also, going to them for information regarding who one's son or relative will marry, or about those affairs which will take place between a husband and wife, and their families (from love, hatred and separation etc), is from the unseen which nobody knows except Allāh.

Magic is from the forbidden affairs, as Allāh said regarding the two angels in *Sūrah al-Baqarah*:

وَمَا يُعَلِّمَانِ مِنْ أَحَدٍ حَتَّىٰ يَقُولَا إِنَّمَا نَحْنُ فِتْنَةٌ فَلَا تَكْفُرْ ۖ
فَيَتَعَلَّمُونَ مِنْهُمَا مَا يُفَرِّقُونَ بِهِۦ بَيْنَ ٱلْمَرْءِ وَزَوْجِهِۦ ۚ
وَمَا هُم بِضَآرِّينَ بِهِۦ مِنْ أَحَدٍ إِلَّا بِإِذْنِ ٱللَّهِ ۚ وَيَتَعَلَّمُونَ
مَا يَضُرُّهُمْ وَلَا يَنفَعُهُمْ ۚ وَلَقَدْ عَلِمُوا۟ لَمَنِ ٱشْتَرَىٰهُ
مَا لَهُۥ فِى ٱلْءَاخِرَةِ مِنْ خَلَٰقٍ ۚ وَلَبِئْسَ مَا شَرَوْا۟ بِهِۦٓ
أَنفُسَهُمْ ۚ لَوْ كَانُوا۟ يَعْلَمُونَ ﴿١٠٢﴾

...but neither of these two (angels) taught anyone (such things) till they had said, "We are only for trial, so disbelieve not (by learning this magic from us)". And from these (angels) people learn that by which they cause separation between man and his wife, but they could not thus harm anyone except by Allāh's

Leave. And they learn that which harms them and profits them not. And indeed they knew that the buyers of it (magic) would have no share in the Hereafter. And how bad indeed was that for which they sold their own selves, if they but knew.

Sūrah al-Baqarah, verse 102

This verse shows that magic is disbelief, and that magicians cause a husband and wife to separate. It also shows that magic in and of itself does not have any effect except by the permission of Allāh, as Allāh is the One who created good and evil.

The evil and harm these people possess has increased, for many people have taken these sciences from the disbelievers, and deceived many weak people through them. Indeed to Allāh we belong and to Him we shall return.

Likewise, this verse shows that those who learn magic only learn what harms them; it will not benefit them. It also shows that they have no alliance or connection with Allāh; this is a grave punishment and shows the immense loss they face in this life and the Hereafter. They have sold themselves for the cheapest of prices. Allāh censors them by saying:

وَلَبِئْسَ مَا شَرَوْا بِهِۦٓ أَنفُسَهُمْۚ لَوْ كَانُوا۟
يَعْلَمُونَ ﴿١٠٢﴾

And how bad indeed was that for which they sold their own selves, if they but knew.

We ask Allāh that he protects and saves us from the evil of the magicians, fortune tellers and all those who deceive people, as we ask Him to protect the Muslims from their own evil, and that He gives the Muslims the ability to stay away from them and apply His law with regards to them so that people can seek respite from their evil. Indeed, He is the most Gracious, the most Kind.

Allāh has placed for His slaves that which will protect them from the evils of magic before it befalls, and that which will cure it after it befalls, as a mercy from Him, and from His kindness to His slaves, and as a perfection of His blessings. We will now mention certain things which protect one from magic before it befalls, and cure one from it after it has befallen. These are things which are allowed in the *sharī'ah*.

Firstly: That which people do in order to protect themselves from the dangers of magic before it befalls. The most important and beneficial thing is to protect oneself with the relevant *du'ās* and remembrances, such as reciting *Āyah al-Kursī* every time after one has finished saying the other remembrances which are said after the prayer. Likewise, it should be recited before going to it sleep. It is the greatest verse in the Qur'ān. It is:

ٱللَّهُ لَآ إِلَٰهَ إِلَّا هُوَ
ٱلْحَىُّ ٱلْقَيُّومُ ۚ لَا تَأْخُذُهُۥ سِنَةٌ وَلَا نَوْمٌ ۚ لَّهُۥ مَا فِى ٱلسَّمَٰوَٰتِ وَمَا
فِى ٱلْأَرْضِ ۗ مَن ذَا ٱلَّذِى يَشْفَعُ عِندَهُۥٓ إِلَّا بِإِذْنِهِۦ ۚ يَعْلَمُ مَا بَيْنَ
أَيْدِيهِمْ وَمَا خَلْفَهُمْ ۖ وَلَا يُحِيطُونَ بِشَىْءٍ مِّنْ عِلْمِهِۦٓ إِلَّا بِمَا
شَآءَ ۚ وَسِعَ كُرْسِيُّهُ ٱلسَّمَٰوَٰتِ وَٱلْأَرْضَ ۖ وَلَا يَـُٔودُهُۥ حِفْظُهُمَا ۚ
وَهُوَ ٱلْعَلِىُّ ٱلْعَظِيمُ ﴿٢٥٥﴾

Allāh! None has the right to be worshipped but He, Al-Ḥayyul-Qayyum (the Ever Living, the One Who sustains and protects all that exists). Neither slumber nor sleep overtakes Him. To Him belongs whatever is in the heavens and whatever is on the earth. Who is he that can intercede with Him except with His Permission? He knows what happens to them (His creatures) in this world, and what will happen to them in the Hereafter. And they will never compass anything of His Knowledge except that which He wills. His Kursī (footstool) extends over the heavens and the earth, and He feels no fatigue in guarding and preserving them. And He is the Most High, the Most Great.

Sūrah al-Baqarah, verse 255

Also, one should recite *Sūrahs Ikhlāṣ*, *Falaq* and *Nās* after every prayer, and recite them thrice after *Fajr* and *Maghrib* prayers. Likewise, reciting the last two verses from *Sūrah al-Baqarah* at the beginning of every night has benefit. They are:

ءَامَنَ ٱلرَّسُولُ بِمَآ أُنزِلَ
إِلَيْهِ مِن رَّبِّهِۦ وَٱلْمُؤْمِنُونَ ۚ كُلٌّ ءَامَنَ بِٱللَّهِ وَمَلَٰٓئِكَتِهِۦ وَكُتُبِهِۦ
وَرُسُلِهِۦ لَا نُفَرِّقُ بَيْنَ أَحَدٍ مِّن رُّسُلِهِۦ ۚ وَقَالُوا۟ سَمِعْنَا
وَأَطَعْنَا ۖ غُفْرَانَكَ رَبَّنَا وَإِلَيْكَ ٱلْمَصِيرُ ﴿٢٨٥﴾ لَا يُكَلِّفُ
ٱللَّهُ نَفْسًا إِلَّا وُسْعَهَا ۚ لَهَا مَا كَسَبَتْ وَعَلَيْهَا مَا ٱكْتَسَبَتْ ۗ
رَبَّنَا لَا تُؤَاخِذْنَآ إِن نَّسِينَآ أَوْ أَخْطَأْنَا ۚ رَبَّنَا وَلَا تَحْمِلْ
عَلَيْنَآ إِصْرًا كَمَا حَمَلْتَهُۥ عَلَى ٱلَّذِينَ مِن قَبْلِنَا ۚ رَبَّنَا وَلَا
تُحَمِّلْنَا مَا لَا طَاقَةَ لَنَا بِهِۦ ۖ وَٱعْفُ عَنَّا وَٱغْفِرْ لَنَا وَٱرْحَمْنَآ ۚ
أَنتَ مَوْلَىٰنَا فَٱنصُرْنَا عَلَى ٱلْقَوْمِ ٱلْكَٰفِرِينَ ﴿٢٨٦﴾

The Messenger (Muḥammad) believes in what has been sent down to him from his Lord, and (so do) the believers. Each one believes in Allāh, His Angels, His Books, His Messengers. (They say), "We make no distinction between one another of His Messengers"- and they say, "We hear, and we obey. (We seek) Your Forgiveness our Lord, and to You is the return (of all). Allāh burdens not a person beyond his scope. He gets reward for that (good) which he has earned, and he is punished for that (evil) which he has earned. "Our Lord! Punish us not if we forget or fall into error, our Lord! Lay not on us a burden like that which You did lay on those before us (Jews and Christians); our Lord! Put not on us a burden greater than we have strength to bear. Pardon us and grant us Forgiveness. Have mercy on us. You are our Mawla (Patron, Supporter and Protector etc.) and give us victory over the disbelieving people."

Sūrah al-Baqarah, verses 285-286

It has been authentically reported that the Prophet (ﷺ) said: *"Whosoever reads Āyah al-Kursī at night, will have a guardian from Allāh until the morning, and shayṭān will not approach him."* He (ﷺ) also said: *"Whosoever recites the last two verses of Sūrah al-Baqarah at night, it will be sufficient for him."* The meaning of this and Allāh knows best is [protection] from every evil.

Likewise, one should often seek refuge in Allāh by saying:

أَعُوْذُ بِكَلِماتِ اللهِ التَّامَّاتِ مِنْ شَرِّ ما خَلَق

I seek refuge in the perfect and complete words of Allāh from the evil which He has created.

This should be said in the night, in the day, when entering a building, in the desert, in the air and at sea. This is because the Prophet (ﷺ) said: *"Whosoever enters a place and says: 'I seek refuge in Allāh with His complete words from the evil which He has created,' will not be harmed by anything so long as he is in that place."*

Also, one should say three times at the beginning of the day and night:

بِسْمِ اللهِ الَّذِي لاَ يَضُرُّ مَعَ اسْمِهِ شَيْءٌ فِي الأَرْضِ وَلاَ فِي السَّمَاءِ وَهُوَ السَّمِيْعُ العَلِيْم

In the name of Allāh with whose Name nothing harms in the earth or the heavens, and He is the All-Hearer, the All-Knower.

It has been authentically reported that the Prophet (ﷺ) encouraged this, and that it protects from evil.

These *du'ās* and their likes are from the greatest ways in which to protect oneself from the evil of magic and other evils. One should strive to preserve them with truth, *īmān*, trusting in Allāh, relying upon Him and opening ones heart to their meaning. It is also from the strongest of weapons with which to repel magic after it has befallen. It also humbles a person in front of Allāh as making *du'ā* to Him to cure these illnesses.

Also, from the established *du'ās* in curing magic and other illnesses, is what the Prophet (ﷺ) would read on his companions:

اللّٰهمّ ربَّ النّاسِ اذْهَبِ الباسَ واشْفِ أنْتَ الشّافي لا شِفاءَ إلاّ شِفاؤُكَ شِفاءً لا يُغادِرُ سَقَما

O Allāh! Lord of mankind, remove this harm, cure for You are the One who cures, There is none who cures except You, a curing which causes the illness to depart.

The incantation (*ruqyah*) that Jibrīl would read over the Prophet (ﷺ) is as follows:

بِسْمِ اللّٰهِ أُرْقِيْكَ، مِنْ كُلِّ داءٍ يُؤْذِيْك، وَمِنْ شَرِّ كُلِّ نَفْسٍ أوْ عَيْنٍ حاسِد، اللّٰهُ يَشْفِيْك بِسْمِ اللّٰهِ أُرْقِيْك

In the name of Allāh I make 'ruqyah' over you, from every illness which harms you, and from the evil of every envious soul or eye, may Allāh cure you, in the name of Allāh I make 'ruqyah' over you.

From the beneficial cures for magic, especially for a person who is prevented from having marital relations due to magic, a beneficial cure is to take seven leaves of green sidr, grind them, place them in a vessel, pour water on it (enough so a person can bathe in it), and recite over it: *Āyah al-Kursī*, *Sūrah Kāfirūn*, *Sūrah Ikhlāṣ*, *Sūrah Falaq* and *Sūrah Nās*, and the following verses:

۞ وَأَوْحَيْنَآ إِلَىٰ مُوسَىٰٓ أَنْ أَلْقِ عَصَاكَ ۖ فَإِذَا هِىَ تَلْقَفُ مَا
يَأْفِكُونَ ﴿١١٧﴾ فَوَقَعَ ٱلْحَقُّ وَبَطَلَ مَا كَانُوا۟ يَعْمَلُونَ ﴿١١٨﴾ فَغُلِبُوا۟
هُنَالِكَ وَٱنقَلَبُوا۟ صَٰغِرِينَ ﴿١١٩﴾

And we revealed to Mūsā (saying): "Throw your stick," and behold! It swallowed up straight away all the falsehood which they showed. Thus truth was confirmed, and all that they did was made of no effect. So they were defeated there and returned disgraced.

Sūrah al-A'rāf, verses 117-119

وَقَالَ فِرْعَوْنُ ٱئْتُونِى بِكُلِّ سَـٰحِرٍ عَلِيمٍ ﴿٧٩﴾ فَلَمَّا جَآءَ ٱلسَّحَرَةُ
قَالَ لَهُم مُّوسَىٰٓ أَلْقُوا۟ مَآ أَنتُم مُّلْقُونَ ﴿٨٠﴾ فَلَمَّآ أَلْقَوْا۟ قَالَ
مُوسَىٰ مَا جِئْتُم بِهِ ٱلسِّحْرُ ۖ إِنَّ ٱللَّهَ سَيُبْطِلُهُۥٓ ۖ إِنَّ ٱللَّهَ لَا يُصْلِحُ
عَمَلَ ٱلْمُفْسِدِينَ ﴿٨١﴾ وَيُحِقُّ ٱللَّهُ ٱلْحَقَّ بِكَلِمَـٰتِهِۦ وَلَوْ كَرِهَ
ٱلْمُجْرِمُونَ ﴿٨٢﴾

And Pharaoh said: "Bring me every well-versed sorcerer." And when the sorcerers came, Mūsā said to them: "Cast down what you want to cast!" Then when they had cast down, Mūsā said: "What you have brought is sorcery; Allāh will surely make it of no effect. Verily, Allāh does not set right the work of the evil-doers. And Allāh will establish and make apparent the truth by His Words, however much the Mujrimūn (polytheists, criminals, sinners etc.) may hate it."

Sūrah Yūnus, verses 79-82

قَالُوا۟ يَـٰمُوسَىٰٓ إِمَّآ أَن تُلْقِىَ وَإِمَّآ أَن نَّكُونَ أَوَّلَ مَنْ أَلْقَىٰ ﴿٦٥﴾ قَالَ
بَلْ أَلْقُوا۟ ۖ فَإِذَا حِبَالُهُمْ وَعِصِيُّهُمْ يُخَيَّلُ إِلَيْهِ مِن سِحْرِهِمْ أَنَّهَا تَسْعَىٰ
﴿٦٦﴾ فَأَوْجَسَ فِى نَفْسِهِۦ خِيفَةً مُّوسَىٰ ﴿٦٧﴾ قُلْنَا لَا تَخَفْ إِنَّكَ
أَنتَ ٱلْأَعْلَىٰ ﴿٦٨﴾ وَأَلْقِ مَا فِى يَمِينِكَ تَلْقَفْ مَا صَنَعُوٓا۟ ۖ إِنَّمَا صَنَعُوا۟
كَيْدُ سَـٰحِرٍ ۖ وَلَا يُفْلِحُ ٱلسَّاحِرُ حَيْثُ أَتَىٰ ﴿٦٩﴾

They said: "O Mūsā! Either you throw first or we be the first to throw?" [Mūsā] said: "Nay, throw you (first)!" Then behold! Their ropes and their sticks, by their magic, appeared to him as though they moved fast. So Mūsā conceived fear in himself. We (Allāh) said: "Fear not! Surely, you will have the upper hand. And throw that which is in your right hand! It will swallow up that which they have made. That which they have made is only a magician's trick, and the magician will never be successful, to whatever amount (of skill) he may attain.

Sūrah Ṭa-Ha, verses 65-69

After he recites what has been mentioned, he drinks some of it, and bathes with the rest, and *inshā' Allāh* with that he will be cured. There is no harm in repeating this twice or more if there is need to do so.

From the most beneficial cures for magic is to search for the place of magic in the earth or on a mountain etc; if it is found and destroyed the magic will be nullified.

This is what we have been able to mention from the affairs which protect one from magic and cure it; with Allāh is all success.

As for curing magic by going to other magicians and worshipping the *jinn* by sacrificing to them, this is impermissible and is from major *shirk*. Hence, one should beware of this and avoid it. It is also impermissible to seek a cure by asking fortune tellers, soothsayers and their likes, and to use what they say, for these people who claim to know the unseen and deceive people disbelieve and are liars. The Prophet (ﷺ) warned against approaching them, asking and believing them; this has already mentioned at the beginning of this treatise.

Allāh is the One who is able to protect the Muslims from all evil, preserve their religion, grant them understanding and save them from all that opposes it.

May the peace and blessings of Allāh be upon His slave and Messenger Muḥammad, his family, and companions.